The Role of the Teacher in Guidance

THE ROL

of the

Edgar G. Johnston · *Professor of Education*
Mildred Peters · *Professor of Education*
William Evraiff · *Associate Professor of Education*

Department of Guidance and Counseling
Wayne State University

TEACHER in GUIDANCE

Prentice-Hall, Inc.
Englewood Cliffs, N. J.

The Role of the Teacher in Guidance

LIBRARY OF CONGRESS CATALOG CARD NUMBER: 59-9186

First printing .... *April, 1959*
Second printing .... *January, 1960*

Printed in the United States of America

78301-C

TO OUR STUDENTS

who have been our teachers

PREFACE

This volume is written for teachers and approaches the question of the school's guidance program from the teacher's point of view. The teacher plays a variety of closely related roles—classroom instructor, member of a staff, ambassador to the school's public, personnel worker. It is to the last-mentioned role that the current volume is addressed.

The authors are here concerned with introducing teachers to the various facets of the guidance function and providing practical help in the day-to-day operation of that function in the school. Attention is directed to understanding the needs of children, recognition of recent findings about child development, ways of studying individual children, the dynamics of group interaction, the relationship of guidance and curriculum, cooperation with parents in encouraging pupil adjustment, and the "team" concept of involving the *total* school staff in a *coordinated* guidance program.

The Role of the Teacher in Guidance is an outgrowth of the authors' experiences *with* teachers and *as* teachers—in formal courses, as consultants to schools, and in the classroom at both the elementary and the secondary school levels. The concepts here presented have emerged from their first hand work in a wide variety of school settings, including participation in specialized phases of personnel work—service as a child therapist, as a school counselor, and as a secondary school administrator.

There have been notable developments in guidance techniques and guidance organization in the past two or three decades. Those developments have been reflected in an extensive and valuable literature of guidance. It is the conviction of the authors of this book, however, that the guidance movement has developed, for the most part, from *outside* the classroom. In this volume there is an effort to move guidance back *into* the classroom, to develop the integral relationship between guidance and teaching and to restore the teacher to his vital role as the primary guidance worker.

The authors wish to express their appreciation to the many teachers, colleagues, and friendly critics who have contributed to the development of the point of view presented in this volume. Especially are we indebted to those students enrolled in the course, "The Role of the Teacher in Guidance" who, over a period of ten years, helped to evaluate the appropriateness of the materials and ideas presented.

The ideas for Figures 8 and 9 came from charts prepared by staff members of the Welfare Federation of Cleveland and presented by Mrs. Olive Banister at the annual meeting of the American Personnel and Guidance Association in Detroit, Michigan, in 1957.

For critical reaction to a detailed outline of the volume we are indebted to Mrs. Sybil K. Richardson of the Los Angeles County School System, and to Assistant Dean J. W. Menge and Professor R. C. Faunce of Wayne State University.

E. G. J.
M. P.
W. E.

CONTENTS

PART I

INTRODUCTION

CHAPTER 1

Guidance Through the Teacher's Eyes

The Teacher's Primary Concern Is Learning

The modern school is a complex organism, and the activities of the teacher in such a school are many and varied. As he faces such diverse responsibilities as planning for group activity in the classroom, writing "anecdotal records," studying test scores to plan work appropriate to pupils of different levels of ability, acting as sponsor of a club, leading a Red Cross drive, discussing with a parent his child's growth, working with other teachers on a committee to improve "citizenship education," he may envy the Hoosier Schoolmaster whose task appeared relatively simple—imparting a limited body of subject matter and maintaining "discipline" by methods appropriate to a rugged pioneer community. The chief requisites for teaching then were a knowledge of subject matter (at least enough to keep ahead of the pupils), ingenuity, and a rugged physique. One of the authors, whose teaching began in such a school, remembers a statement—only half facetious—at his first teachers' institute: "There are only three rules to teaching—make 'em study, make 'em recite, draw your pay." He had never heard of guidance or mental hygiene; psychology was still operating largely in terms of axones and neurones and apperception; and individual differences meant to him only that some pupils were bright, some were dull, and the latter would fortunately soon drop out of school and find jobs.

There is no intention here to cast reflection on earlier schools and teachers. Many schools built up a deserved reputation for inspired teaching and sound education. There were teachers who cared deeply for children and who were able to impart some of their own enthusiasm for learning. The point is rather that the teacher's task was conceived in simpler terms. The recognition of the importance for a democratic society of developing to the fullest the capacities of all its citizens, and the resultant extension of the compulsory school age have brought into the schools thousands of pupils who would not have been the school's concern even thirty years ago. These added pupils vary widely in home backgrounds, abilities, interests, attitudes, and future plans. The growing complexity of our society has shifted to the school many responsibilities which were formerly assumed by the home, the church, or the employer. Recent findings of psychology and other social sciences have given us new insights in regard to the nature of the individual, methods of learning, relationships in groups, and the part emotions play in learning. Teaching in a modern school *is* a complex activity.

It will help to bring clarity out of the confusing multiplicity of activities, if the teacher considers them in relation to the school's primary function, stimulation of learning. Teaching is not an end in itself. Its effectiveness can be judged only in terms of the experiences pupils have which result in modification of behavior—in other words, learning. Three considerations are important here.

First, the scope of desired learnings is much broader than the aim of the traditional teaching of subject matter. Factual knowledge is important, but not nearly so important as understanding the implications of the knowledge acquired. Furthermore, not all individuals need—or *can*—learn exactly the same facts. Kelley's *Education for What Is Real*[1] based on the experiments of Ames of the Hanover Institute, demonstrates convincingly the dependence of new learning on previous experience. No two individuals have had exactly the same experience and no two can get exactly the same learning out of a new experience. This important concept is basic to any real adaptation to individual differences. Many skills are important in modern life and the school has a major responsibility for their acquisition, but more important are attitudes, standards of value, appreciations. Many kinds of learning are involved in the desirable growth of young people which is the school's primary responsibility. Not all of them take place in the classroom or can be provided for by the sequence of assignment, recitation, and examination. The school must be conceived of as the setting for learning experiences, and everything which helps to make that setting educational is a concern of the teacher.

In the second place, learning is not dependent merely on appropriate stimulation. It depends, too, on the condition of the learner. This condition is not just a matter of "primary mental abilities." It is affected by

[1] Earl C. Kelley, *Education for What Is Real* (New York: Harper and Brothers, 1950).

past experiences and present satisfactions. Even the simplest learning of subject matter or skills is difficult for the unhappy child, the one whose past experience has given him no sense of achievement, the child disturbed by emotional conflict, the one who sees no purpose in the tasks he is asked to perform. The successful teacher can never forget that "the whole child" comes to school or that the group of pupils with which he deals includes an infinite variety of different patterns of home background, neighborhood environment, emotional and intellectual and physical characteristics. His goal—effective learning—is dependent on constant awareness of these differences, and adaptation of the learning situation to them.

Finally, learning is individual. Successful teaching can be judged only in terms of the modification of behavior of individual pupils. The old adage about leading a horse to water applies here. If there is no drinking, the expedition was not a success. The readiness of a particular pupil for a given learning experience, the previous learnings he brings to it, the purposes with which he faces a new experience are the determining factors. Conditions adapted to the needs of *each* pupil create effective learning situations.

The Direction of Learning Involves Guidance

From the previous discussion of the nature of learning, it should be evident that the teacher who wishes to be successful cannot overlook the backgrounds, needs, and problems of the pupils who make up his class. The problems pupils bring with them to school vitally affect their ability to profit from the school experience, and the teacher's awareness of these problems and his behavior in relation to them vitally influence the pupil's attitude toward the teacher and toward himself. Assistance to pupils in understanding and handling their problems and in making intelligent choices is guidance, which is inextricably interwoven with the other activities that make up the teacher's role. Without consideration of these factors, teaching (i. e. the stimulation of learning) is bound to be ineffective. Even the most subject-matter-minded teacher must take them into account if he is to achieve his objectives. Whether he wishes or not, *every* teacher is involved in guidance. His contribution may be negative. He may aggravate frustrations, weaken self-confidence, and make solution of the pupil's problems more difficult. His influence cannot be neutral.

This is not to say that guidance and education are synonymous, that guidance is the teacher's sole function, or that there is no need in the school for other more specialized guidance workers to whom the teacher may refer individual problems. We would emphasize, however, that guidance is an important and inevitable part of the teacher's responsibility, directly related to the provision of conditions necessary for effective learning. The relationships of the teacher with other school personnel will be discussed in a later chapter. The point to be made here is that *every teacher is a guidance worker.*

A Modern Concept of Guidance[2]

Guidance as an organized responsibility of the school has passed through a variety of phases in educational theory and practice since the movement originated about fifty years ago with the work of Frank Parsons in Boston. Originally it was viewed as a service to prevent mistakes in occupational choice and was termed "vocational guidance." The term was soon expanded to include educational guidance. It was recognized that vocational choices had implications for educational preparation. When the elective system came into general use in schools and colleges, it brought with it the responsibility for assisting students to make intelligent choices among the items on the educational bill of fare.

Successive influences have modified the concept of what guidance includes and how the school may most effectively carry out this responsibility. It is not within the scope of this volume to present a history of the guidance movement, but it may help the teacher concerned to understand his contribution if we identify a number of the more important of these influences:

The testing movement which developed rapidly following World War I brought to the schools a wide variety of psychological instruments for measuring individual abilities and aptitudes. While tests may be—and frequently are—abused, the testing movement contributed to the widespread recognition of individual differences and has provided the guidance worker with valuable instruments for diagnosis.

The mental hygiene movement added an entire new dimension to the concept of guidance. "Vocational guidance" had been concerned

[2] This section is based, in part, on an earlier work by one of the authors: Edgar G. Johnston, *Administering the Guidance Program* (Minneapolis: Educational Publishers, Inc., 1942), and is published with permission.

primarily with choices to be made—the "distributive aspect" of guidance. Mental hygiene focused attention on the "adjustive" aspect and guidance workers have become increasingly aware of the part the school can play in helping individuals to achieve and maintain that emotional adjustment which represents mental health.

Curriculum study, especially as represented in the Association for Supervision and Curriculum Development, has contributed much to guidance. The concept of curriculum as "all the experiences the child has under the auspices of the school" stresses emotional and social as well as intellectual outcomes of education and focuses attention on the need for guidance integrally related to instruction.

Recurrently within the past three decades we find a concern for "character education" and "education for citizenship." These movements have been influential in clarifying the concept of guidance and developing support for guidance as a part of education. It became clear that "character" cannot be insured by precept or intellectual analysis but involves guidance to individuals in making choices in situations involving personal relationships. "Good citizenship," too, involves choices reflecting a sense of social responsibility. (As formulated in a statement of the Detroit Citizenship Study, "Emotional Adjustment Is the Key to Good Citizenship.")

Among developments in psychology which have notably influenced our concepts of guidance and the application of guidance viewpoints in teaching are *Gestalt Psychology* and the other schools of dynamic psychology, and the interdisciplinary complex characterized as *Child Growth and Development*. From Gestalt comes the recognition that the organism operates as a whole, that physical and emotional and intellectual factors operate in combination and cannot be dealt with separately if progress is to result.

The dynamic psychologies have stressed the uniqueness of individual perception based on the constellation of needs in each person. Motivation then becomes a completely personal aspect of the personality.

Among the dynamic psychologies and perhaps the strongest influence on the mental hygiene movement is Freudian psychology. Too often this school of psychology has been conceived of as the basis for therapy applicable only to seriously disturbed individuals. Actually, Freudian concepts are based on the normal biological development of the individual and have strong implications for the guidance of children. Throughout his work is the concept of education of the "instincts" for the development of a social being able to assess reality, relate himself to others in a positive way and, through the development of an ideal self, exercise conscience. His organization of the personality through interaction of the "id" (the instincts), the "ego" (the reality testing part of the personality), and the "super-ego" (or ideal self) has significant implications for education. Recent writers in the field of psychoanalytic psychology have stressed the meaning of learning and education (Anna Freud, Willie Hofer, Heinz Hartman, Ernst Kris, David Rapaport, Rudolph Lowenstein). Although psychoanalytic psychology has been adopted largely by the fields of social work and psychiatry, with the advent of the "school social worker," its impact is now being felt to a larger degree in education.

Studies in child growth and development have brought together significant data concerning normal patterns of growth in various human characteristics and the wide range of differences among individuals. Such studies furnish educators a basis for determining reasonable expectations in terms of particular individuals. These findings have had a significant impact on the field of guidance.

The field of social work has contributed the concept of the case study and has greatly enriched our understanding of the techniques of interviewing. The child-guidance-clinic movement developed the "case conference" approach to the study of the individual and emphasized the importance of recognizing the multiple factors which shape individual behavior. Mention should be made also of the studies in group behavior carried on by Slavson, Lewin, Lippett, and others. The interactions of groups and the individual members composing them are suggestive of further possibilities in guidance work.

From the impact of these various influences has developed a modern concept of guidance broader and more complex than the earlier aim of "vocational guidance." While there are differences in emphasis on various aspects of guidance, differing concepts of individual roles in guidance work, and emergent "schools" of counseling procedure, there would seem to be a modern concept of guidance with which most workers in the field would agree. The writers of this volume would identify three significant characteristics.

1. *The guidance function is unitary.* There are not separate *kinds* of guidance. It was once fashionable to talk of "vocational guidance," "educational guidance," "recreational guidance," "moral guidance,"

etc. Discussion of guidance today is notable for omission of the qualifying adjective. Problems involving human behavior and aspirations have an uncomfortable way of overstepping boundary lines. Satisfactory occupational placement involves educational decisions, personality traits, emotional adjustment. It may be helpful in working with an individual to recognize that certain aspects of his problem fall primarily in such areas as vocation, health, education, or social relationships. It should be recognized, however, that these are not distinctive types of guidance, but phases of a continuous, unitary process.

GUIDANCE IS NOT DICTATION.

2. *Guidance is not dictation.* The place of adults in helping young people solve problems and make wise decisions is important. The function of the adviser is, however, a facilitative one. The decision is the advisee's. The process by which the student arrives at this decision is important. The process is healthy and constructive as it develops self-understanding and increased ability to meet future problems confidently.

3. *Guidance and instruction are complementary phases of the educational process.* This relationship is epitomized in the provocative title of a recent volume in the guidance field, "Student Personnel Work as Deeper Teaching." [3]

---

[3] Esther Lloyd-Jones and Margaret Ruth Smith, *Student Personnel Work as Deeper Teaching* (New York: Harper and Brothers, 1954).

THE TEACHER'S ROLE IS RELATED TO THE ROLES OF OTHERS.

Guidance—the activity of assisting students in establishing goals, solving problems, and making wise choices—cannot be effectively separated from the direction of learning experiences. The teacher deeply concerned to know his pupils as individuals and to assist them to realize their maximum potential finds his teaching enriched and vitalized by new insights. The functional school curriculum will be based on such insights.

Acceptance of this principle leads to recognition that everyone on the school staff has some responsibility for guidance. It is the viewpoint of this volume that the role of the classroom teacher is paramount.

The Teacher's Unique Role in Guidance Is Related to the Roles of Others

To say that the teacher's role is the strategic one is not to say that others do not have distinctive and important parts to play. Actually, a sound guidance program calls for participation of every member of the school staff. This point is well illustrated in MacKinlay Kantor's poignant story "Valedictory," where the school janitor, retiring after a half century of service, is revealed as an effective guidance worker whose intuitive insights have helped several generations of students over rough spots and have averted a number of tragedies. There are, of course, other resources in the school whose relations to guidance are more clearly evident, with whom the teacher will need to develop a cooperative relationship. He will both receive help from them in understanding and carrying out his own responsibilities and will provide them with the information and assistance to make their specialized contribution more effective.

Chief among these resources are other classroom teachers. Pooling of insights, information about pupil successes and failures, suggestions of types of activity may provide the needed clues in helping a particular pupil learn how to live more effectively with himself and with his peers and to establish reasonable and worthwhile goals toward which to work. In schools where the home-room system is an important guidance agency, each teacher will wish to use the home-room teacher's information to make his own teaching more effective and his relationship with his pupils more understanding. He will also be alert to pass on to the home-room teacher through anecdotal records or personal conference whatever evidences of pupil growth or significant behavior come under his observation. Where core classes have been organized at each grade level, with a longer block of time and major guidance responsibility assigned to the core teacher, other classroom teachers will establish close cooperative relationships with him.

Many schools have a director of guidance (sometimes called a "counselor") whose function is the coordination of the guidance activities of the entire school. It should be possible for the teacher to look to him for help on special problems, suggestions in regard to referrals, and, especially, for leadership in improving the teacher's skills and understanding in working with pupils.

School counselors whose experience and professional study have given them special competence in dealing with difficult problems of pupil adjustment and special knowledge in particular areas of pupil choice are a valuable resource whose assistance teachers should welcome. It is an unfortunate fact that, in some schools, the mutual confidence and respect essential to cooperative action have not been developed between teachers and counselors. Sometimes counselors have been jealous of their prerogatives and have been unwilling to recognize the teacher as a key person in guidance. Sometimes teachers have resented the extra salary or recognition accorded the counselor and have failed to see him as a valuable resource, dedicated to the same goal of success for every pupil, and with special skills to contribute. The result of such misunderstanding is, in any case, inimical to the effectiveness of the guidance program.

A comparatively recent addition to the resources available to the teacher is the visiting teacher who combines the points of view of teacher and social case worker. The visiting teacher can be of special help in cases where problems of pupil adjustment are complicated by parental misunderstanding or neglect. Here, too, there needs to be mutual respect and understanding between teacher and specialist. It is important that the teacher understand something of the nature of the visiting teacher's work and of the time required to make even limited progress in the solution of problems which may have developed over a period of years. It is important, also that the visiting teacher make frequent contact with the classroom teacher to report progress and to discuss supportive activities which may be carried on in the classroom. Otherwise the teacher may feel that he "refers these cases to the visiting teacher and nothing happens".

Perhaps the most important resource to the teacher in guidance work is an understanding principal who looks upon his role as one of leadership and support. Certainly any program will be faltering and ineffective which does not have his encouragement and help. The teacher should be able to look to the principal for leadership in developing his own skills and insights, for provision of necessary conditions and resources (including time!) for the teacher to carry out his guidance responsibilities, for recognition of the teacher's efforts, and that administrative support which gives the teacher a feeling of security.

Other resources available in some school systems include physicians, psychiatrists, nurses, psychologists, placement bureaus, and clinics for diagnosis and treatment of special disabilities. It is important for the teacher to know what resources are available in his own school, to cooperate with them, and to use them to supplement his own activities in pupil guidance. The teacher is one member of a guidance team. It is the point of view of this volume that his role is strategic. In the long run the effectiveness of a school guidance program is dependent on individual teachers with warmth and understanding, secure in their own personal adjustment, concerned that the students in their charge grow not merely in knowledge and skills but in self-understanding, the establishment of purposes, the ability to work harmoniously with others, and the capacity to solve their own problems.

Summary

The teacher's primary concern is learning, the stimulation of which is a complicated process and involves a wide range of activities. To a very considerable extent, learning depends on the experience and background of the learner. An understanding of these factors and the use of procedures based on this understanding make the teacher's task easier. In this he is acting as a guidance person.

From the point of view of this volume, three principles are basic:

1. Guidance is unitary. There are not distinct and separate *kinds* of guidance.
2. Guidance is not dictation. The decision is the pupil's.
3. Guidance and instruction are complementary phases of the instructional process.

All members of the school staff are part of the guidance team; the role of the classroom teacher is basic.

Selected Readings

American Council on Education, *Helping Teachers Understand Children.* Washington, D. C.: American Council on Education, 1944.

Arbuckle, Dugald S., *Guidance and Counseling in the Classroom.* Boston: Allyn and Bacon, Inc., 1957.

Association for Supervision and Curriculum Development, *Guidance in the Curriculum.* Washington, D. C.: National Education Association, 1955.

Gordon, Ira J., *The Teacher as a Guidance Worker.* New York: Harper and Brothers, 1957.

Johnston, Edgar G., *Administering the Guidance Program.* Minneapolis: Educational Publishers, 1942.

Kelley, Janet A., *Guidance and Curriculum.* Englewood Cliffs, N. J.: Prentice-Hall, Inc., 1955.

Kelley, Earl C., *Education for What Is Real.* New York: Harper and Brothers, 1947.

PART II

THE TEACHER LOOKS AT INDIVIDUALS

CHAPTER 2

The Teacher Recognizes That a Group Is Made Up of Individuals

The teacher facing a class for the first time may see the pupils who compose the group as all alike. He may look upon them as passive receptacles of knowledge, as eager listeners, as potential rebels against his authority, as travelers on the road of knowledge who must bridge the subject matter gap from the grade just completed to the grade ahead, as young citizens to be assimilated to the social culture, as growing organisms to be helped to maturity. As he works with them over a period of time, however, he comes to appreciate that each pupil in the group is unique. John is quick to learn, but his attention flags if not interested. Mary is slow and methodical. Jimmy strikes out at anyone who offends him. Joan is calm and stable. Phil is frequently chosen as a leader while Joe is left pretty much to himself. Sam reads at the third grade level and Bill at the tenth. Pupils bring to school differences in home background and parental expectations, in health and physical energy, in concepts of self, in abilities of many different kinds, in personal desires and future plans. The teacher must deal with the unique constellation of behavior which characterizes the individual pupil. Of course there are similarities in pupils of comparable age groups. Individuals of all ages have common characteristics and common problems. These similarities, especially as they derive from the nature of human development, will be discussed more fully in the next section. The point we wish to emphasize here is the unique pattern of the individual. Teachers will disregard this uniqueness at their—and their pupils'—peril.

The facts of individual difference have been pointed out repeatedly in recent psychological literature. These facts have not yet permeated the structure of school organization or methods of instruction. It has

THE TEACHER RECOGNIZES THAT A GROUP IS MADE UP OF INDIVIDUALS.

not been recognized in practice that it is as futile to try to eliminate individual differences as it would be undesirable. The better the teaching, the greater the range of difference in any particular factor such as reading skill or manipulation of numbers. Development for each pupil of his unique combination of abilities and personality traits must be the goal of a school dedicated to the ideal of equal educational opportunity for all. This will demand understand and imagination. The teacher who recognizes and accepts individual differences can do much to adjust classroom procedure to meet them. The issue of *Educational Leadership* for December 1957, is devoted to a discussion of "Trends in Meeting Individual Differences." As Olson points out in the opening editorial: "Individual differences among people are a precious asset." [1] The guidance minded teacher will recognize and act upon the truth of this statement.

The Teacher Recognizes Common Needs

Being human entails definite hazards, poses particular problems which each individual must face in accordance with his own makeup, the experiences he has had, and the cultural milieu in which he has been immersed. The teacher concerned to help each of his pupils achieve success in terms of that pupil's particular pattern of past experiences and present problems will wish to recognize those common

[1] Willard C. Olson, "Trends in Meeting Individual Differences" in *Educational Leadership,* XV, No. 3, December 1957, p. 143.

needs all children—in fact all human beings—have and must satisfy if they are to develop effective, well adjusted personalities.

A number of significant studies of needs have been made. One of the most helpful for teachers is that developed by Louis Raths at The Ohio State University from use of a guidance instrument, *The Wishing Well.* Analyzing the responses of children, Raths identifies eight common needs as follows:

1. the need for a sense of belonging
2. the need for a sense of achievement
3. the need for economic security
4. the need for love and affection
5. the need for freedom from fear
6. the need for freedom from excessive feelings of guilt
7. the need for a share in making decisions, and
8. the need for personal integration of attitudes, beliefs, and values [2]

There is no conflict here with the fact of individual uniqueness. The needs are common. Their satisfaction must be achieved for each individual in terms of his own unique pattern. As teachers we can recognize that unmet or inadequately met needs can inhibit learning. The child who is starved for affection is not in condition to learn the intricacies of algebra or to develop skill in self-expression. Only as the basic need for affection is met are the energies of the pupil released to attack the learning situation with which he is confronted in the class. While the feeling of deprivation may be of long standing and have its origin entirely outside the school setting, the sensitive teacher may be able to identify the real obstacles to learning, and, through a friendly and acceptive attitude may give the pupil the sense of security which makes learning possible. What has been said of the need for love and affection applies to each of the basic emotional needs identified by Raths. Only as the pupil has been able to achieve at least a minimal satisfaction of these needs is his energy free to attack learning situations effectively.

Every teacher can document from his own experience examples of pupils who have demonstrated deprivations in some of these eight areas. He may recognize regretfully that, in many instances, the situation has been aggravated rather than relieved by the child's school

[2] Louis E. Raths and Lawrence Metcalf, "Instrument for Identifying Some Needs of Children," *Educational Research Bulletin,* XXIV, October 17, 1945, pp. 169-77. The point of view is further developed in *An Application to Education of the Needs Theory,* 1949, and *Do's and Don'ts of the Needs Theory,* 1951, by Raths, published by the author, Bronxville, New York.

experience. The child who has no sense of belonging may be further isolated by his peers. A rigid marking system based on "minimum standards" may deprive of the sense of achievement both the pupil who is unable to meet the artificial standards set and the pupil, superior academically, who is never challenged.

Students from families in the lower income brackets provide a disproportionate number of school dropouts.[3] Commenting on the effect of teacher attitudes, Hand has this to say: "Many high school teachers come from middle class origins; very little in either their experience or their training has qualified them to understand the environmental influences, the needs, or the motivations which characterize life at the low end of the economic scale. In consequence, the school program offered by these teachers is too often unappealing to children from such a background."[4]

Fear and anxiety short-circuit the pupil's ability to learn, and carry with them serious dangers to the development of a healthy personality. Too often in the past and sometimes today the school has made fear—of teacher disapproval, of punishment, of failure—the chief motivating force for learning. In the light of modern knowledge of the principles of mental health, there is little justification for such dependence. Positive types of motivation are both more effective and more conducive to the development of a healthy personality. Much the same can be said of the effect on the child of extreme sense of guilt for real or fancied offenses.

The active participation in decisions affecting his welfare is essential to the development of a self-reliant and responsible individual. Lack of opportunity for such participation may result in lack of initiative or in rebellion. Increasingly schools are recognizing the desirability of pupil sharing, both in the out-of-class activities in which pupils play a role of leadership and in classrooms where teachers see the value of teacher-pupil planning of instructional goals and activities.

Finally the child needs to resolve the conflicting sets of standards and values he meets and to arrive at an integration of values in his

---

[3] For the relationship between economic status and school survival see: Harold J. Dillon, *Early School Leavers—A Major Educational Problem* (National Child Labor Committee: New York, 1949), and Harold C. Hand, *Principal Findings of the 1947-48 Basic Studies of the Illinois Secondary School Curriculum Program* (Office of the Superintendent of Public Instruction: Springfield, Illinois), p. 15.

[4] Harold C. Hand, *Principles of Public Secondary Education* (Harcourt Brace and Company: New York, 1958), p. 105.

concept of self. Where standards of the various groups with which he is associated are in conflict—home, school, peer group—it is difficult for the child to arrive at a stable set of ideals consistent with the realities he faces. This "struggle for a point of view" as Leta Hollingsworth calls it, is likely to be most critical at the adolescent period when the young person is confronted with points of view which may be in conflict with the accepted mores of his home culture. This may be particularly serious where teachers of middle class background are unfamiliar with the customs and values of a lower class student group. This point will be developed more fully in Chapter 3.

Children who have been seriously deprived in these eight areas of emotional need may present serious problems of personality adjustment. Where circumstances warrant, it may be desirable for the teacher to refer individual pupils for study by counselors, visiting teachers, or other more specialized workers. It is not the teacher's role to play therapist. There is much, however, that a sensitive teacher can do to alleviate tensions and to provide a comfortable and accepting atmosphere in the classroom. It should be recognized that children deprived of basic emotional satisfactions, just as the victims of malnutrition, are not in a favorable condition for learning. Spelling lists and multiplication tables are not likely to receive priority of attention from an unhappy child. As pointed out in Chapter 1, the teacher's primary concern is learning. In pursuit of that concern he can not afford to overlook the emotional needs of pupils in his classes.

The Teacher Is Concerned with Pupil Growth and Development

In one sense, the teacher's task may be defined as "helping young people grow up." This is another way of saying that our function is that of providing experiences through which young people will develop into mature adults capable of dealing effectively with problems of everyday living. Traditionally—and appropriately—the school has been primarily concerned with intellectual growth. We have come to realize in recent years, however, that there is a close relationship between intellectual and other kinds of growth—physical, emotional, social. Retardation in one area can seriously affect another. We have all known cases where physical immaturity has interfered with a child's social adjustment with his peers. This in turn may interfere with learning. Again, a lack of emotional maturity may prevent a child from dealing effectively with school tasks.

Perhaps we should look a little more closely at the word "maturity." This can be used in two senses. It may refer to the end result as when we speak of an individual as having reached maturity. It may also be used in a relative sense when we refer to a ten year old, for example, as "immature for his age." It is usually in this latter sense we use the term when we look at our pupils. When we talk about "reading readiness" we recognize that some six year olds have reached the stage of physical and intellectual maturity where they can undertake the complicated task of turning marks on a page into meanings, while others will need more "growing" to be ready to embark on this new experience. Good teachers know that the experience can not be forced and that pressure on the child who isn't yet ready to read may only create emotional blocks which will make it more difficult for him to acquire this learning when he is ready.

The teacher will find help in understanding his pupils by acquaintance with some of the findings of studies of child growth and development. Two types of study may prove especially profitable. The first type is that which indicates what is normal behavior or development for a particular age group. The second is concerned with individual patterns of development [growth curves].

The chief illustration of the first is to be found in the monumental studies of Arnold Gesell and his associates at Yale University. With the aid of trained observers, Gesell made records of physical growth and observations of the reactions of children to various stimuli at periodic intervals. Literally thousands of children are included for each age group. As a result, he presents a series of norms for successive stages of development, showing what may be expected in terms of physical, mental, and emotional-social growth.[5] Gesell's descriptions of typical six-year-old or ten-year-old behavior may be very helpful to the teacher in understanding what to expect of children in his class. At the same time, it should be recognized that there is a danger of interpreting "norm" as "goal" and expecting each youngster who has reached a certain chronological age to demonstrate the capacities which Gesell has shown to be typical of this age level. Gesell recognizes this danger when he says:

> No two children are exactly alike, but no two (not even twins T

[5] Arnold Gesell and Frances L. Ilg, *Infant and Child in the Culture of Today* (New York: Harper and Brothers, 1943); *The Child from Five to Ten* (New York: Harper and Brothers, 1946); and with Louise Bates Adams, *Youth; The Years from Ten to Sixteen* (New York: Harper and Brothers, 1956).

and C) grow up in the same way. Every child has a distinctive style or method of growth.[6]

and again:

> The beginning of wisdom in the rearing of children is a realistic recognition of the growth factors which shape his conduct, and the acknowledgment that every child has a unique pattern of growth.[7]

Gesell approaches the study of children from the point of view of a physician. A somewhat similar study of development at different ages is that of Havighurst, a sociologist. He presents the concept of "developmental tasks." According to this point of view every individual at different ages finds himself confronted by the necessity of performing certain "tasks whose nature is imposed by the biological demands of the growing organism and the characteristics of the environment in which he finds himself." Havighurst defines the concept as follows:

> A development task is a task which arises at or about a certain period in the life of an individual, successful achievement of which leads to his happiness and to success with later tasks, while failure leads to unhappiness in the individual, disapproval by the society, and difficulty with later tasks . . . developmental tasks may arise from physical maturation, from the pressure of cultural processes upon the individual, from the desires, aspirations, and values of the emerging personality.[8]

Application of this concept will be presented in Chapter 3.

A third concept which will be helpful to the teacher in understanding the individuals in his class is that of "organismic age" presented by Willard C. Olson. The findings on which Olson bases this concept are derived from "longitudinal" studies of child development. The same individuals are studied and observations recorded at periodic intervals from early childhood through adolescence. A great many different factors are considered—height, weight, development of teeth and bones, muscular development, mental age, school achievement. The various measures are converted into age equivalents and an individual growth curve is plotted for each child in each of the factors considered. From the various measures of individual factors an average is

---

[6] Arnold Gesell and Frances L. Ilg, *op. cit.*, p. 43.

[7] *Ibid*, p. 46.

[8] Robert J. Havighurst, *Developmental Tasks and Education* (Chicago: The University of Chicago Press, 1945), p. 1. A helpful listing of developmental tasks according to age levels is presented by Helen Tryon in Chapters 5 and 6 of *Fostering Mental Health in Our Schools*, the 1950 Yearbook of the Association for Supervision and Curriculum Development.

derived which Olson calls the "organismic age." While there may be considerable fluctuation in the development of the several factors considered, Olson finds that the general over-all development is relatively constant for a particular child. Some children show a consistently rapid rate of growth, others a slower rate. Thus pupils may be identified as "slow maturing," "average," or "rapid maturing." Since the rate of growth for the individual child follows a consistent pattern, it is possible to predict with a considerable degree of accuracy the readiness of a pupil for different levels of learning experience. It is important to note that the slow maturing child is not necessarily less able than the one of similar age who has matured more rapidly. Actually the individual progressing at the slower rate may catch up and surpass his speedier classmate. The old fable of the tortoise and the hare has its counterpart in child development.[9]

Some school systems have developed organismic growth curves as a basis for predicting development of individual pupils. Where this is the case, study of these curves will help the teacher adapt work to the developmental level. Even where these data are not available, the implications of developmental growth curves are important to the teacher. Let us look at several of these implications:

1. Each pupil has his own rate of growth.
2. Growth can not be hurried. It may be retarded as a result of deprivation, but it can not be forced.
3. We can not expect all children in a group to be ready for a particular learning experience at the same time.
4. Organization of curricular materials and instructional procedures which allow each pupil to proceed at his rate of growth are in line with what we know of child development.
5. Predictions about the ultimate achievement of a particular child are hazardous.
6. Marking systems based on comparisons of current achievement are relatively meaningless. To know what achievement means for a particular child we need to know at what rate he is growing and what progress he has made.

Boys and Girls Grow at Different Rates

A further point in relation to growth is frequently overlooked by teachers. This is the well established fact that girls mature more rapidly

[9] Willard C. Olson, *Child Development* (Boston: D. C. Heath and Company, 1949). The teacher will find it worth while to study some of the growth curves reproduced in the volume.

than boys and consequently have an advantage where success is judged by comparative achievement. Girls may be as much as a year advanced by the time they enter school and two years ahead of boys in reaching puberty. The boys catch up eventually, their growth curves rising rapidly in the middle teens, but for most of the period in elementary school and junior high school years, girls are more mature and, consequently, farther advanced than boys. Not only does this affect social

BOYS AND GIRLS GROW AT DIFFERENT RATES.

adjustment and social life, it also is reflected in classroom activity and teacher appraisal. Girls, in general, receive higher marks than boys and are more frequently singled out for teacher approval. Often the basis for this is not superior effort but greater maturity. A recognition of these facts of differential growth will help the teacher to understand sex differences in his classes and to "give the boys a break." [10]

The Teacher Views the School Experience in the Light of Individual Needs

It isn't enough, however, to see pupils as different. Unless we act on our knowledge to modify the experiences pupils have in our classrooms, our recognition of individual differences means nothing. What teachers may do in the classroom to make the learning situation more meaningful for pupils with widely varying needs will be devel-

---

[10] For discussion of differences in growth rates of boys and girls see H. Thompson, "Physical Growth" in L. Carmichael (Ed.), *Manual of Child Psychology* (New York: John Wiley and Sons, 1954), pp. 292-333.

oped more fully in succeeding chapters. It is appropriate here to point out that the relationship between individual needs and the learning the pupil experiences in his day-to-day activities is basic. To understand this and to act on the understanding is to bring about that integration of guidance and instruction which is the essence of good teaching. In the work of such an understanding teacher, instruction provides new insights concerning the pupils who make up the class and these new insights help him to adapt the particular learning situation to each child.

An illustration may help to make this point clear. June, in the second grade, presented a challenge to her teacher. Her reading was noticeably above grade level, yet her achievement in all other subjects was unsatisfactory. She appeared unable to follow the simplest directions, and would not attempt the easiest task without individual assistance. Her behavior was a combination of timidity, helplessness, and defiance.

Miss Watson, her teacher, recognized that further study of June's background was essential if she was to achieve satisfactory progress in the second grade. Analysis of health records showed her normal in every respect, with 20-20 vision and infrequent absences for colds.

A sociogram showed her as not accepted by the other pupils, one of whom characterized her as "too silly." Only two girls listed her as "chosen" and both were second choices. When a new girl moved to the neighborhood and was assigned to June's room, the teacher overheard Carol ask June to "come over to play at my house after you change your clothes." June replied, "Oh, I can't, my mother won't let me go to other kids' houses."

June always came to school meticulously groomed, with hair ribbon, socks, and dress carefully matched for color. The first grade teacher had been criticized by June's mother because she allowed the girl to get her rubbers muddy, "After all I send her to school beautifully dressed and expect her to stay that way."

Parent conferences as a basis of reporting are a practice in Miss Watson's school. The first conference with June's parents was quite revealing and subsequent interviews added to Miss Watson's understanding of June. A difference of attitude appeared—a difference openly discussed before the child. The mother was meticulously exacting and concerned with whether June would "mind" the teacher. Mr. Brown tended to be indulgent, "After all, she's a little girl and needs a lot of help." June is an only child. The teacher realized that this lack of consistency at home had a good deal to do with her lack of self-confidence in school. The parent interview reinforced the impression of lack of social contact with other children of her age. Mrs. Brown didn't approve of the other children in the neighborhood. June's entertainment consisted primarily in going to dinner or the movies with her parents.

The information acquired in Miss Watson's study of June threw a great deal of light on the child's learning difficulties and she modified her instructional procedures to take advantage of the new insights into June's problems.

She was concerned, first, to build a feeling of security in the child and then to help her develop independence. When June burst into tears on facing a new assignment and said "I don't know how to do it," Miss Watson helped her through the steps and then gave her a smile of encouragement when she did the work correctly. Private conversations before school and at recess time gave June the assurance that she was an important person to the teacher and not just "one of a crowd." As the child developed more self-confidence, the teacher was able to throw her gradually on her own responsibility, while at the same time being alert to the ups and downs in June's growth in confidence.

The teacher was careful to give June scholastic material geared to her level of achievement so that she was able to experience success. She avoided comparisons with the work of more capable students and gave June deserved praise for her accomplishments. Miss Watson realized that June's chief need—for scholastic progress as well as for personal happiness—was the taste of success.

The teacher gave a good deal of thought to ways of helping June to gain acceptance from the other children. This was possible in some of the group work where June's superior reading ability could win respect. Where, as in this case, there is good rapport of the teacher with the class as a whole, the teacher's acceptance of a rejected child can make that child more acceptable to the group. Children frequently reflect the attitudes of a teacher they like.

Miss Watson was able, too, to help the Browns to a better understanding of their daughter. Obviously there are limits to what a teacher can do or should attempt in changing parent attitudes. At the same time parents frequently seek advice from an understanding teacher. In this case Miss Watson's warm acceptance of June—and of them—gave the parents confidence in her. Mrs. Brown asked about recent books on child care and took home *These Are Your Children* [11] from the school's professional library. She returned it with a note of thanks saying that both she and her husband had found it helpful and that perhaps they needed to let June grow up.

Finally, Miss Watson found that June had made more than usual progress in academic skills. Reading, already above the norm for her age, was definitely superior, arithmetic and spelling showed marked progress, and the change from manuscript to cursive writing was achieved with no difficulty. Although June was not yet a popular member of the class there was a good deal of progress, too, in social acceptance and friendly relations with other pupils.

What happened in June's case was the result of a constant interaction of guidance and instruction on the teacher's part. Miss Watson studied the available data about June (a guidance function) and adapted her classroom procedures to the individual characteristics revealed (guidance merged with the instructional function). June's performance in the classroom situation in turn provided new insights to add to the teacher's understanding.

> A teacher who effectively integrates guidance with his classroom teaching knows that success in school work is ultimately related to the way a child conceives of himself as a human being, and to the emotional satisfactions he is achieving in his relationships with others.[12]

Summary

This chapter emphasizes the point that pupils are individuals with wide variations in physical, intellectual, and emotional characteristics and that learning is an individual experience. There are common needs to be satisfied and common "developmental tasks" to be performed but each individual meets them in ways which are peculiar to him. We have reviewed some of the recent research in child development, which may help the teacher to recognize what behavior is "normal" for his age group, and to understand the variable rates of growth of individual children.

Finally we have considered the close relationship of guidance and instruction as inseparable phases of the teacher's role.

---

[11] Gladys Jenkins, Helen Schacter and William Bauer, *These Are Your Children* (Chicago: Scott, Foresman Company, 1949).

[12] Camilla M. Low, "Setting Our Sights," *Guidance in the Curriculum,* 1955 Yearbook, Association for Supervision and Curriculum Development (Washington, D.C.: the Association, a department of the National Education Association, 1955), p. 23. Chapters 1 and 2 of this Yearbook are particularly pertinent to the points of view presented in this chapter.

Selected Readings

Association for Curriculum Development, *Fostering Mental Health in Our Schools*. Washington, D.C.: National Education Association, 1950.

Gesell, Arnold and Louis Bates Adams, *Youth; The Years from Ten to Sixteen*. New York: Harper and Brothers, 1956.

Gesell, Arnold and Frances L. Ilg, *Infant and Child in the Culture of Today*. New York: Harper and Brothers, 1943.

———, *The Child from Five to Ten*. New York: Harper and Brothers, 1946.

Havighurst, Robert J., *Developmental Tasks and Education*. Chicago: The University of Chicago Press, 1945.

Hymes, James L., Jr., *A Child Development Point of View*. Englewood Cliffs, N. J.: Prentice-Hall, Inc., 1955.

Morse, William C. and Max Wingo, *Psychology and Teaching*. Chicago: Scott, Foresman and Company, 1956.

Olson, Willard C., *Child Development*. Boston: D. C. Heath and Co., 1949.

CHAPTER 3

The Teacher Refines His Perception

The Teacher Discovers That the Student Has His Own Unique Perception

Many times in dealing with students the teacher finds that the student's view of a particular set of circumstances does not agree with his own. The student may seem to overinvest emotional energy in a particular situation, and the teacher wonders why the student seemed to be so upset or so angry. On the other hand the teacher may wonder why a student is not concerned in some situations where the ordinary person may express a great deal of concern.

At other times one student may express great adulation for the teacher or another student may seem to act as if the teacher were never fair or were always favoring someone else even though reality does not indicate that either form of behavior is called for. After experiencing such phenomena the teacher soon realizes that the student's perception is not the same as his. Indeed, he discovers that the perception may vary from student to student to some degree even though most students will see the same set of circumstances in somewhat the same light. What then makes for this variation and how may the teacher cope with it? How does it come about?

Each young person comes upon the earth equipped with certain capacities and certain needs. The native equipment with which he arrives can be modified little but the way in which the environment deals with the needs of the young person makes it possible for him to use this endowment to its fullest or to a very small extent. Many children who are perceived as slow learners may be children to whom nurture has not been very kind and who, as the result, are unable to use their energies to the advantage of their capacities.

The prototype of the way in which the child will perceive the world is set in his early years in relation to his first teacher, his mother.

Each young being arrives upon this earth a bundle of energy whose main goal is the fulfillment of his bodily needs. In each stage of his development he negotiates his relationships with others on the basis of the maturation of some bodily process. For example, at birth nearly all babies of full term are able to suck, and the early demands of the infant are to alleviate the tension created by hunger. Too, he can experience heat and cold through his skin which is equipped for such a response. His goal is for full pleasure and at this time he has no conception of the mother as a person separate from himself.[1] In the early weeks he begins to be aware that the gratification of his need is dependent upon something outside himself. He might suck and feel that through this process he is going to reduce the tension resulting from hunger, but this reduction is only temporary and the hunger returns only to be alleviated by the bottle or the breast.

One raises the question of what meaning this has for teachers. Learning to delay gratification, to wait, to discover that results are forthcoming is the forerunner of the capacity to bear frustration, a fundamental factor in learning. It is as if the child is constantly giving up the demand for an immediate pleasure for the promise of a future pleasure. "In return for delaying, Mother will approve." Thus the child discovers that it is through some outside agent, namely the mother, that the gratification is eventually experienced. As he moves through each early developmental stage according to his own biological maturation, his tolerance for tension increases. One might say that his tolerance for deprivation increases. However, the learning is dependent upon his receiving adequate gratification and the approval of the mother for giving up the immediate demand. He can do this no faster than his own biology will allow. For example, the most gentle of toilet training cannot be effective until the musculature of the child will permit the retention.

Contrary to the belief of some mothers that early training has been successful, one finds that the training has not taken place in the child as shown by his ability to control but rather is the result of the mother's training herself to recognize the regularity of the timing of bodily processes. In other words, she actually clocks the baby and gets him on the potty at the time he would normally defecate. This does not indicate that he is biologically ready to control his sphincter muscles. He can only do this when nature has made him ready for

[1] Otto Fenichel, M.D., "The Means of Education," in *The Psychoanalytic Study of the Child,* Vol. I (New York: International Universities Press, 1945), p. 281.

the act of retention. Timing of the teaching then will be dependent upon his own organic maturation.

> The nature of the biological equipment of the infant, and the nature of its environment account for the fact that the infant's first reactions are related to indulgence and deprivation experienced at the hand of its mother.
>
> Deprivation, we have said, is a necessary, but clearly not a sufficient condition for the establishment of the distinction between the self and the object. The process of distinguishing has a cognitive or perceptual side; it is thus dependent on the maturation of the child's perceptual equipment.[2]

At this stage of development the conflict lies between an inner demand in the little being and an outer demand from the mother. The child turns then to an investment of love in the person of the mother, the object through whom the gratification is received and who he soon discovers is necessary for any of this wonderful indulgence. This does not mean that he is entirely happy about the whole situation. He is not pleased over the waiting or giving up the demand for immediate gratification and yet he feels he must withhold his displeasure for fear he will lose the beloved object through whom the gratification is received. The groundwork is laid for ambivalence that will continue with him to some extent throughout his entire life.

In the earliest days he was a passive little being to whom the mother ministered but as he develops and can begin to see clearly, he attempts to do to the mother what she does to him. An identity of his own is emerging. His attempt to feed his mother in these early months is not that he feels so altruistic toward his nice mother, but that he is now assuming through the use of his own healthy aggression a self that can do what is done to him. His own ego is coming into being when he discovers that he can use his own energies to cope with reality. At the same time he must constantly make peace with the nurturing figure, whom he needs, by complying with the demands of the mother.

As can be seen, this concept of self, his own ego, his ability to test reality and make some peace between his own inner drives and outer demands does not happen over night, but has been in the process of construction from his earliest days. Throughout these early times he has tried on various ways of behaving in order to bring some peace to himself. He must find ways of avoiding the anxiety over the possible

---

[2] Heinz Hartmann, M.D., Ernst Kris, Ph.D., Rudolph M. Loewenstein, M.D., "Comments on the Formation of Psychic Structure," in *The Psychoanalytic Study of the Child,* Vol. II, (New York: International Universities Press, 1947), p. 20.

loss of the beloved mother whose approval he needs and from whom he receives gratification. Yet his own inner drives are ever present and in and of themselves may constitute a danger to him. As one small boy, who had been kept in a very passive state by the mother, stated, "But there'll be no more me." At the same time, in order to avoid anxiety he must reject his own impulses as alien to him. He then experiments with ways of behaving that will help him to avoid the anxiety that comes with the conflict. He wants to do a particular thing but mother doesn't approve so he says, "Joey not crying, Mama, red chair crying." He may deny that the behavior is his at all or he may take on the opposite behavior and consider the original behavior repulsive. Thus his defenses are being formed and awareness of the original impulses is sent under cover and is no longer a part of his consciousness.

More and more the same manner of handling his life situations is used until it is a repetitive way of behaving of which he is no longer consciously aware. He may rationalize, he may regress to an earlier form of behavior, escape into fantasy, turn to the opposite way of behaving, project the behavior on to someone else or sublimate the original desire into a socially acceptable way of behaving. Whatever means he selects to avoid the conflict, he is no longer aware of why he is doing what he is doing when he meets situations tinged with the original conflict. His defenses become his personal armor. When the teacher asks, "Why did you do that?" and he replies, "I don't know," he well may not know and at this point could not do differently if he wished.

At the same time that his ego is developing an appropriate or inappropriate set of defenses he is identifying with the demands of his parents so that the demands no longer are theirs but become his own demands on himself. His ego-ideal, the person he would like to be, is forming. Even though reality may at times permit certain behavior, if his ego-ideal will not permit it he suffers with guilt feelings even over the desire to do. This development of self with its set of defenses, combined with the development of the ego-ideal gets its final refinement with the discovery of the differences between boys and girls and the child's turning finally to the parent of the same sex with whom he identifies. This implies of course that he has had an adequate balance of gratification and limitation from both parents and extremes of the scale from neither parent. When the balance is upset the child faces real conflict over what he really is as a self.

It is at the height of this identification that he enters school. Even if everything has gone well he is not so sure that the parent of the same sex is not his rival. This, of course, stems from his early feelings of rivalry with this parent. Now his concept of self is beginning to solidify. He is finally finding ways of making peace among his inner demands, the ideal he has set for himself and his recognition of what is permitted in reality. A synthesis of all the functions that will come under the control of his ego is taking place. His perception, his memory function, his motility, his thinking, among other functions come under the control of his ego.

EARLY NURTURE HAS BEEN COLORING HIS PERCEPTIONS.

The development of the defenses is not pathological but a necessary process in the socialization of the human being, but the quality of those defenses, whether they are in the child or the teacher, will color his perceptions of people, of himself, and situations in his life. The amount of energy necessary to keep old wishes in abeyance and to make peace among his inner demands, his ego-ideal, and the demands of reality as tested by his own ego will dictate the amount of energy available for learning. All of his early nurture has been affecting this energy distribution and coloring his perceptions. His own biological make-up will also affect this energy distribution. Thus, if his reality concept of himself is fairly well in line with his ego-ideal, he will not use excessive energy handling guilt feelings stemming from his conscience and out of line with reality. If he has successfully repressed old wishes but not at the expense of his personality, he is able to allow himself adequate gratification and at the same time will be able to move, from direct gratification, in many areas, to ideation and gratification gained through thought or sublimated in some socially acceptable activity. It may be seen then that his learning is dependent upon the stage of maturation of his own biological apparatus, the reaction of the environment, his tolerance for frustration and, finally, on the pleasure he derives from mastery of the situation and the pleasure afforded by the learning itself.[3]

The Teacher Tries to Understand the Student's Viewpoint

The teacher will need then to look closely at the ways in which each student perceives his world. For example, Miss French has Cathy in her fourth grade class. Cathy shows constant fawning behavior toward the teacher. She clings to the teacher and her conversation is filled with many declarations of love. At the same time any demands for production of school work are met with delaying tactics and the attitude, "You can't expect much of me because I'm just a stupid little girl." Cathy's role with the other children is one of constantly playing the fool. She falls out of her seat, utters nonsense sentences, makes facial grimaces and then wonders why the others call her, "crazy Cathy." She complains to Miss French often that the others are mistreating her. From steady observation it is soon found that this ten year old constantly denies that the expressed behavior is hers. She places all blame for her troubles onto the other children. She can read and spell but her repetitive pattern of behavior is one of not carrying out the ordinary demands of the classroom. One thing Miss French has noticed is that this child never seems to get angry with her teacher. It's as if she constantly had to keep peace with the teacher. It is apparent that she is able to learn but for some reason not known to the teacher she puts herself in the position of being a failure. On investigation, even though the teacher has recognized the repetitive pattern of behavior in the child, she finds that Cathy's mother is acting as a tutor every

[3] *Ibid.*, p. 26.

evening at home. Hours are spent at long lists of spelling words and over the reading book. At the same time this mother does not insist that Cathy assume any responsibility for herself. She picks up Cathy's clothes that are thrown on the bedroom floor and each morning goes through the same struggle of trying to get the girl up so she will not be late for school. Miss French now sees that:

1. Cathy has the maturation for the learning tasks.
2. No matter what she does, the environmental reaction is one of expecting her to fail.
3. By not making normal demands on Cathy her mother has not assisted her in tolerating frustration. At the same time Cathy is very much afraid that she will lose her mother's affection as well as her teacher's and must repeatedly tell them that she loves them.
4. Because the mother has taken on so much of the responsibility for the achievement by tutoring and picking up after the girl she has not allowed Cathy the pleasure of her own learning and mastery.

This wise teacher who now begins to understand why Cathy looks at things the way she does begins to work with the mother in such a way that she helps the mother to see that she has a right to expect Cathy to take care of her own things and that she must be the one responsible for picking up her clothes, for getting herself to school on time and for her own learning. Both the teacher and the mother now assume the attitude, "I know that you're capable of doing your own work." This attitude in and of itself is a positive one and a compliment to the child. They no longer express to Cathy how "awful" *they* feel because she cannot do certain things, but rather how "awful" *she* must feel when she isn't able to perform in relation to her own capabilities. By the same premise they no longer take on the pleasure of her mastery and learning but return it to her with, "How proud *you* must feel that you are able to accomplish this." Although neither of them recognize another dynamic factor at this time, it is soon found that Cathy is no longer afraid of her own aggression and beset with guilt over her hostile feelings toward her mother who would not let her grow up. As both the teacher and the mother make consistent and reasonable demands of Cathy and do not keep her in the passive position of being cared for constantly, the child can then express healthy objections and does not have to utilize her energies keeping her normal aggression under cover. She now has the energy available for some self-realization. Although Miss French at no time attempted to act as a therapist, she did discover that Cathy had legitimate reasons for behaving the way she did and by working with the mother to change some factors in the environment she was able to make it possible for the child to find a new energy distribution and a new concept of herself.

This teacher might have tried to protect Cathy from the hostility of the other children by always volunteering to be her partner when the others did not choose her or she could have punished Cathy for not doing her work. Instead, by gathering some information she was able to understand how and why the child's perception was the way it was.

Many times the expressed perception of a child will not be based on the nature of his defenses but will be allied with a reality situation. Frank was in Mr. Jones' fifth grade during the Second World War. The students were studying about the Puritans. In the course of the discussion, Frank spoke up and said, "I don't see any difference between the Puritans and the Nazis." This remark brought forth violent objections from the other children who at the time of war considered anything connected with American history as particularly sacred. Mr. Jones' first impulse was to tell Frank not to be "so smart." Instead he quieted the others down and said, "Let's let Frank explain what he means." Because of the good relationship with the teacher the students were willing to hold off temporarily. Frank then replied, "Well, they wouldn't let anyone who believed something different from their ideas live in the colony. They said they were witches and punished them." Very quickly the children saw the analogy that he was drawing and began to expand the idea. In this situation, Mr. Jones might have passed the comment off quickly and felt that he must now study Frank to see why he behaved as he did. However, in his own security as a teacher he could invite the student to expound further on his idea and discovered that this was a child who was really thinking.

By looking at each case individually and withholding judgment, the teacher will take time to see whether he really understands the way in which situations look to the child at any point of time. He will ask himself if the feelings sent to him as a teacher and to the other students really belong to the child as a person or whether they belong to figures from another point of time in the child's life. However, he will not err by feeling that all positive feelings sent to him by the student belong to him as a person and that the negative feelings belong to the parental figures alone. In other words, just as he assists the students in appraisal of reality, he will also refine his own reality perception.

The Teacher Recognizes That the Student's Present Behavior Is Necessary to Him

In trying to understand the behavior of boys and girls, the teacher will need to ask himself several things. First, he will ask himself if the behavior seen is typical of a particular developmental period. Second, he will want to know if the behavior is the result of a cultural expectation. Finally, he will study the situation to see whether the present behavior is a part of the defensive process built out of the life experiences of the young person.

Developmental behavior. The research of Gesell and Ilg, of Havighurst, Olson, Wattenberg, and others has shown that there are developmental patterns quite common to all children. Havighurst presents tasks in terms of cultural expectations. Olson takes the biological maturation into consideration showing that each child has his own unique constellation. Chapter 2 has presented these viewpoints more fully.[4, 5, 6, 7]

In trying to understand the behavior of boys and girls in the class, the teacher will need to familiarize himself with the developmental expectations for any particular period of growth. For example, he will not expect children of nursery age to have the controls of children in the kindergarten. Again, he will expect a longer attention span of children in the middle elementary grades and expect their partner choices to be members of the same sex. He will expect boys and girls of the early pubertal years to be beset with conflicts related to their glandular development. He will know that at this period the focus is thrown back on the body and that young persons vacillate between escape into the intellectual and into physical indulgence. He will know that there is an approximate difference of eighteen months in the maturation of boys and girls. What then will this mean to him in trying to understand the behavior he sees?

For example, in the case of Cathy, the teacher through observa-

---

[4] Arnold Gesell and Frances L. Ilg, *Infant and Child in the Culture Today* (N.Y.: Harper and Brothers, 1943).

———, *The Child from Five to Ten* (N.Y.: Harper and Brothers, 1946).

Arnold Gesell and Louise Bates Adams, *Youth: The Years from Ten to Sixteen* (N.Y.: Harper and Brothers, 1956).

[5] Robert Havighurst, *Human Development and Education* (New York: Longmans, Green and Company, Inc., 1953).

[6] Willard Olson, *Child Development* (Boston: D. C. Heath and Co., 1949).

[7] William Wattenberg, *The Adolescent Years* (N.Y.: Harcourt, Brace and Co., 1955).

tion identified repetitive patterns of behavior utilized by the child. They were as follows:

1. Fails in work although she knows how to do it.
2. Repeatedly declares how much she loves the adult.
3. Has no friends among her classmates.
4. Plays the clown by uttering silly comments and falling out of her seat.
5. Is very careless about her personal appearance.
6. Blames the other children when things go wrong.

Next then, Miss French looked at this behavior to determine whether it was typical or atypical of most ten year old girls. She found that in every case most girls of this age period do not show these behavior patterns and that they must stem from some psychological need of the child.

If she had found that on the whole these were typical patterns of behavior of girls within this age range, she would then need to ask herself why the behavior was so irritating to her as a teacher or why she perceived it as so unusual. She would also have to keep in mind that there are some children who in the uniqueness of their own biology will behave more like children who are younger than their chronological age and others who will behave more like children who are older.

Quite different from the case of Cathy is that of Stan, a fourteen year old in the tenth grade. Throughout his elementary school and junior high careers, Stan was an excellent student. In the earlier grades he had been double-promoted so that he was a year younger than most of his fellow tenth grade students. His past school record was well known to Mr. Collins, his geometry teacher. Stan was very much interested in geometry and brought in many examples of the nature of proof. He was very excited over the idea of the theorem being the generalization arrived at through experimentation. At the first card marking, Mr. Collins was quite concerned to discover that Stan was barely passing in his English class taught by Miss Gentry. Because of his interest in the boy he discussed the case with Miss Gentry. She stated that she thought Stan was being influenced by Bob who was not a good student and whose behavior in class was quite disturbing to her. He made jokes about everything and one day when she threatened to give him a "pink slip" for after-school-detention he said, "Wouldn't I look silly in a pink slip." When she ordered him out of the room Stan came to his defense and said she "couldn't take a joke."

Although Miss Gentry realized that Bob's case was one to be handled separately she felt strongly about the relationship between the two boys. They were inseparable and Stan constantly played the role of champion for Bob. On the other hand she realized that Bob looked up to Stan and had to admit that although Bob was not a capable student he seemed to try hard in the classes in which Stan was interested. As the two teachers talked over the situation they discovered that Stan did less well in classes where he had a woman teacher. Miss Gentry did not realize that he was a year younger than the rest of the students. When both Mr. Collins and she examined the repetitive behavior of Stan they found it to be typical for his age group. For example, he was in an age period where it is not unusual for students to do much better work in the subjects in which they are interested. They also recalled that puberty is a time of development when, because of the biological changes taking place, the young person must, in a sense, reorganize his concept of self and reorganize the balance between his own impulses, his ideal, and the reality situation. They remembered that it is not unusual for students at this period of their lives to shy away from members of the opposite sex and to seek stronger identifications with adult members of the same sex. They knew, too, that oftentimes boys and girls in puberty have one best friend who becomes a sort of mirror for them. Sometimes the mirror does not behave in a way that is a true image of the individual but rather shows an opposite type of behavior. The mirror then becomes either the impulsive side of the struggling personality or it may be the controlled side. These wise teachers then understood the meaning of the relationship and decided that the best person to help both of these boys would be a man. Miss Gentry found, too, that when she took the "wise cracking" of Bob less seriously, he no longer used it to make her angry. She found that she had been responding in a "face saving" way with the boys and because of her defensiveness she showed these boys a weak spot in her own personal armor that they could use to try out their masculine superiority.

Cultural expectation. In order to understand the way in which a child perceives his world, it will be necessary for the teacher to understand the expectations of the culture from which the child comes. It is a sad commentary that in schools largely attended by children of lower socio-economic groups the children are perceived as less adequate than the children of upper or middle socio-economic groups. The judgments made of children are largely constructed on the basis

of the words that children use and the degree to which the focus is moved away from their bodies. Negotiation of relationships on a body level is largely taboo in our institutions of learning. For example, it is bad to fight; one doesn't demonstrate affection by direct physical contact in public; mention of bodily processes is forbidden. At the same time many children come from cultural patterns where life proceeds largely on a bodily instinctual level and there is such a large degree of direct gratification that there is little energy reserved for ideation or intellectual pursuit. This does not mean that these children do not have the capacities to be developed, but it does mean that they can be helped to delay gratification and find pleasure in the use of words.

Jim, who is in kindergarten settles his disputes with others by his fists. This is a common pattern in his home and in his community. It is hard for him to understand why his teacher doesn't like this way even though other adults whom he knows tell him to "knock the block off" anyone who interferes with his pursuits. His wise teacher understands why he looks at things in this way and yet she must help him to learn new patterns of operation. She says to him, "I know you're angry and it's all right to be angry when you have a reason, but I can't let you hit Mary. You can tell Mary you're angry and she must not interfere with your blocks." The teacher at no time gives Jim the feeling that people don't get angry when there is a justifiable cause, but

IT WILL BE NECESSARY TO UNDERSTAND THE EXPECTATIONS OF THE CULTURE.

rather that he can get relief for his feelings by expressing them in appropriate language. Words then don't become bothersome abstractions but satisfying concepts with real meaning.

Rejection of the culture from which a child comes implies rejection of the base where he has his strongest emotional tie and in and of itself is threatening to the child. Helping him to refine his perceptions of situations and to find new ways of negotiating his relationships makes the behavior his own rather than one imposed from without. Allison Davis [8] has contributed a great deal to the research in this field. He has shown that teachers and counselors have their own cultural norms which they try to impose on their students.

Many children are perceived by their teachers as unintelligent because their word usage is quite different from that of the teacher. Their language patterns, stemming largely from their culture, are such that they, too, perceive what they hear in a different way. A school psychologist was giving a Binet Test to a six year old Negro boy. When the boy was asked what the word "Mars" meant he replied, "You see it's like this. If you wears a new dress, I says, 'Lady, I 'mires your dress.' " The same child, who is a native of New York City, in response to the word "roar" said, "People shouldn't eat rawr meat." These are, of course, wrong responses, but they fit the way the child hears these words in his own cultural group and certainly indicate that this is a child of social sensitivity and one who has been able to learn. Without taking this perception into consideration, think of the many problems his teacher will have in helping this child to read. Think also of the problems that will arise if the teacher's perception of his intellectual capacity is based entirely on his score on this intelligence test alone.

Another example of differences in language pattern occurred in a city in the midwest. The teacher who was a New Englander had shown some slides to her fifth grade class as an introduction to a study of the Panama Canal. As she talked she repeatedly mentioned the "Panamar Canal." When she finished she stepped to the board and wrote out, "Panama Canal." A child raised his hand and said, "Mrs. Foley, you left the 'r' off Panamar." Auditory perceptions are not always the same for student and teacher.

---

[8] Allison Davis, "Child Training and Social Class," in *Child Behavior and Development,* Barker, Kounin, and Wright, editors (New York: McGraw-Hill and Company, 1943), p. 607.

——— and Robert Havighurst, *Father of the Man* (Boston: Houghton-Mifflin, 1947).

Behavior as a part of the defenses. Again referring to Cathy, it was seen that her repetitive behavior was not typical for her developmental period. Further examination showed that it did not stem from a cultural norm but rather from her relationship to her mother. She was not consciously aware that she was continually angry with her mother and felt guilty over her hostility. She could not allow herself to be aware of the hostility, so to avoid the conflict she had adopted the opposite behavior of the over-loving child. However, her hostility "reared its ugly head" in spite of all of the energy used to repress it, namely, through her refusal to learn. Indirectly she was continually punishing herself because the failure reflected on her as well as on her mother. To point this out to the child even if one were quite sure of the dynamics would have been most inappropriate because she could not have behaved differently if she tried. In any event she would have to rebuff such an interpretation because it would threaten her whole psychological equilibrium. She can only change her perceptions when she has gained the insight for herself through new experiences.

The teacher will know that the child's behavior stems from his defenses and that the motivation for that behavior is not available to him on a conscious level. He will know also that even though he may command that behavior to disappear under the threat of punishment it will not be modified by the child himself and become a part of his own internal discipline because giving up this behavior means reviving the conflict of an earlier time. The attendant anxiety would be intolerable to the child. This will not call for a new energy distribution or a refined perception of himself. It will merely mean that the child will find some other way to keep the conflict in abeyance. For example, a teacher and parent succeeded in getting a nine year old boy, under threat of severe physical punishment, to give up hitting out at others, but this did not prevent a new symptom from appearing—that of setting fires under porches.

Although there are developmental characteristics for boys and girls, the wise teacher will know that defenses are normal for everyone and that over and above typical developmental behavior each individual will have his own particular ways of handling his life experiences. His perception, his memory function, his ideation, his motility and, indeed, the quality of his personal relations will stem from the uniqueness of his own pattern of life experiences and his own biology.

Good teaching then, from the guidance point of view, will concern itself with really trying to know how the child perceives his situation.

It will provide experiences for the child so that he has the opportunity to assess reality and become aware of his own perceptions and those of others. It will offer him the opportunity to explore with safety, to disagree and to state why he disagrees, to take responsibility for his own acts instead of having someone else assume that responsibility, and, finally, it will return the pleasure of mastery and learning to him.

Summary

In trying to understand the perceptions of his students, the teacher will ask himself:

1. Is the behavior a response to a reality situation?
2. Is the behavior within the range of the developmental behavior that I may expect from this age child?
3. Is the behavior the result of a cultural expectation that can be modified with new experiences?
4. Is the behavior the result of mechanisms of defense necessary for this child to maintain his psychic equilibrium and his personal integrity?

Understanding the causation is important so that a milieu can be created in which it is possible for each child within his own biological endowment to utilize his energies for his best possible growth. The milieu must contain within it a respect for the integrity of the child and a positive expectation that he has within him the capacity to become increasingly mature through the utilization of new experiences and knowledge. In seeking to understand the perceptions of the child the teacher refines his own perceptions and thereby increases his own maturity. With the children, he selects experiences appropriate to their developmental level, necessary for widening their cultural horizons and of help to the child whose defenses make it necessary to use socially unacceptable behavior or to deplete his energies at the expense of full utilization of his potentials.

Selected Readings

Blos, Peter, *The Adolescent Personality*. New York: D. Appleton Century, 1941.

Buxbaum, Edith, *Your Child Makes Sense*. New York: International Universities Press, 1949.

Cantor, Nathaniel, *The Teaching-Learning Process*. New York: Dryden Press, 1953.

Clifton, Eleanor and Florence Hollis, editors, *Child Therapy, a Casework Symposium*. New York: Family Service Association of America, 1948.

Davis, Allison, "Child Training and Social Class," in *Child Behavior and Development,* Roger Barker, Jacob Kounin, and Herbert Wright, editors. New York: McGraw-Hill Book Co., 1943.

———, and Robert Havighurst, *Father of the Man.* Boston: Houghton-Mifflin Co., 1947.

D'Evelyn, Kathryn, *Meeting Children's Emotional Needs.* Englewood Cliffs, N. J.: Prentice-Hall, Inc., 1957.

Freud, Anna, *Psychoanalysis for Parents and Teachers.* New York: Emerson Books, Inc., 1935.

Gesell, Arnold and Louise Bates, *Youth: the Years from Ten to Sixteen.* New York: Harper and Brothers, 1956.

Gesell, Arnold, and Frances L. Ilg, *Infant and Child in the Culture Today.* New York: Harper and Brothers, 1943.

———, *The Child from Five to Ten.* New York: Harper and Brothers, 1946.

Hartman, Heinz, Ernst Kris, and Rudolph Lowenstein, "Comments on the Formation of Psychic Structure," in *The Psychoanalytic Study of the Child,* Vol. II. New York: International Universities Press, 1946.

Havighurst, Robert, *Human Development and Education.* New York: Longmans, Green and Co., 1953.

Olson, Willard, *Case Method Applied to Recurring Educational Problems.* Chicago: American Council on Education, 1940.

Prescott, Daniel, *The Child in the Educative Process.* New York: McGraw-Hill, 1957.

Redl, Fritz, and William Wattenberg, *Mental Hygiene in Teaching.* New York: Harcourt, Brace and Co., 1951.

Wattenberg, William, *The Adolescent Years.* New York: Harcourt, Brace and Co., 1955.

CHAPTER 4

The Teacher Takes a Closer Look at Some Children

The Teacher Discovers That Misbehavior Is a Symptom

Although all teachers would hope that they were assisting young people to grow and mature in their own unique patterns of development, sometimes they find it difficult to tolerate some types of behavior. Indeed, this is to be expected because the teacher is the product of his own individual biology and experiences. Over and above the difficulties that may or may not arise from the personality of the teacher, there are types of behavior that are more disruptive to the learning situation than others. For example, Wickman[1] conducted a study to determine the types of behavior that teachers thought serious and the types of behavior that mental hygienists thought serious. Teachers tended to rate "acting out" and aggressive behavior more serious than did the mental hygienists. For many years this study was used to show that perhaps teachers were not as insightful or as understanding as the mental hygienists. The fallacy of this interpretation was that the situations for the mental hygienists in contrast to the situations of the teachers were not taken into consideration. Oftentimes, mental hygienists were working in one-to-one situations while the teachers would of necessity be working in group situations. Mental hygienists working in therapeutic relationships were not in the position of constantly having to ally with the controls side of the child. Teachers, in contrast, because of needing to promote learning in the group found that alliance with the controls side of the child was their normal role and overt behavior that disturbed the learning situation would naturally be considered more serious by them.

[1] E. K. Wickman, *Children's Behavior and Teachers' Attitudes* (New York: The Commonwealth Fund, Division of Publications, 1928).

In spite of the fact that any good teacher assists the child with his controls, the teacher who ignores the causes of misbehavior on the part of the child will very rarely be able to help the child to learn academically. When disturbing behavior arises, it is not enough to force it under cover if the learner is to be helped to find a new concept of himself and a new distribution of his energies. As was pointed out in the last chapter, modification of behavior requires an awareness on the part of the individual that the behavior is no longer necessary for him. This does not mean, however, that nothing will be done, but rather we will study the situation in order to arrive at appropriate means for bringing change. The behavior that we don't like is merely a symptom and it is not enough to treat the symptom if lasting change is to be brought about. Temporary means used to check the behavior should not be perceived as the final action. Rather, using many of the means mentioned in Chapters 5 and 6, we will try to discover the cause of the symptoms that we see.

Our first step will be to ask ourselves whether the behavior is truly disturbing to the learning situation or whether we are over-reacting because of some feelings within ourselves. Do I feel this way because I see this behavior as interfering with the learning of the other boys and girls or is this type of behavior just disturbing to me? Does the behavior disadvantage the child himself or does it just make me uncomfortable? In examining our own reactions however, we must not be so hard on ourselves that we always find the blame within ourselves; we must be honest with ourselves if we are to help the students. Recognizing our own feelings makes it possible for us to be concerned with the feelings of others, to create an atmosphere of receptivity so that children can also be honest in the recognition that the behavior belongs to them.

This last point is related to the concept of identification, a most necessary one in learning. The student's wish to identify with the teaching figure makes it possible for him to approach the tasks of school with enthusiasm. Teachers who put all blame for misbehavior on the children make it difficult for the children to identify with them or with the goals of the school, and many times make school experiences sour for the children.

Non-learning and misbehavior are disturbing to teachers. No two cases of either will have exactly the same cause even though the behavior is the same on the surface. Each will be unique in its causation but each time we study a particular case we become more skillful

IDENTIFICATION IS MOST NECESSARY FOR LEARNING.

with the next. It is not enough to say, "He acts this way because of h family background," or "He has a rejecting parent." Study of the cas implies that we must understand what the behavior means to the chil and why he finds it necessary to continue with it.

The Student May Be Untaught

This may sound peculiar to persons engaged in teaching becau they would immediately say that there is no one who is untaugh However, if we as teachers would examine the ways we have dea with some children, we would find that we have had some behavior expectations for a particular child just because we belong to grou in which most children of these ages know these things. Some childre because of their experiences, may not show the behavior we desi because they have not been taught to behave in these ways.

Bobby is a five year old in kindergarten. Whenever he wants som thing he helps himself. It doesn't seem to matter whether the crayo he desires belong to Joe or whether the lunch belongs to Mary. Wh Bobby wants, he takes. During his first days in kindergarten the a was filled by loud protests from the other children, tears and fightin When the teacher felt she would finally have to exclude him from t group she asked Bobby's mother to come for a conference. She explained to her that Bobby looked puzzled, surprised, and actually hurt when she tried to help him to see that he could not interfere with the rights of others. At other times when there was no question about the use of possessions he seemed friendly to the other boys and girls and to the teacher. However, she added that the other children were beginning to avoid Bobby even at these times. The mother looked distressed and finally said, "I'm ashamed to say that that is our fault for two reasons. First, we have moved around so much in Bobby's early years that he has had little contact with other children. He is our only child and both my husband and I have always thought it fine that he was so selfsufficient that he would help himself. Also, I realize that so much of our time has been spent in hotels or small apartments that we would give in to Bobby rather than have him make any noise. I can see now that we were wrong."

The teacher and mother worked out a plan of action for helping Bobby. They decided to be consistent in their demands in school and at home. They agreed that they would both explain to Bobby and would tell him that it would take a little practice on his part in order to accomplish the change. They would be patient but the accomplishment must be his.

In another situation the 8B's were going to give a luncheon party for the graduating 8A's. Whenever they were making their plans Marva would keep absolutely silent. When the girls planned the table setting she withdrew entirely. This was not typical behavior for Marva and Miss Stanton was quite concerned. One day she asked Marva to help her after school and while they worked together she began to discuss the party. Suddenly Marva's eyes filled with tears and she said, "Miss Stanton, I can't come to that party." When her kindly teacher asked why she replied, "I never sat at a party table. I wouldn't know what to do. At home we don't eat together around a table. Everybody helps himself and at school I bring my lunch in a paper and just eat it out of that. I wouldn't know how to act at that party." The girl's anxiety was lowered when Miss Stanton arranged that Marva and she would eat lunch together at a table in the room, with Miss Stanton and Marva planning what they would have, setting the table together and practicing their company manners on each other.

Different mores and modes of behavior oftentimes must be learned by children when they are confronted with the demands of the school. Trouble arises when we take it for granted that all children already know certain things just because these are the expected behaviors in the school.

The Student May Be Reacting to Factors in His Environment

Shirley, a fifteen year old in the tenth grade, suddenly took on the role of constant critic of Mr. Shore, her history teacher. When he suggested that the students preview films to pick those they wished to show for the work of any committee she would say to him, "What's the use of our previewing them. You talk about democracy but you really know which ones you'll make us see." This kind of behavior was startling to the teacher who had had Shirley in the ninth grade and had found her to be a most cooperative student. One day he asked her to remain after class. He tried to discuss the situation with her but she burst into tears and said, "I like you but I can't tell you about it." He talked with her further and asked her if she would like to talk to her counsellor about it if she found it hard to talk with him. She agreed to see her counsellor.

Several days later Shirley told Mr. Shore that she would like to have him talk with her counsellor. She said, "I still can't talk with you about it, but I want you to understand and Miss Roberts said she would explain it to you." Mr. Shore sought out Miss Roberts who told him that there was an amazing series of coincidences that had built up in relation to Shirley. The youngest child in Shirley's family was eleven and her mother was pregnant again. In her pubertal way Shirley was upset about her mother's having another baby and angry with both of her parents over it. She had begun to fantasy that now she would never have time for herself and would have to care for the baby. She didn't dare to confront her mother with this unreasonable thinking, and to punish herself for her ideas had behaved in an unreasonable way, demanding privileges that her father could not grant. In her mind she accused him of being too strict. She then transferred her feelings to her teacher from her father who had so many things in common with him, being also a teacher of history and social studies and having graduated from the same college. When she was able to talk to her woman counsellor and was able to recognize her own feelings she could then allow her well-liked teacher in on the, so far well-kept secret.

Another example of a child's reaction to her environment is illustrated in the case of Anna, a nine year old girl. Anna was tardy nearly every morning and every afternoon. Her fourth grade teacher felt very angry over the tardiness because he could not get Anna to tell him why she was tardy. Along with being tardy Anna had not brought her school supplies and it was already the second week of the semester. He had also sent home a note about the school supplies but to date Anna had not brought them. He finally referred the case to the attendance officer. On investigation it was found that Anna's mother worked and her father was ill. There were four younger children in the home and Anna saw two of those to kindergarten and first grade every day along with four other kindergarten children. The parents of the additional four were neighbors who collectively had promised Anna seventy-five cents a week if she would take the children back and forth. Getting all of the small ones to their respective lines and rooms was quite a task for Anna who was always caught out of her room when the bell rang.

When the teacher had finally gathered all the data he began to see Anna's situation from her point of view. He found that she wanted to earn the money so that she could get her supplies and he also began to understand the fatigue that the child was showing in school, fatigue he had not noticed as such before. He thought she was lazy and he was very angry when she actually had fallen asleep in class. He finally arranged to see the mother on her day off and found that Anna, the oldest, was doing most of the housework as well as caring for the younger ones. The mother told him that the supplies could not be bought until her payday the next week. Later when he understood and began to help Anna by getting her load lightened at home and by supplying her with materials to tide her over until she could get her own, they became good friends. One day he said to Anna, "Why didn't you tell me what was happening?" She replied, "I couldn't because all you did was fuss at me about being tardy and not having my supplies. I was scared to tell you."

From these cases one can readily see that a symptom is not always based in deep psychological causation but may be a reaction of the child to a set of reality circumstances. Another example is a boy, seven years old, who always seemed to be tired when he arrived at school. When his teacher talked with him he said that he had to cut a cord of wood before he came to school each day. His teacher asked him how much a cord of wood was. He paced off a large area in front of the blackboard and also showed her how high a cord of wood would be when stacked up. On investigation it was revealed that the boy's father earned his living by clearing part of his land next to his farm. The father said, "Of course he cuts a cord of wood a day. I have to have some help and when I was a boy in the old country I used to work that way." Through talking with the father the teacher helped him to recall that at age seven he was not expected to do the kind of heavy labor in a short period of time that he was expecting of his son. They agreed that the boy would help him cut some wood but not a cord before coming to school every morning.

Wise teachers try to make themselves aware of the reality circumstances in the lives of their students and will make every effort to reduce extremes wherever they can. One ninth grade teacher helped several boys in his classes by organizing a "breakfast club." The boys came early and cooked their own breakfast. He had found these boys to be low-energy students in his morning classes and discovered that they got their own breakfasts and of course wouldn't bother if they had to eat alone. Their tardiness decreased and their attitude toward school improved. Unfortunately, many of the young people with whom we work often have reality problems that cannot be solved so readily. However, if the student feels that his teacher is concerned over his problems and does try to help in any way that he can, it is likely that the feelings toward the school will be more positive than they would be if the stress in school was just as great as in life outside of school.

THE STUDENT MAY NOT BE ABLE TO RELATE TO OTHERS.

The Student May Not Be Able to Relate Himself to Others

We know that the repetitive behavior used by people is a necessity for them whether it is based in reality or stems from the avoidance of conflict between inner drives and outer demands; but sometimes we feel that by putting a shy or withdrawn student with "nice kids," or an openly hostile one with understanding students, the behavior will magically change. What we do not seem to keep in mind is that these young people became shy and withdrawn or openly hostile because of relationships with people in their lives. They have learned to armor themselves with their present behavior whether it be fawning behavior such as Cindy's or a very tough exterior. They have learned their roles and concepts of themselves through the attitudes expressed toward them in the environment. Parental offerings of affection, rejection, or indifference have shaped the concepts these young people have of themselves and others. These concepts are built up over a long period of years and will take a long time to change. This does not mean, however, that we will give up in discouragement. Instead, we must find out what those concepts are; how much this particular child can tolerate in the way of personal relations; whether the modifications can be made in the classroom situation alone or whether we must ask for help. The damage was done through relationships with others and the repair must come through the same process.

Jimmie was spending his second year in the first grade. His teacher felt that this seven year old was not very bright. When she tried to talk to him he would turn away and shrug his shoulders. If she did receive an answer to a question, Jimmie would stutter badly. However she had heard him talking to his little sister in the hall and he had not stuttered at all. The teacher who had had Jimmie the year before said that she didn't think he would improve. "His brother is the same way. He's two years behind now." However, Mrs. Webster, Jimmie's present teacher, felt that there must be something amiss here because she had heard him say something about "the abandoned house" to one of his classmates and she didn't feel that such words would be in the vocabulary of a slow seven year old. She decided to refer Jimmie for a psychological examination. Although the waiting period was long Mrs. Webster felt it worth while when the psychologist reported that this was a child of superior intelligence who was severely handicapped in his learning because of emotional problems. Jimmie was referred for further help on an intensive basis.

Through the work of the therapist and her own observations, now more closely focused on Jimmie, Mrs. Webster came to realize that this was a very frightened little boy who wanted to be big and strong and to conquer others. However, she finally detected that in his reading group he even let Willie, the boy next to him, get away with biting his ear without complaining. To the therapist this boy looked like a child who had been physically beaten.

From the work of the therapist it was found that this child had not been physically beaten by the parents. The father said, "We never beat him. We always strapped his brother and it hasn't done any good. He's nine and he soils his clothes to this day. We never tried it on Jim." In the course of the work with Jimmie it was found that the father was correct. *He* had not beaten Jimmie but the brother who could not retaliate to the father took his vengeance out on Jimmie by beating him whenever he could. When Jimmie tried to get back at him through words the mother silenced them both by putting adhesive over their mouths and making them sit quietly in a chair without moving. The only one Jimmie felt really comfortable with was his sister who was in the kindergarten. He felt that another sister, the youngest, got most of the mother's attention.

When Mrs. Webster learned to look more closely at Jimmie's productions she found that given a free opportunity Jimmie had been telling her about himself all along. She remembered a drawing he had made of a small figure holding up large barbells. The story he had given her was, "The guy weighs ninety-nine pounds. Each barbell weighs one hundred pounds." She soon saw that his free drawings were all about "crooks," "booby-traps," and trying to escape from the murderers. Here indeed was a very frightened little boy who didn't dare to use any healthy aggression.

Such children cannot be helped in the classroom alone but will require long time individual help.

Sylvia was seventeen and a senior in high school. She was periodically absent from school and when she would return she would bring excuses about being ill. Her home room teacher referred her case to the counselor because she was afraid that Sylvia would fail to graduate even though she knew that Sylvia intended to go to college. When the counselor talked with Sylvia she found that Sylvia was not ill in an organic sense but that at times she was so anxious that she could not go out of the house. Sylvia told her that her mother had taken her to the doctor but he had said that she would get over it if she "put her mind to it." In further conferences with the mother and the girl, the counselor found that Sylvia not only was afraid to go out at times, but that she also had several other problems.

First of all this teen-ager had many compulsive rituals that she went through. At night she would be beset with doubt as to whether she had turned the radio off and would get up and down many times to re-check. Next, she said she couldn't help staring at the clock in class and was afraid that her teachers would find out. And last but not least it was discovered that this girl had only one friend other than her sister. This friend was a Chinese girl at school. This was particularly significant because Sylvia's father would not tolerate any discussion of anything oriental and would not permit Sylvia to bring her friend home. Following an especially violent argument with her father Sylvia had run away and the parents were frantic in trying to find her.

The counselor also discovered that this very attractive girl had never had a date with a boy and that she panicked at the thought of being alone with a boy. The counselor and the teacher recognized that this was not a case that they could handle alone but through conferences with the mother and the girl were able to make a referral so that the girl could receive intensive therapy. The school worked closely with the clinic and with help from both sides they were able to keep this very sick girl in school and help her to graduate.

In both of these cases we have young people who cannot tolerate close relationships with others. If the school tried to bring change in the behavior of either student by persuasion or coercion the results may have been drastic. Giving either of these students pleasant workmates, although a kindly act, would not have solved the problems of either of them. Intensive therapeutic work was indicated in both cases and all the school could do was to be as supportive and as understanding as possible.

At times it seems easier for teachers to be supportive of quiet or withdrawn children but we must keep in mind that the tough and fighting student may also be a person who cannot relate to others without being overcome with anxiety. When we discover such students we know that special help is needed. Unfortunately, such help is not available in all places or long waiting lists make it difficult to get help for young people. In such cases all the teacher can do is to be realistic in a kindly way and not force such students into relationships with others until they show that they can tolerate them. This may mean a long time one-to-one relationship to the teacher or to the one

THE STUDENT MAY NOT BE ABLE TO DO THE SCHOOL WORK.

student with whom they may feel comfortable. One wise teacher handled such a situation in a high school by having the student give his oral reports to just one other student of his choice instead of to the whole class.

The Student May Not Be Able to Do the School Work

Ellen was in Miss Denton's sixth grade. Although the correct age for the grade placement, Ellen was having a great deal of trouble with arithmetic. Although she could read well, she seemed utterly helpless when the decimal system was introduced. At first Miss Denton thought that Ellen just didn't like arithmetic but using some diagnostic tests and analyzing Ellen's work with her, she found some glaring gaps in Ellen's knowledge. First she did not know her ordinary times tables. Second, although a good reader, Ellen did not seem to understand the process of problem solving namely, "What does the problem tell you; what does it ask; what process will I use to solve it?" This splendid piece of detection helped Miss Denton to make arithmetic more palatable to Ellen. First they made a chart of all times tables that Ellen kept in her notebook to refer to whenever she needed. Through using the correct form repetitively and removing the anxiety about not knowing, Ellen soon learned her tables and no longer needed the chart. Second, Miss Denton took a small group of students who all had trouble with the process of problem solving and through practicing the steps of problem solving in an orderly fashion the students began to enjoy the work.

In contrast to the simplicity of Ellen's case the situation for Vince was quite different. Vince was a new tenth grade student in a large comprehensive high school. He had recently arrived from a small rural area where he attended a small high school. According to his transfer he was to be placed in the college preparatory curriculum. Until testing could be carried out he was placed in the courses for which his transfer called. After two weeks he started to truant from school. He had handed in no school work and when he was present he was sullen and would mutter under his breath. Mr. Patton, his mathematics teacher, approached the counselor to see what had been done in Vince's case. Because of the pressure of the opening of school the testing of this transfer student had been put off.

Mr. Horton, the counselor, sent for Vince and in their discussion found that the school work was totally foreign to the boy. Vince agreed to take some tests suggested by Mr. Horton. Through the testing it was discovered that Vince's reading ability was on the fourth grade level and his aptitude tests showed that he was of low normal intellectual capacity. Mr. Horton in consultation with Vince, using the results of achievement, aptitude, and interest tests worked out a general program for Vince. He also arranged for remedial work in reading. Throughout the semester it was found that Vince no longer truanted, was enjoying his shop math course and showed steady improvement in his core class of English and Social Studies.

To guide children properly we see that it is not enough to assume that because young people are placed at a certain grade level that they are able to cope with the school work. Frustration, failure, and constant disciplinary action because of non-learning can create behavior problems. A full assessment of the case is necessary if we are to determine the cause of the behavior.

The Student May Have Special Abilities Which Have Not Been Recognized or Challenged

One evening one of the authors had been invited to moderate a panel for a group of teen-agers. The invitation had come from the teen group who had their own social club at a settlement house. The professional personnel of the settlement had not organized this group. They had organized themselves and then requested a place in which to meet and hold their dances. Their membership was close to fifty and they had earned enough money to buy their own juke box. When their club started, of their own volition they asked a couple in the neighborhood to be their chaperones. This particular evening was "parents' night." They had planned a panel of their own members to discuss "teen problems." The role of the moderator was one of handling questions and comments from the floor. They felt that parents had a right to comment or raise questions.

On the way to the meeting the moderator met a teacher who was from the junior high that most of these students attended. As we walked along he said, "See that girl just ahead, I wish we could get her to show some initiative in school. She barely 'jumps through the hoops' and at times I don't think anyone can get her to assume responsibility." When we arrived at the meeting we discovered that the girl to whom he had referred was the president of the organization. She opened the meeting with all the poise of a mature adult. She introduced the panel and the moderator and then took her place in the audience. As the meeting progressed she stepped out and later we discovered that she had gone to see if everything was going well with the committee on the "eats."

Over coffee later the teacher said, "Was I wrong! I suppose I could excuse myself by saying that she's probably too tired after all this activity to do anything special in school, but I don't think that's the answer. When I look back, I don't think we've ever given her the opportunity to use her leadership."

Many times because of our concern that children will learn what we think they ought to know at any particular time, we forget to focus on the individual and to try to determine whether we are really assisting him in using the special abilities he has. We tend to make assumptions about the capacities of our students without really knowing what they can do.

By contrast it was refreshing to see a sixth grade class returning from the library where the students had been hunting resource materials for a unit on prehistoric animals. Frank had a copy of one of H. G. Wells' books under his arm and the boy with him had some small pamphlets put out by a commercial concern. Both had found reading materials within their understanding and both boys were serving on the same study committee and making contributions within their abilities.

Summary

In addition to a general understanding of the ways in which young people develop their concepts of self and what behavior constitutes healthy developmental behavior we need to take a closer look at some children to discover whether they are functioning as near to maximum capacity as possible. When so doing we will ask ourselves several questions:

1. Does the behavior disadvantage the child?
2. Does the behavior make the learning situation difficult for the other children?
3. Is the behavior only disturbing to me as a teacher?
4. Am I assuming that a child has been taught some things just because I can generally expect that children of this age and of these cultural backgrounds know these things?
5. Do I know anything about the reality situations in which my students live? Are they responding in the only healthy way they know to some trying factors in their environment?
6. Is the causation more deep seated and of such a nature that the child will require specialized help?
7. Do I know what capacities and abilities the children really have?

Finally, we must keep in mind that for any behavior to be really serious it must appear over and over again. When we have identified the behavior that may be disadvantaging the child, we will keep in mind that this is merely a symptom and we will have to study the case in a more detailed way to determine the cause. Then we can devise ways of bringing help to the child. The following chapters offer many suggestions of techniques to help us do a better job of case study and understanding our students.

Selected Readings

Blos, Peter, *The Adolescent Personality.* New York: Appleton-Century-Crofts, 1941.

Cantor, Nathaniel, *The Teaching-Learning Process.* New York: Dryden Press, 1951.

Davis, Allison, and Robert Havighurst, *Father of the Man.* Boston: Houghton Mifflin Co., 1947.

D'Evelyn, Katherine, *Meeting Children's Emotional Needs.* Englewood Cliffs, N. J.: Prentice-Hall, Inc., 1957.

Freud, Anna, *Ego and Mechanisms of Defence.* New York: International Universities Press, 1946.

Havighurst, Robert, *Human Development and Education.* New York: Longmans, Green, and Co., 1953.

Prescott, Daniel, *The Child in the Educative Process.* New York: McGraw-Hill, 1957.

Redl, Fritz, and William Wattenberg, *Mental Hygiene in Teaching.* New York: Harcourt, Brace and Co., 1951.

Wattenberg, William, *The Adolescent Years.* New York: Harcourt, Brace and Co., 1955.

CHAPTER 5

The Teacher Studies Individuals Through Use of Data Collected by Informal Methods

The Teacher Observes the Student in Many Settings

Observation is the most ancient method of studying any phenomenon. It is still a valid procedure. In fact, the scientific instruments of the modern laboratory are essentially tools for refining observations. When it comes to the study of pupil behavior, the teacher will find careful observation one of the most helpful sources of information.

There are, however, cautions to be observed. No observer is completely unbiased. What we select to see in a particular situation is colored by our past experiences, our prejudices, and our own needs. Moreover, "incidental" observation is likely to be "accidental." If observation of pupil behavior is to contribute greatly to understanding the individual pupil, it needs to be planned and to be carried out systematically. The value of reported observations of pupil behavior will be enhanced as the observations of several teachers dealing with the same pupil are brought together. The fact that Bill, whose indifference or aggressive behavior is a problem to most of his teachers, is happy and successful in the science class may be the clue to his adjustment. The pooling of all significant information about a particular pupil will be discussed in consideration of the "Case-Conference Method" in Chapter 12. Carefully planned observations will provide a fruitful portion of that information.

As teachers come to see the value of observation in understanding the behavior of the individual pupils with whom they deal, they will be concerned to develop their skills as observers and to make their records of observed behavior increasingly more objective and more meaningful. The opportunities for the teacher to observe significant behavior are manifold. While the classroom itself provides the most frequently available opportunity for study, there is an advantage in seeing the pupil in a variety of settings—the lunchroom, the playground, the library, participating in a student activity. As Robert Louis Stevenson points out in one of his essays, people not only seem different in different settings and with different companions—they are different. The shy and tongue-tied pupil in the classroom may be an accepted and resourceful leader on the playground. The star pupil may be an outsider among his peers.

The considerations presented above underline the importance of keeping some kind of record of observed behavior. Frequently the significance of a particular example of behavior becomes clear only as it is compared with other incidents occurring over a period of time or matched with the observations of the same "subject" by others. As was pointed out in Chapter 3, organized observation is a necessary tool in determining the typical, repetitive behavior of any child.

The systematic recording of observations need not be the arduous and time-consuming task that some teachers fear. In the first place, no teacher is expected to keep a record of everything that happens. A kind of behavior which is frequently repeated will, over a period of time, build up a picture of typical or characteristic behavior. Such a record may help us to understand the unique personality of this child. How does he seem to perceive himself? How does he relate with his peers? How does he operate when confronted with obstacles to achievement of his plans?

A second type of behavior which is significant is that which is unusual or unexpected. If the boy who has been shy and withdrawn volunteers for a role in a class project, if the "A" student evidences boredom or irresponsibility, such behavior may represent an important turning point in development. Behavior which reflects an unwillingness or inability to face reality is also significant.

The important thing in recording these observations is to describe what happened, not to color the description with our own moral judgments. This is a difficult thing to do but essential if the record is to serve the purpose of helping us and others to understand the child.

In the second place, no teacher will attempt to keep behavior records of all his pupils. At any particular time he may select at most two or three pupils whom he feels that he *needs to understand better*. Which ones seem not to be achieving in terms of their ability? Who are the overly aggressive? the shy and withdrawn? Over a period of time a teacher may study a considerable number of his pupils, but he should limit his systematic observation at any one time to a number he can handle without feeling this study a burden. He need not feel that he is neglecting the rest of the class as he concentrates attention on two or three pupils. As he develops deeper insight and more critical understanding in this intensive study of a few, the entire group will benefit.

In the third place, the records of behavior should be brief. The teacher is not making a case study or writing a life history. The most commonly used type of consistent study of behavior, the *anecdotal record,* is ordinarily a concise report of an incident, so brief that it can be recorded on a 3 by 5 inch card. A teacher may jot down two or three such records at the close of a class period or at the end of the day. This is not an overwhelming task. If consistently followed by the teachers of a school, a really impressive body of guidance information will result.

Finally, the measure of the value of such systematic observation of behavior is the help it provides teachers in carrying out their primary task of stimulating learning. To the extent that these records help the teacher understand individual pupils better, sense more clearly the relationships in the group, and see what factors are obstacles to pupil growth, they represent a saving and not a waste of time. Keeping records is worthwhile only if it helps the teacher do a better job of teaching and guidance.

Accurate observation and objective reporting of incidents are not instinctive. They must be learned. The teacher concerned with understanding children and helping them grow in desirable ways can build up these skills by practice and by thoughtful analysis of his own performance. Ohlsen presents a series of practical suggestions for teacher observation:

—The observer should try to know himself, to understand how his own personal needs and biases influence what he notices and records as significant behavior.
—He should describe the setting in which he observed the child.
—He should record what the child does and says, in as much detail as possible, relating especially those events which reflect how the child sees himself and his problems. He should try to keep a running account of the events in the order in which they occur. Whenever possible, the observer should also note the actions of others which seem to be related to the child's behavior.
—He should observe the child in many different situations—in the

classroom, in the lunchroom, in the halls, on the playground, at school parties, in the community, and in the home. He should observe the child at work and at play, with peers, subordinates, and superiors. He should observe the child during different periods of the day.

—The observer should describe typical behavior as well as unusual behavior. It is important to know what the child does in a familiar setting as well as what he does in a problem scene.

—Most observers find that they need to make some notes while they are observing. Teachers who are carrying on another activity while they observe must make very sketchy notes. However, even sketchy notes help eliminate errors.

—Observers should remember that the record of a single incident tells little about the child, but a collection of reports kept over a period of time by several good observers reveals a significant pattern in the child's development.[1]

Because the *anecdotal record* represents a common plan for reporting teacher observations, it may be worthwhile to describe the procedure in more detail. Essentially the plan is one of preparation by teachers of brief descriptive statements concerning pupil behavior observed. These statements should be factual and as free as possible of evaluative judgment by the observer. In this the anecdotal record differs markedly from rating scales, which are designed specifically to secure adult judgments—by teachers, parents, counselors—concerning qualities of pupil personality. Like a photograph, the anecdote should show what happened, not what the observer thinks about it. It should give the setting of the incident and may include dialogue. In fact, quotation of the exact statement of the subject of observation is an effective way of giving the later reader a feeling "you are there."

Interpretation, the observer's "hunch," as to the cause of the behavior observed or its significance for the pupil's development, may be desirable but should be rigorously excluded from description of the incident itself. Some schools use a form—usually a card or half sheet with place for date, name of pupil, location, and observer—with a separate section for "interpretation." One such form is presented below. Note that this form also calls for "Recommendations" and that interpretations and recommendations are placed on the back of the card, while the face is reserved for description of the incident. In other cases, anecdotes for a particular pupil are recorded on 8½ by 11 inch paper with marginal notation of dates of successive

[1] Merle M. Ohlsen, *Guidance, An Introduction* (New York: Harcourt, Brace and Co., 1955), p. 110.

Pupil__________ Date__________

Location__________

(ANECDOTE)

__________ Observer

(FRONT)

Interpretation:

Recommendations:

(BACK)

FIGURE 1.

observations. The paper may be lined down the middle and the right hand portion used for comments. A sample of such a form is presented below. In many schools, only the anecdote itself is reported. In any case, the essential element is the anecdote, the objective description of an incident.

Anecdotes may be supplied by several teachers and summarized by counselor, home room teacher, or "core teacher." Particularly at the high school level, where a number of teachers see the same pupil in different settings, this is appropriate. However, any teacher may initiate the study of a particular pupil and enlist the cooperation of other teachers as supplementary observers. At the elementary level where a teacher has the same pupil for an entire day, his own observations over a period of time will build up the data for study of the pupil. In either case the collection of anecdotes recorded over a period of

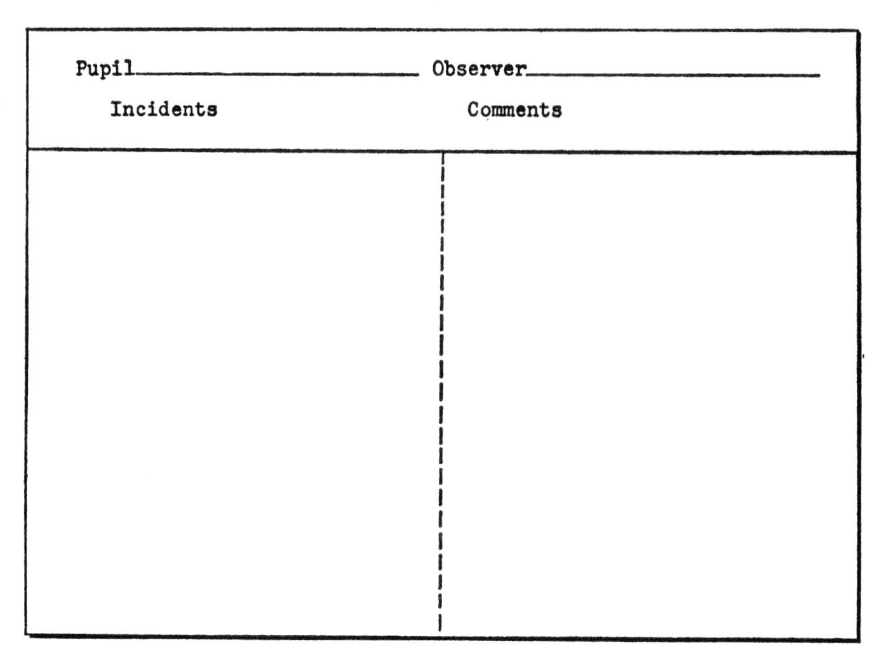

FIGURE 2.

time constitutes an *anecdotal record* or *behavior journal* for the pupil concerned.[2]

It may help to summarize suggestions about the use of anecdotes:

A. *Purpose*

1. To determine whether a behavior pattern is typical.
2. To look for trends in behavior.
3. To look for clues as to the source of the difficulty, e.g., in what kinds of situations does a particular behavior pattern occur?
4. To look for unusual behavior in relation to a particular event or in relation to other personalities.
5. To determine change that is often so gradual that one does not detect it without having regular records over a period of time.

[2] For fuller discussion of this important guidance tool the reader is referred to L. L. Jarvie and Mark Ellington, *Handbook on the Anecdotal Behavior Journal* (Chicago: University of Chicago Press, 1940); to Arthur E. Traxler, *Techniques of Guidance,* Revised Edition (New York: Harper and Brothers, 1957); and to *Helping Teachers Understand Children* (Washington, D.C.: American Council on Education, 1945). The last mentioned reference is particularly helpful in showing how a teaching staff, through group discussion with the help of a consultant, refined their skills in observation and progressively improved their anecdotal reports. This volume, especially Chapter 2, will repay careful reading by any teacher concerned with understanding children better and helping them more effectively.

6. To help us become aware of the kinds of situations to which we as teachers respond.
7. To form a basis for some planned action to help the child.

B. *Writing the Anecdote*

1. It should be a brief statement of a particular situation.
2. It should state exactly what happened.
3. On the whole it should not state qualitative judgments of the child's behavior.
4. It should include exact conversation where the child's comments are significant.
5. It should state exactly who was involved.
6. It should state when and where it took place, e.g., behavior in the organized classroom situation may be quite different from that shown on the playground, in the halls, etc.

C. *Using the Anecdote*

1. Time space between writing will have to be determined by the teacher. Such devices lose their effectiveness if the task of writing becomes a burden.
2. Examine the anecdotes for behavior that might be termed typical.
3. Look for trends in behavior.
4. Look for clues as to the kind of information you would like to have about a child. Watch particularly for those elements that help us to answer, "What kind of person is he?"
5. In the light of the information and what we know of personality development, decide on some hypothesis as to the cause of the behavior.
6. In relation to your hypothesis plan some ways of working with the child.

A number of illustrative anecdotes are presented below. These are not intended as models. In some cases judgments creep into what should be objective reports of what happened. Some are longer than they need to be to catch the significant incident. Varying degrees of insight are revealed. As actual reports by teachers "learning to understand children," they show how teachers in everyday situations can observe and record items of behavior which have significance.

I

Pupil: Larry S. *Date:* 10-29-57

Observer: Mr. R. (Ninth grade science teacher)

Anecdote:

Ernestine had been sitting across from Larry. She said that she would like her seat changed because Larry was bothering her. I asked Shirley if she would like to sit across from Larry. Larry said, "Oh goody. I like Shirley better." Shirley replied by saying to Larry, "I don't like you."

II

An Anecdote from a High School English Teacher

English IV 1:15 P. M. October 15, 1955

Senior students are reading original themes. Dave, a poor student, reads his and when he is finished, Mike T. rises and says, "*You* never wrote that!" Stunned silence for a second, and then Dave says, "I did too!" Mike: "You did *not*!"

I intervened. "Boys, we're not discussing who wrote the papers at this time, but simply the merit of the papers themselves. We'll judge the originality later." The bell rang for change of class.

As Dave left the room, I stepped up to him and said: "Did you really write the paper, Dave?" Not looking at me, he said, "Not all of it, I didn't know how to do it." "You really weren't honest in your work, were you, Dave? You can always get another explanation or extra time after school if you don't understand the assignment. Will you please remember that hereafter?"

"Yes, and can I write another one tonight—my own? To sort of make up for today's?" "Yes, hand it in with the regular assigned work tomorrow."

III

A Series of Anecdotes by a First Grade Teacher

Note:

Robert is eight years old and repeating the first grade. His mother is divorced and remarried. Robert lives with his mother, stepfather, and ten year old brother. His attention span is short and he presents behavior, as well as learning, problems. The teacher is making an effort to learn more about Robert and to gain his confidence.

1-27-57 On the playground today Robert took hats from two of the children and knocked one down. In spite of this aggressive behavior he seems popular with other children.

2-26-57 Robert seems to be interested in Kathy a, pretty, little, blond girl in our class; they spend most of the play time walking around holding hands.

3-4-57 Robert doesn't walk around with Kathy during playtime anymore. I asked him why, and he told me Kathy didn't like him anymore. Later he said he hated all girls.

3-12-57 Sharon asked me how to spell "love" and "marry." I told her and then asked why she wanted to know. "Robert's writing a love note to Marie, the bus guard," was her answer. It is rather typical for Robert to have someone speak in his behalf as he did in this incident.

3-14-57 I met Robert's mother for the first time this morning. Yesterday the children received their report cards and Robert got an "E" in citizenship. Robert's mother wanted to know what he had been doing to deserve this mark. I gave her a rundown of his conduct since the beginning of the semester. She said she could not understand why Robert was such a problem in school; her son, John, was never a problem. She said then that she had given Robert's teacher last semester permission to spank him if he did not behave. I told Mrs. R. that I didn't feel spanking was the answer to Robert's problem; that such a method would only produce surface behavior which would not last. I said I hoped to be able to help him improve with patience and understanding.

Mrs. R. concluded our talk by asking me to let her know in a week how Robert was getting along. I told her that no child will change in a week, but she insisted. I finally agreed, but reminded her not to expect any great improvement.

3-22-57 I sent Robert's mother a note today saying his conduct has improved. I'm not sure it really has but I think Robert is trying.

4-9-57 Robert has asked me several times to come over to his house some day after school to visit his mother. Today was the day. Robert waited for me after school and I drove him home. Mrs. R. seemed a little surprised to see me. She said Robert had told her I was coming but she didn't know when. We sat down at the dinette table and talked about Robert while he went out to play. She seemed nervous and flicked ashes from her cigarette almost constantly. In about five minutes Robert was back in the house. He hung up his coat and brought out a couple of toy cars and played with them on the dinette table. In a few minutes he put the cars away and got some plastic cowboys and Indians. Then in a few more minutes he went back to his bedroom with the cowboys and Indians and came out dressed in cowboy hat, neck scarf, gun and holster. He just showed me his outfit and put them away. The next thing he came out with was a pad of paper and a fourth grade arithmetic book. He barely had time to sit down with this, when Robert's friend, Brian (age 6), came in. Brian sat down at the table also and I helped them make up some arithmetic problems they would be able to do.

During this visit I had very little opportunity to talk to Mrs. R. alone about Robert, but I feel I learned a great deal about his home life. I was there about an hour and his mother never said one nice thing about him but nagged and criticized him constantly for the pettiest things.

4-15-57 A bus guard brought Robert in this morning after the tardy bell rang. "Robert was down in the principal's office; that's why he's late. He was reported for pushing a little girl down on the bus."

I figured Robert had been sufficiently reprimanded for his conduct so I just thanked the bus guard and said to Robert, "Put your coat in your locker quickly, it's time for reading."

As I walked toward the door with Robert, he asked, "Do you still like me?"

"Yes I do, Robert, but I don't like you to misbehave."

Comment:

My visits to Robert's home have given some clues as to why he acts as he does. They have helped to give me a more comprehensive picture of Robert and made me more sympathetic to his problems, and I certainly do feel Robert has problems. He has a stepfather whom he fears, a mother who seems to have little to offer in the way of real love, and a brother who is constantly held up as a model. His need to feel a sense of belonging and of being appreciated at home does not seem to be satisfied.

IV

Pupil: Tom B., age 13

Observer: Mr. E. (Seventh grade teacher)

Descriptive data:

Tom is a low average student. His I.Q. is 91 (Dominion Intelligence Test administered 3-55). He is often inattentive in class and frequently fails to complete work in the allotted time.

Tom's chief problem is, however, social rather than academic. On a sociogram administered 10-56 he was rejected five times and had no choices. On 4-25-57 he was rejected five times and had no choices. On 11-15-57 he was rejected six times and again had no choices.

Tom, like all children, needs attention and has been getting it by doing unacceptable things. He tells stories that are untrue and does odd things.

Tom has the reputation at school both among his classmates and his teachers of being a nuisance. His teacher two years ago made the following remark on his report card.

Tom finds it hard to conform with the rules of classroom and playground.

Tom is doing fair work in class this year. He is reading in the slowest group, but is the best in that group. He is slow in completing work and often leaves it unfinished.

Tom spends a lot of time playing alone. I have often observed him playing by himself apparently quite contentedly. He plays some with his brother and lately he has made a friend in class. He doesn't enter much into ball games in free playtime, but likes to play marbles. He seems interested in nature. He has brought garter snakes, frogs and crabs to class, and seems to like them.

Anecdotes:

3-4-57 This morning I asked Tom for the arithmetic questions which he was to have finished. He said that he had finished them at home and had forgotten his book. After lunch he had his book, and proceeded to look through it. He couldn't find the questions. After he had searched for ten minutes without success I said, "Well, Tom, I guess I'll call your home and see if your mother knows what happened to your questions." Just as I started to the phone he said, "I tore the pages out and told my mother I had all my work finished." I discussed the matter with his mother after school and told her that he would be having a few questions to do each night until he caught up.

3-5-57 First thing this morning Tom said, "I've got my questions done." When I examined them I discovered that they weren't the same questions I had given him. I asked Tom about this in private. He admitted that he changed some of the numbers so the questions would be easier.

3-8-57 Tonight was Open House and Tom's parents were here. His stepmother mentioned that Tom had been working very hard on his social studies homework. I hadn't given him any homework, so I inquired just what it was and she said that Tom has said he was to write a story on Dr. Livingstone and that he has spent several hours copying a story from a book they had at home.

3-9-57 I asked Tom about this story today, and he showed me eight pages of neatly written material. It looked like fairly easy reading, so I asked him if he would like to read it to the class. He looked very pleased and said, "Yes, thank you." I explained to the class that Tom had done some extra work and let him read the story. He read it very well.

3-24-57 Just after dismissal this afternoon three girls came back to tell me that several boys were fighting and that they were really angry. On going out I saw Tom lying on the ground groaning and several boys standing around. The boys told me that Tom had sneaked up behind Douglas when he was bending over to pick up a marble and had kicked him. Bob had then kicked Tom and he was still lying on the ground. I asked Tom, Douglas, and Bob to come into the office. Tom said, "I can't walk," but a minute later was walking with no difficulty. I let the three boys each tell his story and it developed that Douglas had hit Tom's younger brother at lunch time. When Tom saw Douglas bent over he thought this a good opportunity to pay Douglas back. Bob had kicked Tom because he thought Tom was picking on Douglas.

9-16-57 I heard screams from the vestibule this morning before class and went to investigate. Tom was holding a garter snake (about eight inches long) and several girls were screaming. He had a container to keep it in so I let him keep it at school for the day.

10-18-57 Tom came to me tonight after school. He said that Albert was picking on him, and wouldn't let him go home. I went out to see, but Albert had left by this time.

10-24-57 At lunch time today I observed Tom and Douglas eating together. They were chatting together and appeared to be enjoying themselves.

Another instrument which may be helpful to the teacher is the *Rating Scale.* This differs from the anecdotal record in that it provides for judgments or evaluations of various traits or characteristics of pupils, which are deemed important. It is not a substitute for the anecdotal record which is an *objective* report of what happened. In the judgment of the authors of this volume, it has some dangers. (As teachers we have a tendency to be too judgmental anyhow!) At the same time, if appropriate safeguards are observed, it has definite advantages. It makes possible careful consideration at regular intervals of all pupils of a class, a grade, or a school. Where careful consideration is given to the traits to be considered, it may serve to focus attention on desirable outcomes other than academic achievement. Many schools now use some form of rating scale as a supplement to (or substitute for) letter grades in reports to parents.

An extensive form of rating scale—the "Behavior Description" was devised by the Evaluation Staff of the Eight Year Study for use in the thirty schools included in that program.[3] The form provides for rating of each pupil by each of his teachers on the following traits: responsibility-dependability, creativeness and imagination, influence, inquiring mind, openmindedness, the power and habit of analysis, social concern, emotional responsiveness, serious purpose, social adjustability, and work habits. For each of the traits a series of four or five descriptive statements is given and the teacher checks the one which in his judgment best describes each pupil. Rating sheets from all teachers are summarized on the cumulative record card for each pupil. Over a period of years this plan provides an extensive series of judgments about the pupil. A modification of this plan is part of the American Council on Education Cumulative Record Card.[4]

Another well known rating instrument is the *Haggerty-Olson-Wickman Behavior Rating Scale*. This scale is of the graphic type. The descriptions for each behavior judgment are arranged in five steps along a horizontal line, which may be checked at any point. This type of scale permits finer gradations of judgment on the points in question. Comparable graphic scales are used in many college admissions applications to get the high school representatives' appraisal of the applicant. A sample item from the Haggerty-Olson-Wickman Scale will serve to illustrate this form of instrument.[5]

---

[3] Eugene R. Smith, Ralph W. Tyler, and the Evaluation Staff, *Appraising and Recording Student Progress,* Chapter 10 (New York: McGraw-Hill Book Company, Inc., 1942).

[4] *The American Council on Education Cumulative Record Folder for Schools and Colleges* (Washington, D.C.: American Council on Education, 1947).

[5] *Haggerty-Wickman-Olson Behavior Rating Schedule* (Yonkers-on-Hudson, New York: World Book Company, 1930).

Is he generally depressed or cheerful?

Dejected, Melancholic, in the dumps	Generally dispirited	Usually in good humor	Cheerful, animated, chirping	Hilarious
(3)	(4)	(1)	(2)	(5)

The rating scales described may be most helpful to teachers in suggesting outcomes to be desired in terms of pupil behavior, and indicating a method of systematizing judgments as to their attainment. Strang lists the following important principles to be observed in the use of rating scales.[6]

In order that rating scales be of any value at all, they must be based on good observation. The translation of observation into rating scale form is facilitated by following these general rules:

1. Limit the number of characteristics to be rated. It is impossible for a teacher to rate thirty to forty students on many different items.
2. Describe the behavior to be rated as nearly as possible in the form in which the teacher will be likely to observe it. For example, the rating scales developed by Van Alstyne[7] and her associates are organized around situations in which every teacher has opportunity to observe the kinds of behavior to be rated.
3. Provide space in which the teacher may make explanations or give illustrations supporting his rating.
4. Provide space in which the teacher may write supplementary paragraphs to complete his picture of the individual's behavior. It is difficult indeed for a person using a rating scale to reconstruct the student's personality from a list of separate items. The descriptive sketch, on the other hand, emphasizes dominant factors and relations.
5. Allow a long enough period for observation before the rating is made and make it clear that no rating should be made if the teacher does not have adequate basis for making it. No rating at all is much better than a superficial or inaccurate rating.

---

[6] Ruth Strang, *The Role of the Teacher in Personnel Work,* Fourth Edition (New York: Bureau of Publications, Teachers College, Columbia University, 1953) pp. 333-334.

[7] Dorothy Van Alstyne and the Winnetka Public School Faculty, *Winnetka Scale for Rating School Behavior and Attitudes* (Winnetka, Illinois: Winnetka Educational Press, 1935).

Dorothy Van Alstyne and the Francis Parker School Faculty, *Record for Describing Attitudes and Behavior in High School* (330 Webster Avenue, Chicago, 1939).

6. Give clear directions for using the rating scale and offer instruction and practice in improving observations.

7. Arrange to have the rating scale filled out by different persons who have opportunity to observe the student under different conditions.

The Teacher Learns About the Student Through His Productions

In clinical work in recent years there has been effective use of what are known as "projective techniques." Most widely known is probably the Rorschach Test, in which the client is asked to tell what he sees in each of a series of ink-blot pictures. Analysis of responses by a specially trained clinician gives helpful insights into personality structure and adjustment. Another instrument is the Thematic Apperception Test (often abbreviated to "TAT"). This test consists of pictures of people in ambiguous settings. The client is asked to tell the story behind the picture, telling what has happened, who the characters of the picture are, and their relations to each other. Teachers who are familiar with the film "The Angry Boy," will remember the psychologist's use of a picture-story test in an interview with Tommy. Other projective techniques may involve creative activity with art materials or play with toys. In the case of the various projective methods, the common element is the free play of imagination in a relatively unstructured situation and the expression of the way the student *feels* about the situation.

It is not the purpose here to suggest that the teacher is equipped to use these clinical methods in studying pupils in his classes. It may be helpful for him to be familiar with them in a general way so that he may understand better the interpretations which may be made by expert diagnosticians, but applications of these instruments should be reserved for clinically trained personnel. (Administration of the Rorschach is reserved to qualified individuals who have had at least three years of clinical training, and guided experience with the method.) There are, however, sources available to the teacher in his regular classroom work which can be studied to secure some significant insights as to the pupil's background, ambitions, feelings about himself and others, and problems which may disturb him.

Written productions. Stories, compositions, poetry, and other written products by the pupil can lead to deeper understanding when the topics are those in which the pupil exercised a choice, and the relationship with the teacher is such as to encourage free expression. We are not likely to learn much from assigned themes on "What a Daffodil

Thinks of Spring" or "The Poetry of Robert Browning." Many times students will welcome an opportunity to write on topics illustrative of personal experience—"My Most Exciting Adventure," "How I Spent My Vacation," "My Best Friend," "Our Family." Where an accepting climate has been developed and pupils have a chance to suggest topics, they may range the gamut of young people's concerns about life, the problems they face, the ideals they hold. The important thing is that the topics chosen represent the real interests of the student and that the young person feel free to express himself without fear of censure or ridicule. As in the counseling situation, he must have confidence that whatever he reveals will be considered confidential by the teacher.

A somewhat structured, but still informal, method of studying pupils through their writings is the device known as *"My Three Wishes."* The setting for its use may occur naturally in connection with stories read in the elementary grades where fairy stories and others dealing with the supernatural suggest the question, "If you had three wishes, what would you wish for?" In high school classes, in units dealing with personality or plans for the future, students may reveal more of their hopes, fears, ambitions, and problems. The information the teacher may obtain from these free expressions may throw light on problems of concern to the pupil, reveal something of the concept he has of himself, and provide the teacher with clues to facets of behavior which have been difficult to understand.

The *Autobiography* is a more personalized form of pupil writing. Many teachers start the first meeting of a new class by giving a period to introductions including such items as hobbies, interests, places the pupil has lived, unusual experiences, and future plans. Those who know the film "Learning to Understand Children" [8] will remember the scene where the teacher, Mary Brown, uses this plan to get acquainted with the English I class. Some pupils may be shy in talking about themselves, especially when they are new to the group. This, you will remember, was the case with "Ada Adams," the pupil whose progress toward adjustment provides the interest of the film. For pupils, like Ada, who are hesitant to speak before the class, a written account of past experiences may be less threatening. It also gives the teacher more opportunity to study the pupil's background in the light of developing experiences in the class.

[8] *Learning to Understand Children,* Part I, "A Diagnostic Approach," 21 min.; Part II, "A Remedial Program," 23 min. (New York: McGraw-Hill, 1947).

Some writers suggest an outline of specific questions for the autobiography, or a list of items which may be checked. One such form is reproduced in *Child Development and Guidance in Rural Schools* by Strang and Hatcher.[9] Prepared by the Alliance for Guidance of Rural Youth, Richmond, Virginia, this form contains check list and short answer items under seven main headings:

1. First Facts About Myself
2. My Family
3. Our Home
4. My Education Thus Far and Plans for More
5. What I Like—My Interests
6. My Future Occupation—Occupational Preferences
7. Group Contacts

This type of autobiography has the advantage of assuring more comprehensive coverage, since the main items which are likely to be significant are included in the outline. On the other hand, it loses something of the spontaneity and freedom of expression which result when the student writes the story of his life without a specific guide to follow. Probably the most serviceable plan is to follow the freer pattern but to devote some time in class dicussion to the purpose of writing an autobiography, what items might be included, and, possibly, to reading a sample life story. In any case the student should be assured that whatever he writes will be kept as confidential.

The autobiography may be an exercise in an English class but is appropriate in any class where the teacher has established rapport with his pupils and is interested in knowing them better in order to guide them more effectively. An excellent discussion of the values and limitations of the autobiography as a guidance instrument will be found in Traxler.[10]

Of the autobiography, as of the other semi-projective procedures discussed in this chapter, it may be said that its interpretation should be approached with caution. The teacher is not a therapist. It is not his role to diagnose and treat serious disturbances of personality. However, operating within the realities of the classroom situation and utilizing evidence clearly revealed in autobiographies and other written products, the teacher may discover significant clues to puzzling behavior, explanations of apparent indifference, the need to attract attention,

[9] Ruth Strang and Latham Hatcher, *Child Development and Guidance in Rural Schools* (New York: Harper and Brothers, 1943), pp. 199-208.

[10] Arthur E. Traxler, Techniques of Guidance, Revised Edition (New York: McGraw-Hill Book Company, 1956), p. 140.

even if unfavorable. It should be pointed out that evidence from autobiographies and other free expressions by the student should be considered in conjunction with other available data. Information will be most helpful as it serves to identify a *pattern* of behavior. On the basis of such a pattern the teacher can plan activities and relationships which may encourage the timid, provide acceptable outlets for the aggressive, and draw the isolate into the group.

Twenty-four hour diaries or daily logs represent another means by which the teacher may discover what a student considers important. It may be a very revealing experience to the student, himself, to keep such a diary. In its simplest form it consists of a record of what the pupil did throughout a twenty-four hour period, for an agreed period of time, usually a week. An 8½ by 11 inch sheet of paper for each day, with student's name and date at the top, is used. Time of beginning each new activity is indicated in the left hand margin and activities recorded throughout the day. For the teacher, such a schedule may indicate a great deal about social and economic background of the school community in addition to the light it may throw on personal difficulties and adjustments of individual pupils. The daily schedule or diary may be undertaken as a project for an entire class in a unit on personality, budgeting of time, wise use of leisure, or a comparable topic. It may be used with individual students who present problems of adjustment. In any case, it should be undertaken only with the wholehearted cooperation of the pupils involved. As in the case of any instrument the teacher uses, the pupil must be convinced that this is something which will be helpful to him. More extended discussion of this technique will be found in writings by Strang [11, 12] who has been one of the most active proponents of this device.

Personal diaries, especially among adolescents, serve as the intimate confidantes of their doubts and fears, their dreams and aspirations. Over a period of time such a document can bring into clear focus the conflicts and confusions of the adolescent and the emerging pattern of the self concept. *The Diary of a Young Girl* by Anne Frank has sharpened the understanding of thousands who have read the poignant story or have seen it on the stage.

Diaries, however, are very personal revelations. The young person

---

[11] Ruth Strang, *The Role of the Teacher in Personnel Work*, Fourth Edition (N. Y. Bureau of Publications, Teachers College, Columbia University, 1953), pp. 336-348.

[12] Sarah H. Sturtevant and Ruth Strang, "The Daily Schedule as an Aid to Advisers," *Teachers College Record*, 27:37-38, October 1927.

FROM MY DAILY LOG . . . "4 P.M. HAD A SODA WITH JOE AND SALLY."

is usually quite secretive about what he confides to his diary. Only intimate friends are likely to be permitted to look within its covers. Where a teacher or counselor has developed such rapport that the student offers to share the journal with him, a reading of this record can provide insights not likely to be obtained through other media and can contribute significantly to understanding and guiding the pupil. It is not a privilege to be lightly requested. In spite of the contribution the diary can make to the teacher's role as counselor, it is not one of the avenues to understanding which he may expect to use.

Other student productions also provide teachers with insights for guidance. Students reveal themselves in other ways than through the written word. Art is especially productive in opportunities for understanding. Not only are art creations an indication of the interests and abilities of the student. They may reveal much of his personality structure, his inner tensions, his secret aspirations. Frustrations experienced at home, in the classroom, or in the peer group may find outlet in pictures depicting scenes of violence. Deprivations may be reflected in subjects chosen for representation. An art teacher in a midwestern high school suggested to a class that they make self portraits. A Negro girl in the group painted herself with a doll which was noticeably and dazzlingly white. The teacher gained from this incident some insight into the feeling of a member of a minority group in a predominantly white culture.

Student projects may reveal unsuspected talents and habits of work. The boy who has seemed lazy or dull in the English class may show himself in the shop to be a craftsman of skill and high standards of workmanship. A science project may reveal a high degree of ingenuity, scientific knowledge, and persistence. These are evidences which the teacher concerned with helping students capitalize their potential will wish to recognize. Informal dramatizations and "role playing" provide important leads to problems of emotional and social adjustment. These procedures will be discussed in Chapter 10 which deals with instruments for group study.

The Teacher Learns About the Student Through His Interests and Hobbies

Thomas Briggs used to tell his classes that the measure of a liberal education is to be found in the number and variety and depth of the interests it develops. Certainly interest is at the heart of the teacher's task of stimulating learning. A concern with the real interests of pupils is essential if the teacher is to carry out effectively his twin roles of teaching and guidance—the improvement of conditions for learning and assistance to pupils in achieving adequate personal adjustment.

How does the teacher discover pupil interests? Observation of the free play of children and young people is one productive source of

LEARN ABOUT STUDENTS THROUGH THEIR INTERESTS AND HOBBIES.

information. A weekly period may be set aside in class for reports on hobbies. Topics for themes may be based on leisure time activities and avocations. Discussion of favorite motion pictures, radio, and TV programs may reveal present interests as well as provide opportunity for enlarging horizons. They will be revealed in conference and casual conversation. The teacher sympathetically in tune with youth will find them, like Kipling's Elephant Child, "filled with 'satiable curiosity." Interests, of course, vary with age and level of maturation. The teacher will find clues to interests in the concept of "developmental tasks" discussed in Chapter 2. The important thing is to realize that every student is a bundle of energy which must find an outlet and that his interests are the key to its release for learning and constructive growth.

Hobbies, whether of making or collecting things, are a key to student interests. Frequently they carry over into adult life and may influence vocational choices. In this air-minded age many a youthful model airplane builder has later turned his interest and knowledge to use in some field of aviation engineering, in service in the Air Force, or in commercial aviation. Youthful craftsmen have developed skills and standards of workmanship as they have followed an interest in building model railroads, radio sets, scientific instruments. They have read widely and carried out research. Much of this activity has had no relation to school courses or assignments. Talking to a group of teachers, a member of a boys' archery club told of their search for information on making bows and arrows, what was the best wood to use, the different kinds of arrows for different purposes, methods of feathering, and principles of flight. His discussion ranged from the English crossbow to weapons used by the different tribes of American Indians. "And then we read books, not because we had to, but because we wanted to!" was a recurrent refrain. In this statement is a key to motivation of learning.

The range of collecting hobbies is almost infinite. Youngsters are by nature acquisitive, as any mother knows after emptying a small boy's pockets. These hobbies, too, can broaden horizons, stimulate reading, reveal possible vocational opportunities, and build life-long habits for constructive use of leisure time. To the stamp collector geography and history become alive. Rocks or butterflies or wild flowers may open the world of science to an enthusiastic collector.

The wise teacher will use this enthusiasm to stimulate the desire for further growth and to build confidence in the pupil who has found school tasks difficult. The following account illustrates the approach of one such teacher. The story is told by a school visitor who had just returned from a tour of rural high schools.

When I came into that girl's 9th grade public-speaking class, the group was so absorbed in a report being given by one youngster that they didn't give me a glance. The teacher was standing at the back of the room. She didn't have much time for me either. She just pointed to an empty seat. I sat down and in a couple of minutes I was as absorbed as the class. When the student had finished his talk—on the topic "What Does a Citizen Buy When He Pays Taxes?"—the teacher said, "Thank you, Jerome. Are there any questions?" I found myself competing with the kids asking questions. Didn't rattle him a bit to have a strange adult barge in. He knew the answers, too.

Naturally, when the class left I complimented the teacher. She said, "We're all very proud of Jerome. He is a new boy this year. The first few weeks he just sat with his mind off somewhere else. His other teachers found him hopeless, too. Then one day a boy in this class gave a pretty poor talk on the subject 'My Hobby is Airplanes' and Jerome came to life. He hadn't been a very nice member of the class, so I was surprised when he spoke up very *courteously* to point out errors in the speech."

The teacher went on to say that, after class, she asked Jerome some questions about aviation and he said he would bring "some material" next day. She was surprised, for none of his teachers had ever seen him crack a book. The next morning Jerome staggered in with a stack of ten books and told her she could take her time reading them as he had finished with them "except for reference." She found that the books weren't made up of interesting pictures and simple stories for twelve year olds, but were highly technical treatises which were far beyond her comprehension. She told Jerome she "really needed his help" and it took only a little persuasion to get him to give a series of talks on aviation, geared to the level of the class—and the teacher! Jerome hadn't been very popular with the other pupils but now he was accepted as one of the group.

I thought the teacher did a smart thing then. She decided she could now sell Jerome on doing a piece of research on another subject. She said Jerome looked sort of shocked and shook his head. He fished in his pocket and brought out a grubby report card from his previous school. "See, I couldn't get up another kind of report. Like it says here, *I'm a non-reader.*"

The teacher stopped there so I said "Well, what did you do to get that speech this morning?"

"Nothing."

"Well you must have done something."

"No, I just let him go. I thought he would miss being part of the class and he did, and I thought the kids could take care of it better than I could—and they did. They had a fit when he passed up his turn a couple of times, so one day he gave a terribly funny talk on *Toads.* I said, 'Jerome, you must have done some non-reading on toads. He gave me a fishy grin and, you know, the nicest thing happened. From then on Jerome began to take part in *all* his classes."

A final source of information about students which is readily available to teachers is the record of voluntary reading. "Free reading" is a good indicator of taste—if it is *really* free. Many teachers have used lists of books read, often recorded in a graphic device on a bulletin board, as a way of stimulating more or "better" reading. The Eight Year Study of the Progressive Education Association included in the evaluation instruments used a *Questionnaire on Voluntary Reading* to get at the reaction of students to literature read, and a *Record of Free Reading,* in which students' reading was appraised on the basis of range and maturity. Both instruments have implications for guidance. While these are printed forms for use in the study and should, probably, be characterized as "formal methods," the interested teacher can develop informal questionnaires and reading lists to serve a comparable purpose with his own class. Such records are most helpful for guidance purposes as they identify *kinds* of books read—comic books, fiction, biography, history, travel, popular science, etc.—as well as the total number of volumes.

Summary

The teacher can learn much about his pupils without the use of tests or other formal instruments. A number of helpful devices have been discussed in this chapter. Basic to most of these methods is observation of the pupil in the classroom and in other settings. To be most helpful, observation needs to be systematic. Probably the most useful of the informal methods of study is the *anecdotal record,* together with the *behavior journal* or accumulation of anecdotes. Other sources of information discussed in this chapter include the *rating scale, autobiographies,* examples of pupil productions, interests and hobbies, and records of reading.

Selected Readings

American Council on Education, *Helping Teachers Understand Children.* Washington, D. C.: American Council on Education, 1945.

Barr, John A., *The Elementary Teacher and Guidance.* New York: Henry Holt and Company, 1958.

Froehlich, Clifford P. and John G. Darley, *Studying Students*. Chicago: Science Research Associates, 1952.

Jarvie, L. L. and Mark Ellingson, *Handbook of the Anecdotal Behavior Journal*. Chicago: University of Chicago Press, 1940.

Lefever, D. Welty, Archie M. Turrell, and Henry I. Weitzel, *Principles and Techniques of Guidance,* Revised Edition. New York: The Ronald Press Company, 1950.

McDaniel, Henry B., *Guidance in the Modern School*. New York: The Dryden Press, 1956.

Martinson, Ruth A., and Harry Smallenberg, *Guidance in Elementary Schools*. Englewood Cliffs, N. J.: Prentice-Hall, Inc., 1958.

Morris, Glyn, *Practical Guidance Methods for Principals and Teachers*. New York: Harper and Brothers, 1952.

Ohlsen, Merle M., *Guidance, An Introduction*. New York: Harcourt, Brace and Company, 1955.

Strang, Ruth, *The Role of the Teacher in Personnel Work,* Fourth Edition. New York: Bureau of Publications, Teachers College, Columbia University, 1953.

Traxler, Arthur E., *Techniques of Guidance,* Revised Edition. New York: Harper and Brothers, 1957.

CHAPTER 6

The Teacher Studies Individuals Through Use of Data Collected by Formal Methods

Some of the aspects of guidance on which this chapter will touch have probably been more thoroughly discussed in professional ranks and more completely described in the resulting literature than any other aspects. However, no book in the general field of guidance should omit discussion of the cumulative record and the information it contains. In order not to duplicate the efforts of specialists who have written so well and so extensively on this subject, we will explore the ways in which *teachers* may make the most profitable use of information on the student's record.

The Teacher Sees the Cumulative Folder as a Guidance Tool

The subject of the cumulative folder or cumulative record is certain to provoke varied reactions from teachers. A few condemn cumulative records as devices that make teachers high priced clerks; some regard records as necessary administrative evils; others consider them to be valuable guidance tools.

What makes the difference in the way in which teachers view the cumulative folder? No simple explanation will account for these differences; it is probably valid to attribute them to important differences in personality, philosophy, and educational and professional experiences. Perhaps the most logical approach is to concern ourselves with the vast majority of teachers who realistically ask themselves the question, "What can a teacher find in the cumulative folder that will enable him to understand the pupil better and to function more effectively in providing opportunities for the most helpful and meaningful learning experiences?"

A good individual inventory, according to McDaniel and Shaftel, will provide systematic annual recording of these data:

1. Personal (Identification)
   - Name
   - Date of birth
   - Evidence for verifying birthday
   - Place of birth
   - Sex
   - Residence
2. Home and Community
   - Name of parents or guardians
   - Occupations of parents
   - Ratings on home environment
   - Birthplace of parents
   - Language spoken in home
   - Marital status of parents
   - Siblings—names, ages, education
3. Scholarship
   - School marks by years and subjects
   - Special reports on failures
   - Record of reading
   - Rank in class
   - Honors won
4. Test Scores and Ratings
   - Achievement-test scores
   - Interest-inventory results
   - Aptitude-test scores
   - Personality ratings
   - Other test scores
5. School Attendance
   - Record of schools attended, with dates
   - Days present and absent each year
6. Health
   - Height—annual or semiannual measurements
   - Weight—same
   - Hearing
   - Vision
   - Condition of teeth
   - Physical disabilities
   - Vaccination record
   - Disease record
   - Recommendations and referrals by school doctor or nurse
7. Employment
   - Part-time jobs—dates, duties, earnings
   - Summer jobs—same

Employer reports
Work-experience reports

8. Activity Records
   Athletics—team, dates
   Clubs—dates, status
   Student body offices and activities
   Class offices and activities
   Nonschool clubs and activities
   Hobbies and leisure-time activities
9. Anecdotal Records
   (Usually reported on special forms, these brief, occasional, descriptive reports of bits of behavior in specific situations may concern success or problem experiences. Incidents and events should be reported separately from opinion. An accumulation of such records adds to understanding of the student's behavior.)
10. Interview Notes
   (Records should be kept of each interview. Much of the information will be different for each situation, but among the items commonly recorded are the following:)
   Date of contact
   Reason for Interview
   Interest and plans expressed
   Nature of problem discussed
   Action taken
11. Follow-up Record
   This part of the record may contain periodic reports of employment, education, satisfactions, and problems.[1]

If the kinds of data mentioned above were selective in nature, well-organized in structure, and objectively presented, teachers would be provided with a valuable guidance tool. To develop and maintain a folder which fits such a description necessitates a broad approach to the whole problem of cumulative records. Teachers, guidance specialists, and administrators need to work cooperatively on this matter to determine such things as the kinds of data needed, the techniques to be employed, frequency of collection, and responsibility for recording.

The Teacher Unifies Available Data

At this point we can begin to explore ways in which teachers may use the information about each student that the school has made a

[1] From *Guidance in the Modern School* by Henry B. McDaniel and G. A. Shaftel. Copyright 1956. Reprinted by permission of the publishers.

systematic effort to obtain. The areas to be stressed are personal and family background, health, attendance, scholarship, activities and experience, and test data.

Personal and family background. The child's ability to cope with his developmental needs cannot be understood or handled by the classroom teacher in a very understanding fashion if the teacher is not aware of the subculture in which the child is growing up. The kindergarten teacher is the first member of the faculty to experience the importance of knowing what a child's family life is and has been. He recognizes the importance of knowing such things as with whom the child is now living (both parents, one parent, foster home); the family attitudes toward education; methods of parental control. The information may vary as the child progresses through the school system; the need for it doesn't.

In an elementary school, when the pupils are to encounter their first male teacher, the school could utilize both information from the records and the previous teachers' experiences with the children in considering whether or not certain boys and girls have a greater need for identification with a male figure. In junior high schools some boys and girls may have a particular need to establish satisfying relationships with adults of the same sex. Throughout the time a child attends school, teachers are aware of the influence on the child of the parental attitudes toward education, the positive and negative ones, the laissez faire attitude, the pressuring attitude. Teachers know that they cannot generalize adequately about the diverse directions in which students are influenced by their personal and family backgrounds. Of one thing a teacher can be sure; the more awareness he has of the background, the more understanding he will be and the more likely to plan his classroom procedures and experiences on an individual or small group basis, rather than always planning the same experiences for a whole class.

Health. It would be ideal if every school child could have a complete physical examination every year, but we all know that at present school systems cannot afford such professional examinations. The only regular checking done in some school settings has been the simple general check-ups that teachers themselves perform. These are not likely to be very accurate. Most children, unfortunately, get no medical or nursing service until they become ill. Others attend schools which are equipped with audiometers for hearing tests and Snellen charts for sight testing. But sight and hearing tests are not the only kinds of check-ups necessary if the teacher is to determine whether the students are well enough to have energy available for learning. The general physical well-being of a child is extremely important. It cannot be determined by merely looking at the child. Some children are naturally more pallid than some others. Some students are slenderer and others naturally heavier.

The most valuable tool that can be used by the teacher for a test of general health is the Wetzel Growth Grid.[2] This grid is a single 8½ by 11 inch card that can be used successfully from kindergarten through high school. It will show the teacher whether a child is pursuing his own growth in a normal fashion based on his unique body type. All the teacher needs in the way of data for the chart is the height and weight of the child taken twice a year. One side of the chart reserves a space for the age, weight, height, the date of recording and the developmental level arrived at by using the card. The center of the card is divided into body type channels: "Obese" or channel "A_4"; "Stocky" or channels "A_2" and "A_3"; "Good" or channel "A_1", "M", and "B_1"; "Fair" or channel "B_2", "Borderline" or channel "B_3", and "Poor" or channel "B_4". These channels are superimposed on a graph with the weights down the side and the height across the top. Finding the point on the chart where the measure of height meets the measure of weight, the teacher makes a dot. This dot will then be in one of the channels. The first measure will not give us the complete story. When the student is weighed and measured again after six months, a line is drawn between the first dot and the second. This shows us whether the child is moving along in his own body type channel. These lines are called isodevelopmental lines and are numbered. It is from these numbers that we determine the developmental level. If the child is growing well he will gain six points for every six months.

It is not enough to determine the developmental level. This score is carried over to the right side of the card where the "Age Schedules of Development" or "Auxodromes" are recorded. This side of the chart has a series of lines superimposed on another graph. The developmental score is on the left side of the graph and ages are across the bottom. The ages range from five to eighteen. Here again, the teacher finds the point at which the developmental score and age meet and

[2] Norman C. Wetzel, M.D. is the author of the Grid titled, "Grid for Evaluating Physical Fitness." It is published by the NEA Service, Inc., 1200 W. 3rd St., Cleveland, Ohio.

makes a dot. After six months the next dot is recorded and the two are connected. The growth curves are printed on the card and if a child's growth curve parallels one of these curves we may say that he is growing at a consistent level. The curves are the same for boys and girls up to age nine. After this age the curves for girls are accelerated and level off at puberty. The curves for boys do not accelerate until about ages fourteen or fifteen.

The value of this card is that we need not be concerned about the general health of a student who is pursuing his normal course on both graphs. The "Age Schedules of Development" side of the card will screen out those who need a special medical examination. The parents can then be notified and some remedial help can be given. Another decided advantage of the Grid is that as soon as children are able to read and write they can record their own data on the cards. The card gives the boy or girl a graphic picture of his own growth. All the major data are on one side of the card. The reverse side of the card has space for a continuing health record. The initial expenditure for the card is made only once, at entrance into school. This then becomes a health record that can be kept with the permanent record cards for the entire school career. Many pediatricians have adopted the cards in their own practices; school systems where the Grid is used feel that it is one of their most valuable tools.

Attendance. Maintaining attendance records can be a time-consuming task for classroom teachers. Often it is viewed as an administrative chore that is required to insure that the school receives an accurate financial apportionment from the state—an apportionment which may be based upon the average daily attendance at the school.

If we are to view attendance records as a guidance tool, we need to look at what attendance, or more correctly, failure to attend, means to the student and to the teacher. The meaning it has for a particular student may be determined by the cause for the absence. However, real causes are not always apparent or even easily discernible, and in some cases the causative factors will bear no relationship to the meaning of the absence. The child's relationships with his classmates and with his teachers may play an important part. Some children feel the need to belong and to identify with the group much more than others. In early elementary grades it may be the teacher toward whom the child looks to see if he has been missed after an absence. The longer a child has been absent the greater may be the need for the teacher and the class to help him reestablish his sense of belonging and feeling of identification with the group. The teacher as group leader plays an important role in helping each student feel that he has been missed. In addition, any prolonged absence from school provides the teacher with an opportunity to work with the class in sending *greetings* as well as assignments to the child. In some situations it may even be quite appropriate for the teacher to visit a child.

The boy or girl whose record indicates that he doesn't attend school regularly should be studied to see how the school, particularly his teachers, can help. Chronic truancy is a factor that is associated positively with the tendency for students to drop out of school at an early age. More important, it is closely identified with delinquency. It is true that a child who is in school may or may not be doing an effective job of learning. However, the child who is not in school is denied the opportunity to be one of those who may learn effectively. When a student is absent quite often, the teacher needn't develop guilt feelings. His role is to be aware of the student's problems and make a genuine effort to provide him with classroom experiences that help meet his present as well as his future needs.

WHAT DO SCHOOL MARKS REPRESENT?

Scholarship. A good place to start would seem to be with the question, "What do school marks represent?" If we were to interview teachers, we would get responses such as "achievement," "effort," "interest," and "growth." But, ask two teachers what they mean by any one of those words, and more important, how they measure it? You will get little agreement. This seems to indicate that when we look at grades we want to be careful not to pay too much attention to any single grade, but rather concentrate on patterns of grades. This then becomes *one* factor that we can consider not only in looking at previous achievement, but also as a basis for future planning. The child who enters the sixth grade with consistently low marks in certain areas should probably not be expected to begin his studies in those areas at the sixth grade level.

Another guidance aspect to be derived from a look at grades is the information it gives teachers about previous successful school experiences. Few boys and girls continue to be motivated toward learning those things at which they regularly meet defeat, especially when defeat is viewed by them as low grades. What thoughts must go through the mind of a youngster entering junior high school knowing almost as surely as he knows his name that in his classes he will be asked to read books that he can't read, to take tests that he doesn't understand, and that, as a result, he will receive low grades. The teacher who foresees the possibility of this kind of situation arising is in a position to forearm himself not only with understanding and patience, but also, from a realistic point of view, with a wide range of classroom materials and teaching procedures that consider the needs of all the students.

Activities and experiences. The record of a student's activities and experiences both in and out-of-school may provide the classroom teacher with a new view of the pupil's interests and potentialities. The clubs which a student has joined, the sports which he enjoys playing, the jobs he has held, the places he has visited, the experiences which he has had, all contribute in varying degrees to the student's life. There are times when the teacher can offer an opportunity to explore some aspect of a student's experience in a new setting.

School experiences should not be isolated from other life experiences. A student who has very little or no feeling of success in school may be helped if some successful experience he has had outside of school can be brought into the activities of the classroom. Similarly, a bright student may be having a great deal of success in school in terms of grades, but his desire to learn may be dulled by what is to him the drabness of school work. If he has developed stimulating projects outside of school, there ought to be some way for him to continue to expand his interests and to interpret some of them to his classmates. A stamp collector's hobby can often be utilized in social studies; arithmetic takes on a new perspective for a coin collector or for an aspiring young athlete; visits that individual students have made to other towns, states, and countries have limitless possibilities for the teacher of geography, language, arithmetic; the jobs that a student has held and the job he now holds offer a wealth of material for almost any class. The record of the activities and experiences does not tell the teacher what meaning they have had for the student, but it can suggest new possibilities for revitalizing the curriculum and stimulating student interest.

The Teacher Uses Different Kinds of Test Data

This is probably the time to state explicitly a very important guidance point of view. No individual can really be understood by using data that we have collected about him, in isolation from the total picture of the person. School data need to be pooled with other information on the child's life experiences. When we recognize that we can seldom collect sufficient data about a school child in order to have a total picture, then we can realize how important it is not to judge a student on the basis of some isolated evidence, but to view all the data that we have accumulated over a period of time. If there is any area in guidance to which this last point particularly pertains it is testing.

There are at least three phases associated with a school's testing program. They are selection, administration, and use of tests. We are not going to concern ourselves with the first two phases except to state that teachers should be involved in the selection process, and that, if teachers in a particular school are to administer the tests, then an in-service training program should be provided for those teachers who are not familiar with test administration.

The testing program from kindergarten through the twelfth grade has become one of the most important data gathering devices in school today. That is to say, more and more tests are being given, and more and more scores are recorded. What has this meant for the classroom teacher? In most cases we have probably failed to help teachers see how they can use the test results professionally and effectively.

To begin with we need to rethink about the functions of tests in schools. The primary function is undoubtedly that of prediction. One of the first tests used in many schools today is a reading readiness test. Its purpose is to help us to know which youngsters are ready to begin certain reading experiences. As a child progresses through the grades he will be given a variety of tests labeled "aptitude," "achievement," "interest," and "adjustment" or "problem inventories." The one thing that all these have in common is that they are intended to help us in a prediction of some sort.

A teacher in an elementary school usually sees test scores that fall into two main categories: scholastic aptitude and achievement. When students enter the secondary school they may be given more scholastic aptitude and other kinds of specific aptitude tests, perhaps an aptitude test battery; they may take interest tests which are more correctly titled "interest inventories" rather than tests; they will probably take more achievement tests; and they may be asked to take some form of paper and pencil personality test or problem inventory. High school teachers encounter the results of a greater variety of tests, but teachers at all levels need to be aware of the valid uses of test results.

Scholastic aptitude or "intelligence test" data. "Tests of general scholastic aptitude have long been known as intelligence tests. There is now a tendency to favor the terms 'academic aptitude test' or 'scholastic aptitude test' rather than 'intelligence test,' because to many people 'intelligence test' implies a measure of native ability." [3]

The scholastic aptitude test score has become the device that many teachers use to predict the learning ability of the students in their classes. This practice is legitimate only if we are willing to make two extremely important assumptions. The first is that the test score is valid, that is, it is a true measure of the student's ability to do school work which will be scholastic in nature. A single test performance should be viewed with a great deal of caution, particularly in early elementary grades. In addition, test validity may be doubtful if the individuals tested are products of culturally limited backgrounds. Too often no real attempt has been made to enrich the lives of these students to enable them to overcome their verbal handicaps. Results on successive tests over a period of time may provide us with a more legitimate basis for assessing the student's aptitude.

The second assumption is that the performance that we want to predict is primarily verbal in nature. This seems to be a legitimate assumption.

Scholastic success is the most important educational goal in the minds of many students, parents, teachers, administrators, and others in the community. No one in education wants to stifle intellectual growth. What we often need to be reminded of, however, is that intel-

[3] Arthur E. Traxler, *Techniques of Guidance* (New York: Harper and Brothers, 1957), p. 53.

lectual growth does not take place in a vacuum. It is accompanied for every child by physical, social, and emotional growth. Standards of scholastic growth in terms such as increased desire to learn and ability to handle concepts and facts need not suffer because teachers begin to recognize the importance of other learnings. As teachers we can refuse to admit the value of the concomitant learnings in education but we can never ignore the fact that other than academic learnings are present.

There are many scholastic aptitude or group verbal tests, and the majority are reliable, but the results from different tests are *not interchangeable*. As Cronbach points out, "Not only have authors used different standardizing groups but they converted scores to 'I.Q's' which resemble Binet I.Q.'s only in having a mean of 100." [4] With standard deviations varying from about 10 to 26, Good states that "a very bright youngster might have, taking extremes, an I.Q. of 130 on one test and an I.Q. of 178 on another. Or, a child might have an I.Q. of 80 on one test and be judged a bit subnormal, and have an I.Q. of 48 on another and be classified as an imbecile." [5]

Some teachers have been known to label students according to their test scores. There are even instances where teachers have written test scores in their grade books opposite the students' names. The fact that some teachers are not professionally objective or at the moment not well trained to handle test results does not mean that all teachers should be denied test scores or should not utilize them. Every school has an obligation to set up a program that enables its faculty to recognize that test scores should be viewed cautiously but can be used intelligently when planning learning experiences for and with children. The teacher's role is not to interpret the test score to the individual unless he has developed a counseling relationship and is qualified to interpret tests on an individual basis. His role is to view the test results as another basis for understanding both the individual student and the class, and to plan learning situations accordingly.

It may be helpful to the reader to take a brief look at some representative group verbal tests in Table 1.

Other aptitude data. Many secondary schools now offer their students a variety of aptitude tests. The primary purpose is usually to

---

[4] Lee J. Cronbach, *Essentials of Psychological Testing* (New York: Harper and Brothers, 1949), p. 175.

[5] Warren R. Good, "Misconceptions About Intelligence Testing," *University of Michigan School of Education Bulletin,* May 1954.

TABLE 1

REPRESENTATIVE GROUP VERBAL TESTS [6]

Test; Publisher	*Grade Level*	*Time*	*Features*
ACE Psychological Examination; Educational Testing Service	9–12; College	65 min.	L score (linguistic) Q score (quantitative) T score (total score)
California Test of Mental Maturity; California Test Bureau	Kgn–1 1–3; 4–8; 7–10; 9–adult	90 min. or two 45 min. per.	I.Q. and Mental Age equivalents for the language test, the non-language test, and the total score
Henmon-Nelson; Houghton Mifflin	3–8; 7–12; College	30 min.	Easily administered
Kuhlmann-Finch; Educational Test Bureau	One for each grade 1–6; 7–9; 10–12	25 min. for all but sr. high which is 30 min.	Not easily administered; less verbal in content for early grades. Attempt to minimize cultural differences
Ohio State University Psychological Test, Form 21; Science Research Associates	9–12; College; Adults	120 min.	Power test, not a speed test; may be best single test score for predicting academic success in college
Otis Quick-Scoring; World Book	1–4; 4–9; 9–12; College; Adult	30 min. or 20 min.	Easiest and most economical to score. May not be very valid for lower grades
Terman-McNemar Test of Mental Ability; World Book	7–12	40 min.	Measures verbal ability exclusively

predict success in some future subject and possibly some future occupational area. One would be hard pressed indeed to find research that would justify aptitude tests as a basis for determining future occupational success. However, many schools have found that they can use certain aptitude tests for predicting scholastic success in some subject-matter fields. This is not a single-teacher project but one for an entire school under the direction of someone in the school system who has an adequate understanding of the process. An *expectancy table* is a device whereby students' test scores are related to grades in courses. This is based on the assumption that the best guess we can make

[6] The tests listed here and in subsequent tables in this chapter are reviewed by O. K. Buros, editor, *The Third Mental Measurements Yearbook* (New Brunswick, N.J.: Rutgers University Press, 1948), and *The Fourth Mental Measurements Yearbook* (Highland Park, N.J.: Gryphon Press, 1953).

about a student's probable scholastic success is what students with similar abilities have accomplished before him. The main advantage of the expectancy table would seem to be that it offers specific relationships for use by the teacher who has the task of explaining the results of tests to other teachers, students, and parents. Some of the dangers in test interpretations are considered later in this chapter.

Table 2 contains a list of representative batteries for differential testing of abilities.

TABLE 2

REPRESENTATIVE BATTERIES FOR DIFFERENTIAL TESTING OF ABILITIES[7]

Test; Publisher	*Grade Level*	*Kinds of Scores*
Differential Aptitude Tests; Psychological Corporation	8–12	Verbal reasoning, numerical ability, abstract reasoning, space relations, mechanical reasoning, clerical speed and accuracy, language usage
Guilford-Zimmerman Aptitude Survey; Sheridan Supply Co.	Adolescents and Adults	Verbal reasoning, numerical, perceptual speed, spatial orientation, spatial visualization, mechanical knowledge
Primary Mental Abilities; Science Research Associates	Age levels: 5–6; 7–11; 11–17; College Freshmen	Verbal, word fluency, number, space, reasoning, memory
USES General Aptitude Test Battery; United States Employment Service	Adults	General intelligence, V, N, S, P, clerical perception, aiming, motor speed, finger dexterity, manual dexterity

Achievement test results. Achievement testing has had a controversial history in education. It is interesting to note that "the first systematic comparison of school attainment was made by an educational crusader, J. M. Rice, in 1897. Rice was convinced that the pressure for perfection in certain types of achievement was leading to faulty emphasis in education, and prepared a test of spelling ability to determine what results could be expected. His test was given in twenty-one scattered cities and showed that, regardless of the time devoted to spelling, the test scores of eighth-graders were about the same in all cities. He showed further that although children in some cities were superior in spelling during early grades, presumably because of stress on that subject, such differences vanished by the end of schooling. It is ironical that Rice hoped by such evidence to show that the time

[7] *Ibid.*

spent on formal learning could be reduced, saving more time for an enriched curriculum." [8]

In many educational programs achievement testing has had the disturbing effect of putting the curriculum in a strait-jacket. In essence, the test has determined the curriculum. Teachers have been forced to provide the same learning experiences for every student regardless of community and pupil needs. Students may be motivated to study by this procedure. However, they often limit themselves to studying just the material on which they feel they will be tested. Some students may even spend more time figuring out techniques for taking different kinds of tests than they devote to the material to be studied.

MISUSE OF ACHIEVEMENT TESTS . . . BASIS FOR EVALUATING TEACHERS.

One of the more important misuses of achievement tests is the one whereby test results become a basis for evaluating teachers. When teachers are compared according to the test achievements of their students; when schools are compared similarly; then we have succeeded in making the test the master of the learning process, and teachers and administrators anxiety ridden pawns in the game of determining who can do the best job as a machine for imparting someone else's preconceived notion of what is good for all boys and girls to know.

[8] Cronbach, *Essentials of Psychological Testing*, pp. 272-273.

The concept of *curricular validity* is particularly pertinent to the area of achievement testing. "A test has curriculum validity if it measures fairly the extent to which pupils have learned what the curriculum was intended to teach them." [9] What the curriculum intends to teach boys and girls is not measurable by any single test or even by any group of standardized tests in existence today. This is perhaps the most important generalization for teachers and administrators concerned with achievement testing, and it becomes clearly discernible when teachers and administrators place their objectives alongside their tests.

Achievement tests can be useful. The newer forms of achievement testing focus attention on measures of behavior such as ability to apply principles, reasoning skills, and ability to interpret data. An awareness of the particular aspects of an achievement test plus the performance of his students on that test should help a teacher avoid the kinds of learning experiences that are beyond some of his students. They may also suggest some experiences for those who have a high degree of ability to reason and interpret. This is one reason why so many schools have moved in the direction of using achievement survey tests at the beginning of the semester. Teachers and administrators can then use test results as an educational rather than a training tool. Table 3 describes some representative achievement test batteries.

Interest inventories. Teachers have at least three methods for finding out what a student's interests are. One way is to look at the student's stated interest. What does he say that he is interested in? Another way is to observe the student in action or to study what he has done previously. How does the student manifest his interests? A third way is to look at the results of an inventory of his interests. Teachers in the elementary grades cannot make use of interest inventories, because there are none with any validity for that level. Ordinarily it isn't until late in junior high school that interest inventories begin to have some utility.

When used correctly as a guidance tool along with other data about an individual, especially data regarding aptitude, interest inventories do have some value. Unfortunately there has been a great deal of misunderstanding by many people in education on two issues regarding interest inventories. First, what do scores on interest inventories reveal, and second, what constitute valid procedures for using the results with students?

[9] *Ibid*, p. 274.

TABLE 3

REPRESENTATIVE ACHIEVEMENT TEST BATTERIES[10]

Test; Publisher	*Grade Level*	*Content*	*Features*
California Achievement Test Batteries; California Test Bureau	1–3; 4–6; 7–9; 9–14	Reading, arithmetic, language	Easily administered, scored and recorded
Cooperative Achievement Tests; Educational Testing Service	High School	English tests (Mechanics of expression, effectiveness of expression, reading comprehension), vocabulary, dictionary, general math, social studies, natural sciences	Offers a variety of subject matter and other kinds of achievement tests
General Educational Development Tests; (USAFI) Educational Testing Service	High School College	Mathematics, expression, interpretation of reading materials in social studies, natural sciences, and literary	Have been used to grant servicemen high school diplomas; reading ability may be too important
Iowa Tests of Educational Development; Science Research Associates	High School	Nine tests: Basic social concepts, background in natural sciences, expression, quantitative thinking, reading materials, etc.	May be best battery for measuring general education
Metropolitan Achievement Tests; World Book	1; 2–3; 3–4; 4–6; 7–8	Vary according to level; attempts to include all subject matter according to level	Stresses mastery of subject matter, not problem-solving ability
Stanford Achievement Tests	2–3; 4–6; 7–9	Skill subjects: reading, language, arithmetic, spelling, etc.	Subject matter content may not be up to date

It is extremely important to recognize that interest inventories are self-reports, not tests of ability or achievement. The student is letting us know, through the indirect fashion of a paper and pencil test, the interests he has (at a particular time) in common with people in certain occupational categories. Some people have likened interest inventories to personality inventories. However, this is an erroneous impression. Whereas a subject will often conceal his attitudes and feelings in an adjustment inventory, he can more easily be motivated to provide an honest self-report regarding his interests. There are clinical aspects to interest inventories, but they are seldom openly threatening to a student. Teachers, of course, will not want to use interest inventory

[10] O. K. Buros, *op. cit.*

results as diagnostic tools in a personality assessment, since teachers are not hired or qualified to function as clinicians.

Interest inventory results are intended to help students as they look to the future. They provide another aid whereby the student can decide what his future will be as he considers course work in school and possible future occupational goals later. Homeroom teachers, teachers of group guidance units, and teachers who function as counselors may have recourse to the use of interest inventories.

This kind of test may be administered to students on a group basis and scored by them. Unfortunately many schools have followed the easy way of interpreting results only on a group basis. There is no substitute for the interpretation of test results on an individual basis. Limitations of time do not justify the misuse of tests. Adolescents may be told in a group what interest inventory scores represent, but many of them will go home with misinterpretations as to the meaning of their inventory profiles. As they talk with their families or friends they may fail to distinguish ability from interest or interest in an occupation from interests similar to the interests of some people in that occupation. Table 4 contains a description of four representative interest inventories.

TABLE 4

REPRESENTATIVE INTEREST INVENTORIES[11]

Test; Publisher	*Age Level*	*Content*	*Features*
Brainard Occupational Preference Inventory; Psychological Corporation	Adolescents; Adults	Seven fields subdivided into areas	Has brevity
Kuder Preference Record; Science Research Associates	High School College	Ten areas including a verification score	Self-scoring; may initiate student's consideration of occupations
Lee-Thorpe Occupational Interest Inventory; California Test Bureau	Adolescents	Artistic, business, etc.	May provide leads to interviewing rather than curriculum
Strong Vocational Interest Blank; Stanford	Adolescent and Adult; men, women	400 items covering wide range of interests	Empirical keys relating students' choices to those of adults in different occupations

Problem inventories. This area of testing is the one that needs to be viewed for teacher use more cautiously than any other. Many per-

[11] O. K. Buros, *op. cit.*

sonnel workers get quite concerned at the thought of classroom teachers with limited backgrounds in testing using any kind of adjustment or problem inventory test.

The clinicians are aware that in this kind of paper and pencil test expressed problems are not often the real problems. They also recognize that importance needs to be attached not to a problem, but to a patterning of problems. However, we feel that there are at least two legitimate uses of this kind of test by classroom teachers.

The use of an instrument such as the Mooney Problem Check List or the SRA Youth Inventory can be justified when it is viewed as a means for discovering common problems. A teacher may be interested in the problems of her class, or a faculty may want data on the problems of its entire student body. Here then we have an opportunity to provide data that will enable a teacher or an entire faculty to study and understand their groups better. In this fashion the inventory is being used as an educational tool that will help relate a school's program more realistically to the needs of the students which it serves. If the instrument is to be used primarily for studying and understanding group problems, it may be desirable to administer it without asking students to sign their names or in any way to identify themselves. By eliminating any possible threat to the individual the data are likely to be more reliable and valid.

The problem inventory can be utilized on an individual basis also. Some inventories have a question at the end, "Is there someone in school with whom you would like to discuss any of your problems?" Responses to that kind of question serve as excellent leads to later interviews by the teacher or referrals by the teacher to whomever the student has mentioned.

The Teacher Understands the Responsibilities Involved in Test Interpretations

In recent years the authors have noted an alarming trend in many schools where good testing programs have been established on paper. The pressure of time and the lack of understanding regarding the need for careful interpretation have resulted in test results being interpreted on a group basis with students being given their test profiles to take home and discuss with their parents. Skilled counselors who interpret test data in carefully qualified fashion to students and parents *on an individual basis* are aware of the problems that arise because of the uncertainties involved in the way in which the student or his parents will perceive the results. Most psychologists would not give a client a test score unless they could interpret the score so that the client would understand it. If the latter is true of test interpretations to individuals, can any school justify mass interpretations of test results? No consideration of expediency justifies such an unacceptable practice.

Sometimes teachers and counselors feel that students and parents need to be made aware of certain realities. The teacher or counselor may regard his position as that of the objective scientist reporting the facts—just the facts. On the other hand, the student or his parents may be viewing the interpretations with a great deal of emotional involvement. The dilemma that is posed results from the fact that there are *two* realities. The first is the professional responsibility of the tester to learn the truth (assuming he knows what truth is in this instance) and report it; the second is that tests have emotional significance for individuals, and the teacher or counselor is there to promote the welfare of the student. This means that responsibility cannot be viewed just as giving students and parents realistic interpretations, but also should include helping them resolve emotional conflicts which the test interpreter may have aroused.

Summary

Cumulative records can be useful guidance tools for classroom teachers. An effort needs to be made on a school wide basis to develop the best procedures for obtaining the data, recording them, and locating them so that they are easily accessible for use by the classroom teacher. The kind of data that are collected in a fairly formal fashion by almost all schools are personal and family background, health, attendance, scholarship, activities and experiences, and test scores. These data can be utilized by the classroom teacher as an aid to studying and understanding the individual students and the class. At times the data may suggest needed curriculum changes and also changes in the student-teacher relationship. The cumulative record is not meant to be used to give teachers a favorable or unfavorable reaction toward a youngster. It is intended for use by teachers who are trained to use the data in a professionally objective manner. As teachers increase their knowledge and understanding of those whom they teach, they should be able to function more effectively.

Selected Readings

American Personnel and Guidance Association, *The Use of Multifactor Tests in Guidance.* Washington, D.C.: American Personnel and Guidance Association, 1957.

Buros, O. K., editor, *The Third Mental Measurements Yearbook.* New Brunswick, N.J.: Rutgers University Press, 1948.

———, *The Fourth Mental Measurements Yearbook.* Highland Park, N.J.: Gryphon Press, 1954.

Cronbach, Lee J., *Essentials of Psychological Testing.* New York: Harper and Brothers, 1949.

McDaniel, Henry B. and G. A. Shaftel, *Guidance in the Modern School.* New York: Dryden Press, Inc., 1956.

Super, Donald E., *Appraising Vocational Fitness by Means of Psychological Tests.* New York: Harper and Brothers, 1949.

Traxler, Arthur E., *Techniques of Guidance.* New York: Harper and Brothers, 1957.

CHAPTER 7

The Teacher Works with Individual Students

As teachers tend to work increasingly with students on an individual basis both within and outside the classroom setting, questions arise as to the nature of this teacher-pupil relationship. Almost all teachers do some work with individual students. Our concern here is with understanding the role of the teacher who works with a student apart from the rest of the class. Is this just an academic relationship? Does the teacher ever occupy a counseling role? Should he accept the counselor's role as one of his functions? Is it possible to discover a point at which the academic relationship becomes a counseling one? These and other questions are of great concern to more and more educators. The trend toward job specialization at times tends to lessen the effectiveness of the guidance programs in the schools. This is not to decry the definite need to designate specific personnel as counselors and to provide adequate time and facilities for counseling. What curbs the effectiveness of a guidance program is the tendency on the part of many—particularly those who have never been classroom teachers—to define the teaching and counseling functions as if they were mutually exclusive.

The Teacher Views His Possibilities as a Counselor

Some people resist the concept that teachers can function as counselors. Too often the argument centers on an all-or-nothing basis. "All teachers are counselors" or "A teacher cannot be a counselor." The authors agree with the idea that it would be desirable if all teachers were counselors, but we recognize that this situation doesn't exist today. However we do feel that teachers can function as counselors. We believe that counseling has different degrees of intensity, and that the kind of counseling which is a legitimate function of personnel in educational institutions can, in many instances, be performed by classroom teachers as well as by the person with the title "school counselor." In many universities, especially in the master's degree program, a large percentage of the majors are not contemplating future careers as school counselors but are concerned with being able to do a better job of teaching.

The counseling that goes on in a school setting *is not psychotherapy.* The latter statement may embroil the authors in disagreement with others in the field of guidance and counseling. In the end it probably would be dismissed as semantic quibbling over the concept of psychotherapy. Our position however is that teachers, teacher-counselors, and counselors function with children who are reality-oriented and who are not deeply disturbed emotionally. The counseling process in the schools involves education, not re-education. There is a difference between the school situation and a strictly therapeutic one. "The school counselor," McDaniel has pointed out, "is concerned primarily with normal people," and "works in an institution which has development and learning as its chief objectives." [1] The authors would be inclined to agree with Arbuckle's statement that "the teacher-counselor does not refer at the first sign of any disturbance." [2] However, recognizing one's ability to function effectively and professionally imposes a necessary limit on the kind of counseling that can be done. As Gordon has said, "The teacher-counselor cannot be all things to all students. He must be clearly aware of his limits and use referral processes when the counseling situation seems to be going 'out of his depth.' " [3]

This book has not been written to train teachers to become counselors. Therefore we have not included detailed descriptions of the counseling process nor enumerated the attitudes and skills needed in order to be a competent counselor. It would take more than a brief chapter to relate adequately all the things which are involved in the intricate process of counseling. The teacher's concept of himself, his role as counselor, his attitudes, and his skills, the student's self-concept, his concept of others, his defenses, the counselor's ability to function as a counselor from a variety of orientations such as clinical, client-centered, or eclectic, all these represent important elements of the counseling process. A great deal has been written in the area, and

[1] McDaniel and Shaftel, *op. cit.*, p. 120.

[2] Dugald S. Arbuckle, *Guidance and Counseling in the Classroom* (Boston: Allyn and Bacon, 1957), p. 113.

[3] Ira J. Gordon, *The Teacher as a Guidance Worker* (New York: Harper and Brothers, 1956), p. 279.

anyone interested would do well to do extensive reading from the selections listed at the end of this chapter. Teachers desiring to function as counselors should keep in mind the primary function of a counselor which is to do what is best for the pupil, and, through counseling, to help a student increase his self-understanding and learn how to solve future problems more effectively than he is solving his current ones.

The kind of counseling possible in schools has been defined by McDaniel and Shaftel "as a series of direct contacts with the individual aimed at offering him assistance in adjusting more effectively to himself and to his environment." He then goes on to state "this very broad definition places emphasis not so much upon the techniques employed as upon the *relationships which exist between counselor and client*." [4] The point of view of the authors is that the teacher's relationship with his pupils in a classroom often leads to possibilities for establishing good counseling rapport.

The Teacher Develops Opportunities Through the Curriculum

Classroom situations vary in the extent to which teachers are able to work with students on an individual basis. Some teachers have just one class for a whole year. Others may have five classes for half of a school year. If we look at the time possibilities alone, the former teachers might have as many as one thousand hours with one class, and the latter less than one hundred hours. Obviously the teacher who has more time to spend with fewer students is in a better position not only to recognize the characteristics which make a student an individual, but also to work with him.

Elementary school educators have been the leading advocates of providing teachers with more time to work with fewer students. The growth of the core curriculum movement in the secondary schools has been given a great deal of impetus with the recognition that getting teachers to feel responsible for more than intellectual growth is not realistic unless they are provided with the means of perceiving and working with students individually. This is not to imply that the majority of high school teachers can not or should not attempt to work with their students on an individual basis. It is probably impossible to conceive of any classroom situation where a teacher would not need to do some individual work with each student.

[4] McDaniel and Shaftel, *op. cit.*, p. 120.

Almost every classroom teacher at some time or other finds it desirable to establish with at least some of his students an individual relationship to consider academic questions. The degree to which a teacher develops opportunities for individual contacts through the curriculum is undoubtedly closely related to the manner in which he operates as a teacher. If he tries to utilize the experiences of the members of the class, allows them to assume some responsibility for their learning, and concerns himself with what these new learning experiences mean for his pupils, he is going to be confronted with a variety of opportunities to talk with different students individually. The initial relationship between a teacher and a pupil may be centered around some aspect of the curriculum. The student's perception of the teacher will play an important part in the development of any future relationship.

The Teacher Promotes the Classroom Climate That Makes a Counseling Relationship Possible

A teacher-pupil relationship does not always have to start via the teacher or with an academic situation. Many times students go to teachers to discuss a variety of problems. The teachers to whom students go represent a cross-section of grade-levels, courses taught, and teaching methods.

How can this happen? Aren't students supposed to perceive teachers as authoritarian and limiting adults? Is it impossible for a teacher to promote the kind of emotional climate in the classroom that would lead an individual pupil to be able to see the teacher as a non-threatening adult and someone to whom he can go with some of his problems? Kelley had fifteen students in a core curriculum class fill out a youth inventory and then asked them, "With whom would you like to talk over these problems?" Five named the core teacher, two, their guidance counselor, three, other teachers; of the other five, two named a specific parent, one, a minister, and two, people in the community.[5] Many school teachers have long been familiar with the same kinds of data. They have recognized that students are selective in their choices of the adults with whom they are willing to discuss their problems. It seems then that students tend to seek out that person in the school with whom they feel they might have a secure relationship.

What promotes this kind of relationship? To label it as good teaching would be true but not helpful. Students have to be able to perceive

[5] Janet A. Kelley, *Guidance and Curriculum* (Englewood Cliffs, N. J.: Prentice-Hall, Inc., 1955), p. 387.

THE CLASSROOM CLIMATE MAKES A COUNSELING RELATIONSHIP POSSIBLE.

teachers in a certain light, and their perceptions are usually based on feeling tones. What the teacher says is probably not as significant as the attitudes he conveys. The teacher must be sensed as having genuine respect for the individual. He needs to be regarded as an accepting adult rather than a judgmental one. He has to be thought of as one who will understand the student. *Respect for the individual, acceptance, and understanding* are demonstrable to students not as techniques but by the way in which the teacher operates as a human being.

The Teacher Finds Time for Informal Conversation with Students

Counseling has been conceived of by many as a process that is limited to a formal setting. However, who is to say what kind of situation is best at all times? We know that we improve counseling the closer we can bring the time a student feels like talking about something to the time that we arrange to talk with him. The student who has a problem and wants to talk about it now may be deterred by his inability to get an early appointment. The sequence of events within the total milieu which leads to particular kinds of behavior and feelings on the part of the student, creates opportunities for teachers that often cannot be provided in formal interviews. These may occur in the classroom, in the hall, in the cafeteria, or on the playground.

The situations which follow were real and illustrate how opportunities may occur. Note that the counseling skills of these teachers are seldom those of the expert counselor. However, we have here examples of teachers to whom students came, and this opportunity to help the student was recognized and utilized. (The letter "T" refers to the teacher, the letter "S" to the student. The teacher's comments are enclosed in parentheses, while those of the authors are in brackets.)

I

Informal Interview with a Thirteen Year Old Boy

What the teacher knew about the boy prior to the interview: Jim is in the eighth grade and has maintained a good academic standard though his full capabilities do not seem always to have been realized. His scholastic aptitude scores on two different tests taken in the earlier grades seemed to indicate verbal ability slightly above average. Jim had two physical difficulties: (1) poor eyesight—with a strong correction in glasses; (2) overweight—had been overweight for the last three years, but had just recently dieted and lost twenty five pounds so that his appearance was normal for his age. The father is an airline pilot and the mother has returned to college to become a teacher. Jim's grandmother has lived with his family for the past year.

The Interview:

(The following meeting took place in the cafeteria where I was on duty. The student seemed to approach me uneasily at first. As the conversation went on, I realized the boy had a definite problem, and actually was seeking help and understanding. Thus this meeting certainly became an interview though not in a place conducive to a good interview situation.)

S: Hi, Mr. King.

T: Hello, Jim, what's on your mind today?

S: Nothing much—I was just over there (pointing to a group of 8th grade girls seated at a table in the cafeteria. Most of the other kids had left the lunchroom). Boy! We really have some pretty sharp girls around here, haven't we? (Surprised by this remark from the student. Studious appearance—not the type usually interested in girls at this age and the type the girls seem to go for.)

[Sometimes we teachers don't know what our students are really interested in or concerned about.]

T: Yes, I would say that we have a lot of pretty girls.

S: That Jo Ann is the one I really go for.

T: You really like her, eh?

S: Ya, but she don't go for *me*. (Student looked down at feet while making this statement.)

T: How do you know?

S: She won't even talk to me. I say 'Hi' to her and Sharon and they both say, 'Get out of here.' (Long pause. Student was not looking at me. The long pause seemed more uncomfortable for me than for the student, but I felt he had something more he wanted to say.) She doesn't care if I live or die so what's the difference? (This last statement was full of emotion. I thought, "what a childish statement. He's not meeting the situation very realistically.")

T: I don't believe she feels that way at all.

[Teacher does not seem too understanding here of the student's problem or his feelings. In spite of this the student continues to reveal important feelings about himself.]

S: Sure she does—she goes for Jack. You know him. I guess it's just me. (This seemed to be stated with the implication that Jack was not a good guy for her to know. Jack is 13, tall, strong, loud, an athlete, and very forward with the girls.)

T: You feel you don't have a chance with Jo Ann.

S: Nope, the sharp girls go for the big wheels around here. (Short pause.) What can you do about it? (Considerable pause) (This question did not seem to be put to me but to the world at large.)

T: Could you be using the wrong approach to these girls?

S: I don't know. The other guys just stand around and whistle at them when they walk by. That's not the way to get a girl. Maybe I'm behind times, old-fashioned or something. You know—the guys stand outside of Barton's and whistle at girls and say things to them especially in front of adults who are walking by. They call, 'Hi Grandma' to older women and 'Pops' to the old men. I think sometimes girls have funny ideas about the guys they want to go out with.

T: You mean you feel the girls tend to want to go out with the guys who aren't good?

S: You don't know the number of girls we have who go out with bad guys at night in cars doing the wrong things. Your teen code didn't change that any.
(This statement seemed to be made very challengingly.)

T: Maybe these kids didn't have the proper guidance as they were growing up.

S: Ya, take Jean. She didn't have any guidance. Only guidance she's had has been at school. Now she's teaching her younger sister all the things she learns in those cars at night. (At this point the student entered into a long account of the bad reputation his class has gotten as a result of the actions of kids like Jean.) Guidance is all right, but too much is junk. That's the way my grandma is. Like when I stayed to watch Mr. Star fix his car the other night. I got home at 5 o'clock and she gave me a hard time. Since my mom works she thinks she's the boss around the house. She even tells my mother and dad what to do. (Considerable pause.) Everything was all right until my grandmother came to live with us. (Unfortunately, at this point the bell rang and I had to proceed to my next class. I felt that we were about to make some significant progress. He asked if he might talk to me again, and I assured him that he could any time that I had free. We are to have lunch together this Friday.)

[Even though many of the teacher's responses were centered on the student's statements rather than the feelings underlying them, it can readily be seen that the student was in a mood to talk, and in the process he revealed a great many anxieties—not atypical for an early adolescent—and he disclosed at the end of the interview some strong feelings about his grandmother. The teacher has learned a great deal from this conversation and is in a much better position to give him the understanding and help that may be needed.]

II

Informal Interview with a Thirteen Year Old Girl

What the teacher knew about the girl prior to the interview: Barb is attending a special education program for youngsters with orthopedic handicaps. She has scoliosis or curvature of the spine. Her intelligence is reported to be dull normal. She is the adopted daughter of a boarding mother. Barb had been moody for a few days before this conversation took place. I was aware that she was going to have surgery and suspected that this was the reason for her moodiness.

The Interview:

T: Barb, is something bothering you today? You look kind of depressed.

S: No, nothing's wrong.

T: O.K., but if you want to talk something over remember that we have all the time that the kids are resting.
(Barb left, but a few minutes later another youngster came to tell me that she was crying. I asked her to tell Barb that I would like to talk with her. Barb returned.)

T: Sit down, Barb. Do you feel like talking or do you just want to sit here for a while?

S: (Stopping her crying) I don't want to go.

T: To the hospital, you mean?

S: Yes, I don't want to go again.

T: This is the second operation on your back, isn't it?

S: Yes.

T: Are you worrying a lot about it?

S: Not a whole lot. I guess I'm scared.

T: Were you afraid the first time?

S: No. (Pause)

T: Do you know why you are afraid?

S: I just don't think I'll make it.

T: You won't make it?

S: No. . .

T: Can you tell me what you mean.

S: I just won't make it, that's all.

T: You feel that you might not come through the surgery?

S: Yes. I almost didn't the last time.

T: You had trouble the last time.

S: My mother told me that I almost died. I had to have a lot of blood transfusions.

T: Barb, almost any type of surgery means that the person has to have blood transfusions. Ask Miss Stone. She used to be a nurse.

S: But my mother told me that I almost died.

T: Did the doctors say anything about it?

S: No.

T: Did you ask them?

S: Yes, but I didn't get any answer.

T: You're afraid of this operation because of the experience you had with the last one.

S: Yes.

T: I thought that the doctors said this was going to be a very simple operation.

S: Yes. It's supposed to be like a pin scratch.

T: Did you mention these fears to the doctor when he told you about this operation.

S: No, I was afraid to because my mother would say I was being a baby.

T: Then you didn't have a chance to talk to the doctor.

[Teacher has been missing some good opportunities to get at the girl's feelings, and has just now overlooked what may be one of her real concerns, her relationship with her mother.]

S: No.

T: Have you talked to your mother about it?

S: I tried to, but she said I was silly and that I was too big a girl to act like that. She got mad when I started to cry in the doctor's office.

T: You cried when the doctor told you that you would have to have another operation?

S: Yes, but my mother got mad and yelled at me for crying.

T: Have you talked to your mother about your fears since then?

S: Every time I try to talk about it, she tells me I'm silly and for me to grow up.

T: Would it help if I talked to your mother.

S: Oh, no. She'd get real mad at me.

T: You think about this a lot, don't you?

S: I try not to, but every time I do, it doesn't work. Right in the middle of my work I start to think about it. I try not to, but I just can't help it.

T: And you don't think I could see your mother?

S: No. She'd probably get real mad.

T: Well, Barb, if it gives you any comfort, I know the doctor said that it would be a very simple kind of operation, and there would be no chance of anything happening to you. Will you be sure to come and talk to me about this again if you feel yourself getting disturbed.

S: Yes . . . It feels better 'cause I told somebody.

T: You can go back in and get some rest, since there is still some time left.

[This teacher is probably too oriented to giving direction to his conversations with his students, but he still manages to learn a great deal about the girl's fears regarding the impending operation, her feelings about the relationship with her mother, and the way she is perceived by her mother.]

III

Informal Interview with a Girl in the Seventh Grade

What the teacher knew about the girl prior to the interview: Kay is thirteen and had an I.Q. score of 82 on an Otis administered in the sixth grade. She is in a homogeneously arranged group with students of her ability. In achievement, she rates low in this group. Most of her classmates are twelve years of age. She has been in this group and school for only twelve weeks.

Kay is of average height, tending to look heavier than some of her peers since her immature waist line has not yet begun to recede toward its more mature appearance. Her hair is dark brown, slightly curled at the ends by an unset permanent wave. Her features, particularly her eyes, are small—the eyes being set close together, the mouth tiny.

Kay's record indicates that she has two brothers, ages eighteen and twenty. The records mention no sisters. She lives with her parents and brothers.

First Interview:

(It is three-thirty in the afternoon. Kay comes into the science room. She approaches the teacher who is engaged in planting cuttings in a planter table at the back of the science room.)

S: (Hesitantly): Do you . . . ah? Carol told me to come and ask you if you like my haircut. Do you like it?

T: (Smiling): It looks very nice. Did you have it done by anyone special?

S: (Smiling briefly): My mother and I went to this hairdresser last night. She's a lady mother knows. It's funny. Do you know? My mother and I both have a funny hair line. See. Back here. It grows way down here. (She puts hand on back of neck to indicate the low hair line.)

T: (Nodding understanding and encouragement): Uh-huh. Yes. I see.

S: Well, this hairdresser says its hard to cut when it's this way. She says it's funny we both are exactly the same. It has to be clipped way up. (She turns and points again to the shaved and shingled hair line at the back of her neck.)

T: It really does look neat. I like it. I guess you do, too, don't you?

S: (Grinning): Yes, I do. It's just like my mother's. We had the same haircuts.

(Pause) (The teacher takes another cutting from the jar at hand, and places it in the planter.)

T: Would you like to try one?

S: Oh, could I?

T: Certainly.

S: (Kay is busily working the dirt in the planter): Mrs. Carlson, did you . . . , have you . . . , Well, were you ever . . . I mean . . . Did you ever feel uncomfortable around people? The kids call me fat.

T: (Speaking slowly and seriously in a confidential tone of voice): I guess you mean one can feel uneasy around someone or some people.

S: Well, yes. At home I feel fine and easy and like I belong. Here at school I don't. I don't know . . . (Pauses and seems to be thinking and concentrating on problem.)

S: (Going on slowly): My mother says she feels that way sometimes. She says everyone does. Do you?

T: It's as if school is not such a familiar place as home, perhaps.

S: I don't know. At home my mother is there; my sister and I. My mother is short. We're all short. Mrs. Carlson, do you think I'm short?

T: (Without hesitation): You feel you are shorter than the other girls?

S: (Seriously): Well, no. But they say I am. They always call me short and fat. (Pause)
I don't know. At home my mother is short and my sister is there. We're all short. I feel O.K., but here the kids tease and I feel different. . .

T: (Picking up trowel and digging a trench, repeating): You feel that you are different from the other girls in your class.

S: At home we don't mind that we're short. We have fun. My sister is older than I am, but we're all there together and I feel good. Do you think I'm fat?

T: I guess you feel as if you really belong when you're at home.

S: That's right. None of these kids were my friends in sixth grade. Maybe that's why I feel this way.

T: (Thoughtfully): M-hm. You're feeling, perhaps, that you have not become really well acquainted with any of your new classmates.

S: Maybe that's it. I really don't know.

T: (Planting last cutting): Well, there that's in. Is it really four o'clock. We'll have to get along. Will you come in again to let me know how you're getting along?

S: (Eagerly): O.K. I'd like to. I'll go now. Good night, Mrs. Carlson.

[The teacher has focused on the girl and allowed her to select the topics for discussion. From this has emerged the beginnings of a good adult relationship for the student. It has also given the teacher insight into Kay's difficulties with her peer group.]

Second Interview with Kay:

(Kay had been seated next to Carol until the time of the first interview. Noting that she had chosen one day to sit next to Jeri Lee in class, the teacher had suggested she might change her seat to this one if she preferred. Kay had appeared eager to do this.

It is again three-thirty, a week later when Kay comes into the science room.)

T: Hi, Kay. Did you have a good day?

S: (With a slight smile) Pretty good. You look nice in that outfit Mrs. Carlson.

T: (Noting Kay's new spring cotton dress with its too low, gathered waistline): You look nice and springlike yourself. Is yours new?

S: Yes. My mother was downtown and bought it yesterday.

T: (Smiles, pauses for a few seconds. She is washing beakers, funnels, and other laboratory equipment.) Would you like to give me a hand with these? When they're wiped, we'll store them on this shelf. (This activity is being carried on in a science storage room containing sink, counter, and cupboards. Kay puts down her books, picks up towel, and begins to polish the glassware and stack it on the shelf indicated.)

S: I like sitting next to Jeri Lee in science. (Pause) I'm doing better in it now too.

T: I guess you feel more satisfied with what you do. It's as if you know what to do and when to do it.

S: Yes. (Smiles quickly and briefly). Jeri Lee doesn't tease like Carol did.

T: (Nods in understanding.)

S: (Pause) It's hard to get to know the kids in junior high. They're all different. Some come from one school, some from another.

T: Junior high is sort of a mixing bowl where everyone is shuffled up, I suppose.

S: My mother keeps telling me it will soon feel the same as sixth grade. She says she felt strange when she moved to our new neighborhood.

T: Do you remember how you felt when you first began sixth grade?

S: We had Mr. Grant. I was real scared. The kids said he was tough. But he wasn't.

T: (Pause) I suppose when you became acquainted with the class and him you felt better about it.

S: I wasn't scared anymore. I liked helping do things. I help my mother a lot at home.

T: You like to do things. I imagine it makes you feel good to know you help.

S: I don't know. I feel good if my dad says he likes the cookies I bake. Where does this go? What is it?

T: That's a crucible. It's kept in this drawer. (Student and teacher have been leaning on the counter as they talked.)

S: I like to do things for people.

T: People are fun. Aren't they? (Smiles and Kay returns smile. Pause)

S: I think I'll ask Jeri Lee to come to my house some day. She asked me to sit by her.

T: You feel you know her better now than some of the others.

S: Well, yes. (Speaks slowly, hesitantly.) But she doesn't tease me any more. She said she likes my new dress.

T: It's as if you enjoy being with Jeri Lee now.

S: Yes, more than some of the others.

T: Let's feed the fish before we go home.

(They walk together to the aquarium, sprinkle fish food over the water, watch the fish for a few minutes before Kay speaks.)

S: Science rooms are fun. Can we look at those bugs some day?

T: Surely. Come back again soon. Won't you?

S: O.K. Mrs. Carlson. I'd like to. Good night.

T: Good night, Kay.

[The teacher utilized in the classroom some of the things she had learned about Kay. This interview points out some of Kay's reactions, and indicates that her adjustment to her peer group, although still beset with difficulties, has improved. The girl sounds less tense. A good counseling relationship would appear to have been established.]

IV

Informal Conference with a Girl in the Eighth Grade

What the teacher knew about the girl prior to the interview: As a teacher-counselor in my school I had had several opportunities to get acquainted with Tanya. She was slender and slight, and she loved dramatic gestures. Previous interviews had been held at the request of the mother because of difficulties Tanya had with several girl friends. In one of the interviews Tanya had said, "I have a high IQ and an eleventh grade reading level, you know." Tanya's grades were mostly C and D. Her relations with her peers were such that when I allowed Tanya to come into my journalism class, the girls in the class came up to me afterwards and protested. Tanya had never really seemed to accept me as a counselor, and in the beginning it appeared that I would not have a good relationship with her in class. After several months an opportunity to talk with Tanya on an entirely different basis came up. It is important to understand the background however from which the conference emerged.

A Summary of the Discussion on the Feature Story:

The eighth grade journalism students were beginning their study of the newspaper feature story. Because the definition included the phrase "appeals to the reader's emotions," the teacher explained to the students that they would first have to define and discuss "emotions" before they could get very far in the lesson.

The children knew what an emotion was—a strong feeling that a person has.

The discussion and behavior that followed when they started to name the various emotions were typical of their thirteen year old age group. The mere mention of the word "love" brought forth the usual giggles, wise-cracks and raucous laughter until the teacher explained that from the journalism point of view, "love" included liking, admiration for and respect for —and that boys could like (or dislike) other things besides girls—for example, animals, pets, parents, brothers and sisters—and even teachers.

Everybody seemed to like pets so we discussed our feelings for pets. We were back on safe ground again.

With this "feeling" tone established, the teacher passed around clippings of feature stories from the metropolitan dailies, which included stories about the closing of the zoo and the animals' reactions to the people they saw, the death of the baby Siberian tigress and the lonesomeness of the surviving brother, the curtains in the Royal Oak dog pound, the pathetic story of the father who had only three dollars with which to bury his six children burned to death in a fire, etc. The children read these stories silently, occasionally pointing out some phrase or expression they particularly liked. The emotional effect the reporters had striven for was there.

Tanya's reaction was much the same as the other children except at the beginning. She made the statement that she just couldn't read this story because sad stories made her cry. The children seemed absorbed in their reading and no one made any comment. Tanya then read all the stories and there were no tears.

We were now ready to discuss emotions. The children made a list of the various feelings and talked freely about anger, jealousy and envy as well as others.

Near the end the teacher made a summary of their statements:

> An emotion is a feeling that comes from the inside.
> Everybody has these feelings.
> A person would be pretty dull if he didn't have any feelings.
> Some are good and some are bad—at least not-so-good.

The majority refused to accept the idea suggested by one student that even bad emotions might be good for one.
You just have to learn to control the bad ones.
The control comes from reasoning the thing out.

The teacher concluded the discussion with a remark that it was good to talk about emotions because emotions would play an important part in their lives the next few years in the process of growing up. When these feelings came, it would help to recognize them as emotions, admit it, at least to themselves, not to let these feelings worry them, and to go on from there.

We studied next the mechanics of feature story writing.

Four Days Later:

The editor assigned Tanya a story for the local newspaper the day before. She covered the story, checked the details, and wrote the story during the class period.

Tanya no longer gets as far away from the teacher and other students as she did when writing a story. She sat at the table where the other children were writing, but on the fringe, however. She kept busy all the hour, working calmly and quietly. She seemed to be finished near the end of the hour, but she made no move to put her work away when the other children did. The dismissal bell rang and the other children left. I was standing at the doorway. Remembering how difficult it was for Tanya to hand her writing to me and that I always had been standing when she did, I slipped quietly into a chair at the table where she was. Tanya remained in her seat and handed the story to me.

The Interview:

(Through all this conversation that follows Tanya talked quietly. There was no wringing of hands, no exaggerated intonation, no facial grimaces.)

S: Well, here it is. Oh, dear, I wish I could get over the awful feeling I have every time I hand in anything I write. (Pause)

T: You enjoy writing but you don't like to hand it in?

S: Yes, I've checked this carefully. I know I have the 5 w's in the lead. The names are spelled correctly because I checked them from the flat files. But yet I hate to hand it in.
I'm such a sensitive soul. I'm this way in all my classes when I have anything that's my own writing to hand in. I just can't bear to have anyone laugh at me. (Pause.)

T: Has anyone ever laughed at you, Tanya, to give you this feeling?

S: I've thought and thought about this. I guess it is just some block that has developed through the years. I've gone back over the things that have happened in the past, trying to bring it out in the open, but I can't ever recall anyone laughing at or making fun of my writing. I guess it's just because I have such an unhappy home life—I can think of no other reason, but then it just doesn't tie up with this.

T: Things aren't going well at home, Tanya?

S: No, not at all. I just can't get along with my mother. Things are getting progressively worse. Last night we had a particularly difficult time—a little worse than usual.

I was playing with my little sister and we were getting along fine. All at once, she ran screaming to my mother that I had stuck her with a pin. My mother believed her although there wasn't a pin in sight. I tried to explain to my mother that I admitted I was jealous of my little sister —(sighing) it took me so long to recognize these feelings for my little sister as jealousy—I admitted being jealous, but I definitely was not sadistic. She knows I just can't stand seeing anyone hurt or suffer. No matter how jealous I am, I would never hurt my little sister.

My feelings were so hurt because she didn't believe me, I started to cry. Then she accused me of deliberately starting the tears to get the sympathy of my father, screaming that I was driving deeper and deeper the wedge between my father and her. That just isn't so—I just cry because I am so deeply hurt.

Then the other night she had to go out and couldn't be there to eat with us. She was just going out the door when I came in. She told me my dinner was in the oven and she left. I was starved so I ate what was in the oven. (Tanya broke down and sobbed at this point.) How was I to know that my father had not eaten yet? She didn't say so. I had eaten the lamb chops she had fixed for him. What a scene she put on when she came home.

There are times when I actually think I hate my mother—but then again I don't believe I really do because I am so concerned about her. I try to look at these things from her point of view. Her actions just don't seem to be based on any logic. (Pause)

T: Are emotional reactions based on logic?

S: No, these are expressions of feelings, aren't they? I know my mother had a very unhappy childhood. Her parents always preferred her brother, my uncle. All their love and attention was centered on him. They sent him to college. My mother felt out of it. (Pause) I know my mother is aware of what she is doing. She said to a friend of hers over the telephone the other day that she knew what children were for—just somebody upon which the mother could vent her feelings of an unhappy childhood on—the vicious circle goes round and round. (Pause)

T: Did your mother know you were listening?

S: Definitely she knew. I was quite near her and had been for some time. I believe she was—I believe she was trying to explain to me why she was acting the way she was—only she said it to her friend. I thought this might be the time to talk things over with her. I tried. But my mother and I have no common ground. I can talk to my father. He listens, but all he says is that I must learn to cooperate with my mother better. What an empty word, "cooperate"! When I asked him "but how"? he just shakes his head and looks sad.

I am trying to talk him into letting me drop ballet lessons. I've come to hate my ballerina teacher so. She hits me and slaps me around. She always did that, but somehow, I just don't like that anymore. (Pause)

T: Now that you are growing up, that type of discipline is no longer satisfactory?

S: It hurts my feelings. Dad never did approve of that type of discipline, either, but he says he has invested so much money in my dancing lessons, he doesn't want me to quit now. And that's another thing that hurts—regarding it as purely a cold business deal.

That's not being fair to my dad. He really says to wait another week—that he wants to be sure this wasn't just another adolescent whim. (Tanya smiles at this and pauses.)

T: Your father seems to have an understanding of 13 year old girls. They sometimes get the idea, when things are not going just right, that they want to do, or don't want to do, certain things. Then they think differently the next day or week. Don't you think your father wants to be sure that this is what you really want?

S: Perhaps. I do know that since he has paid in advance for the lessons for the next two weeks, I have an obligation—those are his words—to go through with it, for two more weeks anyway. Look at the time! I feel so good about getting this out. Now if I can just remember that these are emotions and accept them as such. You know—I don't feel any guilt feelings at all telling you all this. My mother forbade me—after the big scene of going to the visiting teacher with my party troubles—she absolutely forbade me to tell anything about our family troubles to strangers. But you aren't a stranger, are you?

T: Not now, Tanya. But that's for you to decide, really. Growing up and all the feelings that come with it—the desire for independence—all create problems in the home between children and their parents.

S: Yes—me with my guilt feelings and my mother with hers—they sort of collide. Don't worry about me telling my mother about this conversation. I learned my lesson when I tried to repeat some of the things that were said when I talked to the visiting teacher. Goodbye now, and thanks.

[This is an excellent illustration of a teacher who was able to create a good emotional climate in the classroom and to use the curriculum as a means of paving the way for a counseling relationship. In addition it demonstrates that there are times when a counselor is in a better position to counsel when he functions not as a "counselor" but as a "classroom teacher."]

The Teacher Arranges Time for Formal Interviews

It would be highly desirable for every teacher to have a planned interview with each pupil, a friendly discussion about the pupil's progress, his feelings of success, where he feels he needs to improve, his likes and dislikes about school, his aspirations. When the importance of the teacher's "learning about the pupil in order to teach him" has come to be appreciated fully by the supporting public, class sizes and teacher schedules will be adjusted if the ideal is to become a reality. While this situation does not exist in most school communities, many teachers do find opportunities for pupil conferences with some pupils and find that the increased understanding of the pupil is reflected in better teaching. Such interviews are particularly helpful with pupils who are new to the school or the class, those who have been absent for an extended period of time, pupils whose achievement does not appear consistent with abilities, and in cases where there is some evidence that out-of-school conditions are affecting the pupil's adjustment in school. The formal interview does not always have to be initiated by the teacher. As stated earlier, with the right emotional climate in the classroom and with good teacher-pupil relationships the teacher will find many students initiating requests for interviews.

THE TEACHER ARRANGES TIME FOR FORMAL INTERVIEWS.

The realities of the classroom being what they are, most teachers are not in a position to have many interviews while teaching classes. This means that teachers who believe in sitting down in a one-to-one relationship with students may have to provide for occasional meetings before or after school. The following two interviews show how one teacher took the time to work with one of his "problem" students by talking with him after school.

I

(To visualize Bobby, the child in question, picture a twelve year old boy, plainly dressed, blue-eyed, blond, curly-headed, robust-looking, five feet four inches tall, weighing approximately 110 pounds. By comparison with his group, Bobby is older, sturdier, and brighter than many of his classmates. He has a Detroit Intelligence Test rating of C (average), as of February, 1956. Bobby has been a discipline problem since coming to my school in the 3A. Not only has he had trouble with his teachers, but also with the police. One day last week I asked Bobby if he would mind having a conference with me after school. He made no objections. The following is the initial interview I had with him.)

First Interview—April 17, 1956:

S: Can I come into the room now, Mr. Bart, the kids have all left?

T: Sure, Bob, come on in, I'll be with you in just a few minutes, then we will go upstairs to the teacher's lounge. (About ten minutes later Bob and I proceeded to the teacher's lounge.) Sit down Bob, and make yourself comfortable.

S: This sure is a nice chair.

T: I'm glad you like it. Well, Bob, I'm glad you could make this appointment today.

S: Am I here because I did something wrong again?

T: No Bob, I thought we could just get to know one another better.

S: I'd like that!

T: Bobby, what do you do for fun at home?

S: In the evening (he replied with a sigh) I play with Mickey. He's my best friend. (A long pause.)

T: Is he older than you?

S: Oh, he's sixteen, but I'm almost as big as he is.

T: What do you play?

S: There ain't much for us to do, sometimes we play ball. (Again a long pause.)

T: Do you belong to the Boy Scouts or the Y.M.C.A.?

S: Well, I used to belong to the Boys Club, but I don't go there anymore. (Again there was a pause.)

S: On Sunday I usually go to the show if I can get the money from my father.

T: Do you see your father often? (I knew that his parents had been separated. I asked the question to see whether he visited his father because he missed him.)

S: No, not unless I want to get money for the show. He's always slapping me.

T: You do not visit your father often because you're afraid he will slap you.

S: Yes, lots of times he slaps me, but he doesn't always catch me. (Angrily) (Bobby began to fidget in his seat.) Aw, nuts! I'm hungry!

T: Well, Bob, since it's getting on towards dinner time, let's stop now, but we can come here and talk again next Tuesday, if you want to?

S: Sure, Mr. Bart, (enthusiastically) I don't mind staying after school and besides, you promised to drive me home.

(After my first interview with Bob, I noticed that he had begun to demand more of my attention, but, fortunately, in a more positive manner.)

[The beginnings of a good adult, male relationship for this boy. However, not sufficiently well established that he was willing to continue talking about his feelings toward his father. Teacher uses good judgment and doesn't pursue this any further.]

Second Interview:

(The second interview with Bobbie was tentatively scheduled for April 24, 1956, a week after the first. However, he told me that he had a baseball game with some of the "kids" after school. I told him to play baseball, and we would have our talk the following week. He seemed very pleased with this arrangement and he asked me if I could watch him play. Having watched the game for a while, I was glad to see how well he was getting along with the other children. The following conversation took place the next week.)

S: (Coming in the room) Can we go upstairs and sit in those nice chairs, Mr. Bart?

T: Sure, Bob, in a few minutes we'll go to the teacher's lounge. (About five minutes later we went upstairs to the teacher's lounge.)

S: Tomorrow, I'm going to play baseball again. I sure have fun! I don't play too well, but John said he would teach me to be a good batter.

T: I like baseball, too. It's a great sport. Maybe, after school Friday, I can give you some tips on how to field and bat.

S: Gee, Mr. Bart that would be swell! My "old man" wouldn't help me. He never does.
(He used the term "old man" with great anger in his voice.)

T: Bobby, the last time we talked together, you told me that you do not feel like visiting your father very often.

S: Yes, my father gets mad very easily.

T: Do you feel your father would be more friendly if you would come to see him when you didn't want money for the movies?

S: I don't know. (A puzzled look.) (Long pause.)

T: Now, Bobby, suppose you were a father and you had a son who only visited you when he wanted money, would you like it?

[Teacher is moralizing and being quite judgmental. This is very questionable.]

S: No, I guess not (rather sullenly) but he has it coming to him. He was terribly mean to my mother. Anyway I hate him! (At this last statement, he began to cry. A long pause followed. I was not exactly certain just how to treat this emotional outburst.)

T: Right now you hate your father because he has been mean to you and your mother.

S: I don't like him, but he really isn't so bad anymore. He does give me money for the movies. Gee, I sure wish I had a dad like Mickey, my buddy.

T: Would you like your father better if he were like Mickey's father?

S: Yeah!

T: What makes you feel Mickey's father is so nice, Bob?

S: Gee, Mr. Bart, Mickey's father takes him places. They go on picnics, and they go swimming and they go to drive-in movies together. You know, his father even helped him build a keen looking toy sailboat that really goes in the water. (Replied with enthusiasm.)

T. You have asked your father many times to take you places and to help you make things, like Mickey's father, but he refused?

S: Well, now I ain't exactly asked him that. I was always sure he'd say no, anyway. Maybe, I should ask him if he'd go swimming or maybe even play baseball with me. I'll ask him this Saturday.

T: Why don't you, Bob!

S: Mr. Bart, if I could buy an airplane would you help me build it?

T: Would you like that?

S: Gosh! I sure would! You mean you're going to build me an airplane? (Bobby's eyes sparkled.)

T: Yes! Will you help build it?

S: Well, I ain't so sure I can, but I'll try, if you will help me. Gee! If I learn how to build model airplanes I won't have to sit around then all weekend doing nothing.

T: I'll drive you home now, Bob, it's getting late.

[Teacher became judgmental and quite directive, but his good relationship with the boy seems to have remained intact. These interviews were initiated by the teacher, but focused on the student—his feelings and his desires. As teacher stated prior to second interview, Bobby was now demanding more of his time, but in a more positive manner.]

II

Formal Conference with a Boy in the Third Grade

What the teacher knew about the boy prior to the interview: David is a third grader, active and interested in school. He has maintained a consistently high scholastic rating in all grades, and according to sociometric data, is considered a popular boy.

(David asked if he might talk to me after school concerning a problem the baseball teams in our class were experiencing during recess time. The meeting lasted about fifteen minutes.)

S: I don't like to be a tattletale, but I'm not happy about what's going on.

T: Yes—

S: Well, you know how much fun we've been having with our baseball teams. (Long pause.) It's the first time we've ever divided into teams and played baseball at school, and now Kit is spoiling it. (Short pause.) Remember what you told us. If the teams had any trouble, the captains should get together and decide what to do.

T: Yes.

S: Well, Kit keeps telling Gary not to give in when Bill and Gary are trying to settle a problem.

T: You mean whenever the captains (Bill and Gary) get together to decide, maybe on a play, Kit tells Gary not to give in?

S: Yeah! And Gary listens to him, and then Bill goes along with anything Gary says. It ain't fair. I've been thinking of quitting the team. (Short pause.) Maybe I'm not being a good sport and all that, but wouldn't that make you mad? If Kit wouldn't be so bossy, everything would be all right. (Pause)

T: In other words you feel if Kit did not interfere with Bill and Gary while they're settling things, everything would be all right?

S: Yeah! Sometimes I don't agree with the captains, but that's OK. Like you always say, everyone can't be pleased all the time. (Long pause.) I know sometimes I get excited and mad, but I don't interfere. (Short pause.) I've talked to Kit, but I get nowhere. I don't want to quit the team but I get hopping mad at Kit, and lately we've been getting into more arguments.

T: You feel that the fact you sometimes don't agree with the captains' decision is all right, but what you become mad about is when Kit makes the decision for the captains.

S: Yeah. (Short pause.) I thought maybe you could talk to Kit about not interfering and leaving the problems to the captains. (Short pause.) I don't want to quit, especially now since you told us we could play the fourth graders next week. I just can't wait! My brother Chuck is on their team, and I would just love to beat him.

T: Then you really don't want to quit, especially now since you're playing the fourth graders next week, but you feel it would help if I would talk to Kit about not interfering?

[Teacher probably made a wise decision not to follow up the feelings regarding the brother, but to focus on his previous feelings regarding the conflicts in baseball.]

S: Yeah. Or maybe at the baseball meeting you could talk about it? (Long pause.)

T: Yes, it could be brought up at the meeting tomorrow. (Another pause.)

S: You know, I've been thinking. If the guys are willing we could choose an umpire, let's say for a week at a time. Then maybe it would solve everything. What do you think of that? Then Kit couldn't interfere.

T: You think by choosing an umpire to decide on the plays, the problem of interfering would solve itself.

S: Yeah, I think so! Maybe at tomorrow's meeting I could ask the guys what they think about choosing an ump for our games.

T: Yes, tomorrow's meeting would be a good time to ask.

S: I guess you won't have to talk to Kit after all if the guys choose an ump.

T: Yes, talking to Kit might not be necessary now.

S: See you tomorrow then. Bye.

[It is evident that a good relationship already exists between the teacher and the student. The teacher appears to have handled the situation in a fashion that enables the boy to come up with a possible solution of his own rather than having to rely on the teacher to settle the problem.]

Summary

In this chapter we have discussed the idea that some kinds of counseling constitute a legitimate function for classroom teachers. The teacher's counseling role is not a therapeutic one, but does aim at offering the student assistance in making more effective personal and environmental adjustments. There are many avenues by which the teacher can create counseling possibilities. Opportunities may emerge through the curriculum. If this is to happen, the classroom climate must be such that the students can perceive the teacher as an adult with whom a satisfying relationship is possible. Each teacher will have to decide for himself whether he can utilize opportunities for informal interviews with students or if he will have to set aside some time for formal meetings. The classroom teacher, in functioning as a counselor, does not obviate the need for school counselors. The latter are needed to serve as consultants to the teachers, to work with those students who have been unable to relate with the classroom teachers, and to handle those cases beyond the ability of classroom teachers.

Selected Readings

Arbuckle, Dugald S., *Guidance and Counseling in the Classroom*. Boston: Allyn and Bacon, 1957.

Hamrin, S. A. and B. Paulson, *Counseling Adolescents*. Chicago: Science Research Associates, 1950.

Marzolf, Stanley S., *Psychological Diagnosis and Counseling in the Schools*. New York: Henry Holt & Co., Inc., 1956.

McDaniel, Henry B. and G. A. Shaftel, *Guidance in the Modern School*. New York: Dryden Press, Inc., 1956.

McKinney, Fred, *Counseling for Personal Adjustment.* Boston: Houghton Mifflin Co., 1958.

Ohlsen, Merle M., *Guidance, an Introduction.* New York: Harcourt, Brace & Co., 1955.

Rogers, Carl R., *Client-Centered Therapy.* Boston: Houghton Mifflin Co., 1951.

Shostrom, E. L. and L. M. Brammer, *The Dynamics of the Counseling Process.* New York: McGraw-Hill Book Co., Inc., 1952.

Tyler, Leona E., *The Work of the Counselor.* New York: Appleton-Century-Crofts, 1953.

Warters, Jane, *Techniques of Counseling.* New York: McGraw-Hill Book Co., Inc., 1954.

Williamson, E. G., *Counseling Adolescents.* New York: McGraw-Hill Book Co., Inc., 1950.

PART III

THE TEACHER LOOKS AT GROUPS

CHAPTER 8

The Teacher Finds He Must Know the Group as Well as the Individual

After studying various individuals in the group the teacher finds that there are still behavioral factors emerging that do not seem to stem from the individual personalities of the children who make up the class. For example, it seems a little difficult to understand why the class can be working along on some project, and seeming to work well, when all of a sudden an unusual amount of talking or moving around occurs. What seems to be going on? Or, on the other hand, why is it that the group which ordinarily ignores the clowning of Joe, now seems to think that he is so funny? What made the group so restless from the time they arrived this morning? What has happened to the fine sharing of materials that was going on yesterday? Today, members of the group seem to be overly possessive of their belongings. When we planned the paper drive it seemed as if anything that Marvin said was picked up very quickly by most of the group and yet there were several who objected to any suggestion that he made regardless of its worth. Where is the real "oneness" that was expected of this group?

On closer inspection it is soon discovered that this is not one solid group with equal amounts of loyalty to the situation. One individual whom the teacher studied is definitely not liked by the other boys and girls and yet she does her work well and always complies with any request made of her. She brings in excellent materials for their group study and yet the others do not seem to want to use these materials. She was put in that particular group in the hope that the others would soon learn to like her and to recognize the contribution that she has to make. Why doesn't it work as anticipated?

When we organized our groups it didn't seem wise to permit all those boys to be in one group because they would be sure to make more noise than is necessary for carrying out their plans. Now it seems as if they had really set up a very good plan and have divided the tasks without a great deal of trouble. All this in spite of the extra conversation.

There must be some other factors in groups that one doesn't recognize no matter how extensive a study of individuals has been made. What are these factors and how do they come about? Most of all, how do I, the teacher, cope with these factors so that the learning situation can be the most conducive to success?

THE TEACHER DISCOVERS THAT THE CLASS IS MADE UP OF MANY GROUPS.

The Teacher Discovers That the Class Is Made Up of Many Groups

It is soon discovered that the collection of individuals that make up this class do not all have the same commitment to each other and to the situation. Marvin, Jim, Joe, and Frank always come in and out together and when Marvin makes a suggestion, the others all agree with it readily. The other boys in the group seem to want to belong to this same little clique and they also turn to Marvin for approval. They try to please him and yet he doesn't seem to court their favor. He seems to have a great deal of influence over the others.

The girls too seem to have some specially chosen people. Sally, Cheryl, Jane, and Lillian seem to stick together but not as tightly as the boys. Marie and Fran are with these girls part of the time and then at other times they are by themselves. Sue Ann never seems to please them no matter how much material she brings or how much she helps the teacher around the room.

With extended observation it is soon discovered that this class is made up of several sub-groups with varying relations to each other. Even though these groups are broken up for study projects they still seem to gravitate to each other or turn to each other for approval or criticism. There would seem to be three major cliques in this particular class with several students not in any of these cliques but definitely paired off in friendship. In addition, there are several boys and girls who don't seem to fit into any of the groups. Will is quiet and the students don't seem to know whether he is present or not. When Sam begins his clowning the others act disgusted and tell him to, "Turn it off." At other times they seem to encourage Sam in his clowning. What makes this change in role?

Research shows that the capacity to give and receive affection is related to one's perception of himself and that this perception in turn affects the position one holds in various groups. Other studies show that the unique make-up of groups can affect the behavior of individual members. In other words, groups form constellations of sub-groups dependent upon the needs of individual members of the group and upon unique needs inherent in the group itself. *One might say that individuals need to use the group for some needs of their own and that the group needs to use individuals to satisfy some needs that it has as a group.*

Good teachers for a long time have tried to bind groups together in a oneness of loyalty to their class and its standards because they felt that this was the most effective way to improve the learning situation. In part they have been right because groups can unite on the basis of acting out hostility as well as for altruistic purposes. Each individual brings his own set of defenses to the group and in the group finds reinforcement for his own controls or reinforcement for acting out some feelings that he would not dare to act out on an individual basis. The process of identification is present again. Not only do people find what they are as persons through the original identification with the parental figures but the process is constantly being refined through identification with one's peers whether in school or in the neighborhood. The strength of the binding depends on the degree to which one's original needs in this direction were met or denied. School groups are particularly important because they may reinforce some skewed perceptions of one's self or can refine such perceptions through new identifications. Thus we meet the process of individuals using the groups for the gratification of their own unconscious needs. On the other hand reality factors that press upon groups may make it necessary for the group to use individuals to change the state of affairs so that life for the group may become more comfortable.

In this process sub-groups emerge in the larger classroom group. The size of the sub-groups seems to depend upon the developmental growth period of the particular constellation of boys and girls, upon the climate set in the situation by the leader, and upon the degree of communication among group members. Thus each classroom group may be made up of several sub-groups, several pairs or trios, and a number of isolated individuals who seem to have no particular membership in the group.

Each larger classroom group seems to have a limit to the number of individuals who can be bound together. Some individuals make no impact upon the group at all, while others seem to have strong influence with the larger group or are definitely rejected by the group. Groups seem to have the need to place certain people in positions of influence and others in positions of rejection. When these individuals are removed from the group others soon take their places. Recognition of the reality of group structure would seem to aid the teacher in creating a good learning situation. What then are the crucial factors in working with the group in general?

1. Sub-group allegiances will be present. Research in the structure of groups has shown that all groups contain sub-groups or cliques.[1] Members of these sub-groups have stronger ties to each other than they have to the rest of the members of the larger group.[1, 2] These

[1] Mildred Peters, *A Study of Social Acceptance, Rejection and Isolation Among Children from the Second Through the Tenth Grades* (Unpublished doctoral dissertation, Ohio State University, 1945).

[2] Ronald Lippitt, Norman Polansky, Fritz Redl, and Sydney Rosen, "The Dynamic of Power," in Dorwin Cartwright and Alvin Zander, editors, *Group Dynamics* (N.Y. Row, Peterson and Co., 1953), pp. 462-81.

members seek out each other outside of the classroom and will make every effort to communicate with each other inside the classroom. The numbers within the sub-groups will vary but they are always clustered around one individual except where the sub-group is reduced to two or three members. Quite often it is possible to have a group of four or five all of whom choose each other mutually. This is especially true of boys' groups.

It must be remembered that such groups are not ability groups in the sense in which many teachers are used to working. For example, these will not be children who will be reading on the same level. These members are attracted to each other on some emotional basis. Even when they first come together, individuals will tend to have a stronger attraction for some members of the group than for others.[3]

All members of the class will not be included in these cliques. On he whole, however, most students will have membership in a sub-group even if it is with only one other partner.[4, 5]

Where teachers become aware of the cliques in their classes they oftentimes feel that the classroom work will be improved by breaking up the sub-groups. This will not improve the situation. Instead, acceptance of these groups, allowing them to work together, assisting hem to formulate their own group goals and ideals may avoid the acting out of taboo behavior that group action often makes possible.[6]

Mr. Stevens had an eighth grade English class in which there were wo major cliques; one was made up of a group of five girls and he other of six boys. Mary Jane seemed to be the leader of the one roup. At least she was the one around whom the others used to luster when they came into class. John seemed to be the center f the boys' group. Mr. Stevens decided at the opening of the semester hat he was going to have "no nonsense" in his class so he arranged he seats so that these groups were broken up. Shortly after the first week, he discovered that when he presented ideas for a unit of work Mary Jane would raise some objection to them and was generally ollowed in her criticism by the others, not only of her own clique ut by the boys. To add to the difficulties Jim, a boy who did not

[3] Roger Barker, "The Social Interrelations of Strangers and Acquaintances," in *ciometry*, 1942, Vol. 5, pp. 169-79.

[4] Mildred Peters, *op. cit.*

[5] Helen Jennings, *Leadership and Isolation*, Second Edition (N.Y.: Longmans, reen and Co., 1950).

[6] Ruth Cunningham, *Understanding the Group Behavior of Boys and Girls* (N.Y.: eachers College, Columbia University Press, 1951).

seem to have much status generally, began to clown. Although Mr. Stevens tried to suppress Jim he soon found that Jim was being encouraged in his clowning by John's clique. They had no particular regard for Jim but there was definite evidence that they were using tactics to disrupt the class. Finally, Mr. Stevens decided to try a new tactic. He discussed areas of literature with the group and let them decide in which areas they would work. With their help he set up the topics and allowed them to make their choices. It was not at all strange that the clique members chose the same areas of study. In addition, some other members of their class also chose the same topics. The groups then began to set up their own ways of working, time limits, and methods of reporting. Of course, there was talking among group members but the few side conversations that took place were not nearly as disturbing as the note passing and clowning of the earlier era.

2. Individuals need group identification but cannot stand the extreme loss of their own identity. In our society we tend to identify persons by the groups in which they hold membership. People join clubs and other voluntary groups not only for the interest in a particular sport or other activity, but also because of the identity which membership gives them. Man is a member of a group from the time he is born and it is in the initial group, the family, that he first finds his own identity. In this primary group he is more than just a member of the group; he also has a definite role identification that no other member of the family has. To live as a family, members must give up some of their own narcissistic needs for the support and nurture they gain from the others in the maintenance of their roles. Oldest, youngest, boy, girl, "like mother," "like Uncle Joe," regardless of how the individual member is identified he is still a unique totality different from the totality of any other member of the family. Where this uniqueness is denied him his perception of himself becomes skewed, he finds it hard to relate himself to others and harbors resentment whether he shows it openly or not. As a member of a group he must still hold on to that uniqueness.

To become a member of a group he gives up some of his own ego for the group but group membership must not so threaten him with loss of identity that he is always just one of the crowd. If the teacher so structures the class activity that there is no individual recognition of contribution, students will find their own unique ways for gaining recognition. Loss of identity can be avoided by clowning, talking out, or other devious ways.

An eight year old girl in a third grade found her own unique way for recognition. She was a member of a class that did everything as a class. The teacher, though well meaning, placed "our class" far beyond the individuals who were members of that class. Added to this attitude was one of "my children." Work productions were either identified as those of the class or shown as the work of "my children." Although this little girl asked to go to the lavatory at the same time each day there was so little concern for individuals that the teacher did not recognize what was happening. One day the kindergarten teacher stopped the third grade teacher in the hall. She said, "What about this health contest you are having in your room that we all have to enter?"

"Health contest?" queried the third grade teacher, "I don't know what you're talking about."

"Well," said the kindergarten teacher, "That cute little blond, Alice, has announced it to all the lower grades and said that we'd have to keep charts and check for clean hands, brushed teeth and so on."

Needless to say, the third grade teacher was aghast. This little girl whom she hardly knew had developed a large enterprise for herself. She had impressed the other teachers so well that they took her announcements to their classes seriously. The only thing that disturbed them was that they felt that one of their colleagues was making a lot of work for them. For the first time, this teacher became aware that there was no room for individual recognition in that class except through grades on the report cards.

3. Some individuals are not ready to become group members. As was mentioned earlier in this chapter, the individual's capacity to give and receive affection which is definitely related to the student's perception of himself makes it possible to be a good group member or not. As the result of life experiences some individuals are not ready for group membership. They may be openly anti-social in behavior or may find it necessary to withdraw from contact to avoid anxiety. To force them to be social or to participate with others may make it too difficult for the individual or may be asking too much of the group. Even adults find it hard to accept hostile people.

Jean was an eleven year old in Miss Smith's room. She hit out at others, marred their papers, broke their crayons and in general made life difficult for the young people around her. Miss Smith knew that Jean needed to feel accepted so she put Jean into the regular work groups in her room. In her own kind way she felt that by assuming that the hate was not there she could make up for the years of deprivation that this child had suffered. One day she came to her supervisor in tears saying, "I guess I'm a failure as a teacher." In order to help her the supervisor visited her class and discovered that Jean would call out remarks in Polish that the teacher did not understand but the remarks were either funny or frightening to the other children who understood the language. She roamed the room at will and interfered with the activities of others. The result was that members of the group had had to find their own ways of showing the teacher that just accepting the behavior was no way to live as a group. Some who had been well behaved before began to adopt Jean's behavior even though they didn't like her. They did this partly out of fear of the girl and partly to make the teacher take hold of the situation. Others were so perturbed by the behavior that threatened their own controls that they withdrew into an extremely quiet state.

When Miss Smith was helped to see that this was not a child who was ready for group membership she referred her for outside individual help but worked with her on an individual level in the classroom with the attitude that, "I can't let you misuse others in this way and I would not allow them to do this to you." The result was a feeling of greater security on the part of the other children as well as Jean, who actually was frightened of her own impulsivity but felt that if she was perceived by all adults in her environment as "bad" that she must live up to it and thereby receive punishment.

Working with such children on a single basis gives them the feeling of the individual concern of the adult and a chance to find security in a single personal relationship with an adult who is consistent but understanding and at the same time to discover that all adults are not limiting without giving approval for the successful withholding of impulsive behavior.

Many times a very shy or withdrawn child who cannot tolerate group membership can be reached in the same way or can be helped to work with one person with whom he seems to feel fairly safe.

4. Individuals have different roles in the group. Some boys and girls are high influence figures while others are definitely rejected or have made no impact on the group at all. The influence figures are highly chosen by many of the children and are usually only two or three in number in the average class. The rejects are those children who are generally rejected by many children. They will usually be only one or two. If these children are removed from the group others take on these roles or rather are assigned these roles by the group. The number of children who will be the isolates, those not really known by the others, will vary in number according to the size of the class and the degree of interaction encouraged by the teacher. Large classes have more unknowns than smaller groups. Classes in which students work entirely as individuals and are not invited to communicate with the others will have many isolates.

Because the solidifying of groups does not begin to emerge until about the third grade and the children are still more strongly under the influence of the adult than either the pre-adolescent or adolescent groups, teachers of the early elementary grades are more likely to know who are the influence figures. However, the positions in groups may be identified by close observation and through more formal study means that will be explained in Chapter 10.

SOME STUDENTS ARE MORE INFLUENTIAL THAN OTHERS.

The Teacher Discovers That Some Students Are More Influential with the Group Than Others

In observing the group it is soon found that the students in general ccept the ideas of some boys and girls more readily than those of thers. These young people are not always the highly active or the nost vocal. Yet, when they propose an idea or put on it their stamp f approval or disapproval, the group seems to side with them readily. t will be noted that students turn to these young people to determine hether they approve of what has been said or done. It is not that ney seek out others but rather that the others seem to want to communicate with them. They may even meet the approval of the group when their behavior is not in compliance with the stated rules.[7]

If another person were to act out the same piece of behavior, he would find immediate disapproval on the part of the group.

This group phenomenon has special significance for the teacher. Most teachers fear the contagion of behavior. They are afraid that if a young person is ill behaved that this behavior must be stopped or soon the whole class will begin to behave in the same way. Research shows us that these disliked children cannot normally influence the behavior of others except in certain circumstances. Only highly-chosen, strong-influence figures can divert an interested class. Such behavior is easily brought under control by the teacher who has good relations with his class and concerns himself with the interests of class members. Such influence is exerted by these leaders sometimes to add liveliness to the program or to break an air of seriousness.

It cannot be assumed that these influence figures will be able to involve the whole class in the run of fun. An influence figure of one sub-group may not meet the approval of an influence figure of another group. For example, a boy leader may not meet the approval of a girl leader and vice versa. This will depend upon the chronological age of the group and their social maturity.

Experienced and sensitive teachers soon recognize the social positions of these leaders and do not make large issues of temporary behavior contagion because the allegiance of the group is more likely to be in favor of these leaders than that of the adult in charge. Rather wise teachers will utilize this leadership by involving these young people in the planning of activities and will make provision for their leadership to be used in a positive way.

The Teacher Finds That He Is Not Always the Actual Leader of the Group

Oftentimes, an adult assigned to a group as its teacher assumes that he then becomes the highest influence figure in the group. The degree to which this is true will depend on many other factors which will be discussed in Chapter 9. A teacher new to the group is not necessarily a leader of the group at all except that he has been assigned the role by the administration. What have the other students said about him before? What behavior of his did they observe in the school before he

[7] Polansky, Rosen, and Redl, *op. cit.*

THE TEACHER FINDS HE IS NOT ALWAYS THE ACTUAL LEADER.

was assigned to this class? How do they feel about teachers in general? All these factors will modify the degree of acceptance of him in his assigned role.

Even when the teacher is highly accepted by the group in general he will find that group resistances to his leadership will emerge. If he ignores the influence positions of their natural leaders he will soon find that the contagion of behavior is on the increase and it becomes necessary for their own influence figures to "put him in his place." If he so jealously guards his role that any competition is a threat to him he will find that he soon loses the loyalty of the group, a loyalty he probably never had.

On a large city playground attended by almost two thousand children daily it seemed as if Mr. Dante did nothing but walk around. However, the attendance was high, activities were in full swing, courts were well marked and all safety precautions were being taken. If one looked closely he saw that activities were managed by the young people themselves. Boys were umpiring the ball games, girls were refereeing the volley ball games, another group of youngsters had a rhythm band under the direction of a young accordion player and Mrs. Antonio, a neighbor, was showing another group of children how to weave willow baskets. Here was evidence of the highest utilization of the leadership present. The times that Mr. Dante was called upon were either because some young people needed an additional judgment, because they wanted him to see what they were doing, or to share some plans they had made for their activity. This does not imply that Mr. Dante had an absence of group organization but rather that the plans were so well worked out with members that they were carrying out their own organization and utilizing their own leaders. His ability to share his leadership role made him truly the leader of the group.

By the same premise, if the teacher's needs are such that he must bind the group to him as "my children," he will find that they resent this dependency position and only the extremely dependent students will tolerate it. This type of group climate created by the assigned leader demands too great an ego loss from group members as pointed out earlier in this chapter.

The teacher who is aware of group leadership will utilize and nurture that natural leadership for the formulation of group plans and the development of group conscience. He will assist these boys and girls in learning some of the ways of good leaders. An attack on the leaders is interpreted as an attack on the group. The wise teacher shares his leadership acording to the maturity of the students and remains secure in his own adult role, feeling gratified when the students are able to assume leadership of their own.

The Teacher Discovers That Reality Circumstances Can Change the Climate of the Group

Even though the sub-groups of a larger group are identified and the natural leaders utilized in creating a good learning situation for the students, sometimes reality circumstances will alter the group structure or climate.

Mr. Robin had a new seventh grade. He decided that this year he would try to be really democratic with this class and involve them in pupil-teacher planning with a focus on their own interests. He proceeded to discuss the plan with the students and found that even though they seemed to like him as a person he was getting very little response from the students. He could not understand this and thought, "Perhaps all I have been taught about students wanting to learn when offered an opportunity to plan their own work is not true." Students would say, "Why don't you decide?" After mulling over the problem he decided to try to get at the source. He talked with several students informally and soon discovered that these students nearly all came from an ethnic group where the adults made all of the major decisions for the young people. The attitude in most of the families was one of, "Young people should be seen and not heard." He found that his ways of working were so alien to the cultural conditioning of the students in both their homes and in their past school experiences that they thought him slightly "crazy" when he turned to them for their ideas and invited them to participate in the planning. To them this was an invitation for license. It soon became evident to him that this must be a gradual process of teaching these young people to discover the safety of their own ideas in relation to the adult. They discovered that this was not an invitation to "do as you please" but that they developed a definite plan for operation and evaluation. They had to ask themselves, "What is it that we want to do?" "How will we go about doing it?" "How will we know whether we have accomplished our goals?" The problem, then, was merely one of knowing the background of the group and understanding why a way of working was alien to them.

The teacher of an algebra class thought she was utilizing the natural leaders of the group and yet could not understand why she did not seem to gain the cooperation of these leaders. A visit to the class revealed the following. The class entered the room and sat down in their rows of seats. As soon as this was done the teacher said, "Chairman, call the roll." He did. Next she said, "Chairman, check on contributions for the paper sale." This he did. This was followed by excusing this chairman to his seat and asking another chairman to take over. Teacher: "Chairman, assign the problems." He did. Teacher: "Chairman, assign board spaces." He did and the students went to the blackboard to work their problems. They then took their seats. Teacher: "Chairman, point to problem one." The chairman went to the blackboard and stood with his finger pointing to the first problem while another student explained the problem from his seat. When this was completed he repeated the process by pointing to the second problem at the instruction of the teacher. Needless to say, he looked very bored and several of these ninth graders giggled. Here was a teacher, disappointed with the responses she was getting from the students although from her viewpoint she was going through all the mechanics of utilizing their natural leaders. What she had not examined was her own reluctance to relinquish any of the leadership to the students.

Another example of a reality circumstance occurred in a fifth grade. The students were giving criteria for the selection of committee members. As they gave them the teacher wrote them on the board. After enumerating five or six the teacher stopped and said, "Now we will select the members based on these criteria." With that two or three boys slumped down in their seats and looked very disgusted. Instead of telling them to "sit up straight" she turned to them and asked them the difficulty. Sam said, "Ah, every time we pick a committee we use the same old criteria." Still not being defensive, she asked him what he would do. He replied, "You always stop when we get the criteria that you want. Why don't we put down, 'kids who never had a chance to work on a committee'?" This wise teacher recognized that Sam was correct and being sensitive to the responses of the group she was able to rectify a situation that was realistically disturbing to the students.

Regardless of the degree to which we seem to study the group we cannot always make the assumption that the difficulty lies with the group and not the reality circumstances of the situation. For example, groups that experience a very rigid and punitive atmosphere in one class are likely to let down from the tension in the next class when they are with a teacher with whom they feel comfortable. Groups expected to accomplish work far beyond their ability or that they do not understand will soon unite in group resistance and utilize every means to break up the situation. Groups confronted with pressure to accept behavior of individuals that is threatening to them will have to create enough disturbance so that the adult will have to step in and put a governor on the behavior of that individual. The general atmosphere of the school as a whole and within the community of which the school is a part will make a great difference in the operation of any group. Each classroom group is an integral part of the school as a whole and also brings with it influences from the community at large.

Summary

The teacher soon discovers that the large classroom group is not "one group" but is made up of sub-groups with varying degrees of allegiance to each other and to the teacher. These groups have their own natural influence figures and it is soon found that the assigned leader, namely, the teacher is not necessarily the recognized leader of the group or groups. Individuals in the group will need to use the group for their own psychological needs and in turn circumstances in the group will affect the way in which the group needs to use individuals. Contagion of behavior in groups can only stem from high influence figures unless a group is bored, frightened or feels that they are being misused. The extent to which lines of communication are opened in the group will affect the degree to which the teacher will know group members and sub-groups. Communication and the size of the group will affect the number of isolates. There is a limit to the number of influence figures or rejects that a group can tolerate.

Guidance-minded teachers will know that it is not enough to know individual members of the class but will know that there is a group personality that oftentimes will transcend the personalities of the individual members.

Selected Readings

Cartwright, Dorwin and Alvin Zander, editors, *Group Dynamics.* Evanston, Ill.: Row, Peterson and Co., 1953.

Cunningham, Ruth and others, *Understanding the Group Behavior of Boys and Girls.* New York: Teachers College, Columbia University Press, 1951.

Jennings, Helen, *Leadership and Isolation* New York: Longmans, Green and Co., 1947.

Sullivan, Dorothea, editor, *Readings in Group Work.* New York: Association Press, 1952.

Thelen, Herbert A., *Dynamics of Groups at Work.* Chicago: University of Chicago Press, 1954.

Redl, Fritz and William Wattenberg, *Mental Hygiene in Teaching.* New York: Harcourt, Brace and Co., 1951.

Wittenberg, Rudolph M., *So You Want to Help People.* New York: Association Press, 1947.

———, *How to Help People.* New York: Association Press, 1953.

CHAPTER 9

The Teacher Sees Differences From Group to Group

As was stated in the last chapter, we soon discover that the classroom group is not a single group but is made up of sub-groups of varying sizes. Even if the teacher were to analyze the sub-group structure of his class he would find that this alone would not explain some of the group behavior that he sees. Even if he were to use a high degree of pupil-teacher planning in the class there would still be some behavioral patterns that he would find hard to explain. What are these factors and how do they affect group operation?

DEVELOPMENTAL GROWTH MAKES CHANGES IN GROUP BEHAVIOR.

The Teacher Recognizes That Developmental Growth Makes Changes in Group Behavior

In studying school groups it is soon found that the developmental period in which a particular group of boys and girls happen to be will make a difference in the behavior of the group and the way in which that behavior is best dealt with in the classroom. For example, children of five and six will not have the strong group allegiances of the older children. At this stage they are moving away from their families and beginning to develop strong identifications with their peers. However, they are still caught up in the struggle for an identification within their own families and trying to make peace with the parent of the same sex. They aren't so sure about their own positions in relation to their siblings and the first uprooting from the family circle.

At this period they still have deep need for the approval of adults. The friendships they make with other children are changing. One day Mary may be Lila's best friend and the next tells the others not to talk to Lila. The little girls find it easy to identify with the woman teacher but the small boys who are struggling with their own masculine identifications oftentimes will band together in mischief to ward off all the females. In their group play children of this age will replay the family situations and their own roles as if to reassure themselves. The sub-groups within the class are not solidified and the teacher is more likely to see pairs of friends emerging. Sometimes this makes group organization difficult because the tendency is toward parallel play rather than working or playing in larger groups. The problems for the teacher at this period are not so much those of group structure but rather assistance with controls within reasonable limits and help in learning to share with others.

The middle years, from seven to ten, bring new group phenomena. The identification of boys and girls with members of their same sex creates a "boys for boys" and a "girls for girls" world, in and out of the classroom. When left to their own choices in the second through the fifth grades, the children are not likely to choose partners of the opposite sex and this creates problems for the teacher who wishes to hurry co-education. These group characteristics sometimes create arguments or the acting out of behavior that individuals would not do alone.

Miss Mundt's fourth grade seemed to be ready to start the day when

Mary Jane arrived in a new dress. Because Mary Jane was well liked, the girls made such comments as, "Gee, is that cute." With this Mike, who was one of the boy leaders, said, "Oh girls are silly. All they do is primp and want fancy clothes." A grand argument followed. The subject: "Which are sillier, men or women"? Miss Mundt felt hopeless at first but decided that she had better let the group get some of these feelings out. She assisted them by making two columns on the board, one for "men" and the other for "women." Into the lists went such things as, "Women wear make-up," "Men use smelly shaving lotion," "Women spend a lot of money on hats," "Men spend a lot of money on fishing and golf equipment," and on and on. After a considerable period of time the children themselves saw that this could go on and on and they also discovered with the help of Miss Mundt that they were making generalizations that did not always hold true.

The separation of the sexes at this age is marked. Progressively the girls consider the boys rough and dirty and the boys would rather not be in any activity than to be identified with one considered feminine. In spite of this, they band together readily on an "us kids" basis to bedevil the nice teacher with giggling and squirming campaigns. It's group against group most of the time in class and on the playground, teasing, tormenting, and once in a while uniting in a common uprising.

In part the differences are emphasized group-wise because of the developmental differences between boys and girls. The natural feminine passivity makes it easier for the teacher, but the very passive learning seems to be a threat to the development of the boys' masculinity. As a result small boy-gang outbreaks of wild behavior are not unusual in the lavatories and on the playground. The wise teacher recognizes these differences and capitalizes on them in classroom planning.

The large advantage for the teacher whose class is in these middle childhood years is that it is a time of the final formation of the ego-ideal and the solidifying of ego controls. These are the real conscience building years. The children of this age, on the whole, welcome assistance with their controls but fear the punitive adults who make identification impossible. These adults almost force boys and girls of these ages to gang up with their own groups at the expense of the adult. The kindly, mature teacher who helps the group to formulate its rules of behavior and assists the children in the incorporation of controls finds teaching a pleasure. These teachers make room for boy groups to be more active and to learn through exploration.

The refinement of the ideal self comes about not only through the incorporation of the values of the parents as a part of the self, but through identification with values of teachers whom the children prize as their friends but who can also take children's criticisms when they are deserved. When we relax enough with groups of this age and show them that we respect their opinions, welcome their suggestions, and at the same time behave in a consistent manner, we encourage the sequence of, "I like you," and "I would like to be like you," so necessary for the identification with adults.

The ideal is not only developed through personal relations in the group but also through their own code of behavior. Groups of this age demand clearly stated limits; limits that they have a part in defining. When the teacher makes demands within the agreed code of behavior, groups of this age cooperate very well. However, if at any time the boys and girls feel that the teacher is unfair, either by making sudden rules or ignoring the original agreement, group resistance results. This age group is most rigid in expecting agreement with the group code for both the teacher and for themselves. An occasional stepping out of bounds is allowed the influence figures in the peer group but not for anyone else unless the group has need to use an individual to disrupt the activity. This will occur in times of stress or disappointment with the assigned leader, the teacher.

The pre-pubertal years of ten to twelve bring new group problems to the classroom. The girls in their acceleration of maturation are now moving in the direction of interest in boys and are physically outgrowing their masculine classmates. Groups of this age may contain a goodly number of tom-boyish girls who seem to be in constant competition with the boys or on the other hand a fairly large number of girls who are imbued with romantic fantasies and flirtations with the boys.

At times the boys will tolerate the tom-boyish girls and include them in their team games, treating them as if they were not girls at all but other boys. The result can make for tensions in the classroom and especially for tensions among the girls. The tom-boy group thinks the flirtatious behavior of the feminine group is disgraceful and almost immoral and the feminine group oftentimes will band up to isolate the tom-boyish girls. As a result there is an outbreak of tears, "She's talking about me and setting the other girls against me," or "They're too high hat and we don't want to work with them." These emotional flare-ups interfere with the smooth operation of groups in the classroom and cannot be ignored. On the other hand if the teacher makes a large issue of the tensions in front of the whole class, nothing is gained. Quietly talking with small groups alone or creating temporary separate work teams allows those of the same social maturity to work together. Allowing the small groups to choose their own work partners will often stave off these crises. Even wise planning will not avoid some of this group behavior but teachers who know the developmental characteristics of this age group are fore-warned and not easily upset when the behavior appears.

The pubertal years bring their own group problems. The girl is already in the "best friend" stage and cannot conceive of joining any activity if her "mirror" friend is not a part of that activity. This phenomenon is readily recognized but not so easily handled in the classroom because the pairs then find it difficult to concentrate on anything except outside interests. Group work suffers and more declarations of war are formulated by the girl groups who are sure that the adult demands are unreasonable.

However, it is not the girls who suffer to the greatest degree in school groups at this period. Because the change in individual and group behavior comes earlier for the girls, it seems to be better tolerated than the change within boys. By the time the real change is being initiated in boy groups, the girls are settling down in part and unfortunately most group activity in schools is geared to the development of girls rather than to that of the boys.

Boys, too, take on the "best pal" but because the passive situation of the school is an even greater threat to the masculine development at puberty, the boys are more likely to act out in an overt way in class and in school and soon find disfavor among teachers. Boy groups are often perceived as "delinquent" or as "vandals" rather than groups going through the pubertal change. The lipstick using, preening, narcissistic behavior of girl groups seems to be tolerated as "a group of girls going through puberty." The behavior of boy groups at this period is oftentimes perceived as a greater threat to authority and, as a consequence, is dealt with more drastically. When one examines the dropout and failure rates in the ninth and tenth grades and discovers that the majority of these are boys, one may be sure that we have not learned how to deal with boy groups at this period of their development.

Because groups in these years resist adult authority, oftentimes teachers will feel that if they behave as teen-agers with their groups they will establish better rapport with them. Nothing could be further from the truth. The students do like teachers who can joke with them and who don't make large issues out of every little run of fun, but the teacher who abandons his adult role becomes an emotional threat to this age group. The cause of many of the classroom discipline problems among beginning junior high and high school teachers resides in this area. Why does the group need to create chaos when the teacher tries to be a teen ager? First of all these young people need to use their group identification as a way of moving away from adults and to create a world of their own in which they have an identity. If the adult invades this world he leaves them nothing of their own. Secondly, this is an age when all young people are having difficulty controlling their impulses to some extent and they expect to gain through group controls, but they also use the group to dilute the guilt they would suffer if they carried out certain impulsive behavior alone. Here they need the adult to assist them in hanging on to their own impulsivity. They also need the understanding teacher, who behaves as an adult, as a target for both their positive and negative feelings. They can safely move these feelings from the parental figures through other adults in their environment and finally out to a comfortable one-to-one relationship with their own age mates, particularly with the opposite sex. The best teachers of this age group utilize these group identifications through a high degree of pupil-teacher planning, but also assist these students, on the group level, through the incorporation of cooperative evaluation practices in the classroom, to become their own judges.

Throughout the pubertal years and into the adolescent years, although the main group affiliations remain boy and girl groups, cooperative work between the groups increases. Girls and boys have their special girl or boy friends as their comfort with the opposite sex increases. It is not unusual in the high school to find that groups that seemed most bothersome at the ninth and tenth grade levels are able to work in a very cooperative and responsible way in the eleventh and twelfth grades. Although the adolescent still needs his group affiliations he has less need to use his classroom groups to gratify some of his emotional needs. Later adolescent groups in the high school and early college years gain more of their group gratifications in their extra-curricular activities. Pursuit of learning in the later adolescent groups can be followed on either an individual or group level.

Throughout the years from age seven into adolescence the subgroups tend to increase in size. In the second and third grades there may be little cliques of three but by the time boys and girls are in the fourth and fifth grades the sub-groups enlarge progressively until in some high school classes where the group has been together for a long time, ten or twelve members may be united on some basis.[1, 2] The change in clique size will dictate a progressively changing manner of working with groups in the classroom as the students move chronologically.

Teachers who work with any developmental group over a period of time soon learn that there are developmental characteristics of groups as well as of individuals. Special difficulty arises when classes contain a great spread of ages. Where some of the students are as much as two or more years retarded, although the academic achievement rate of the older students may not be beyond that of the others, the social group behavior or needs may be quite different.

2-

The Teacher Recognizes That Each Group Has a Personality of Its Own

As was said earlier in relation to a study of individual personalities, namely, that knowledge of the individuals who make up the group does not necessarily give one understanding of the functioning of the group, it might also be said that knowledge of one group does not mean that one automatically understands every group. A teacher may have one group of a particular developmental age and find that another group of about the same age and the same type of young people with the same methods of working may behave quite differently. The unique constellation of needs of individuals who make up the group and the way in which those needs are met or not met, unique properties residing in each group, and the position of the group in relation to other groups will make each group behave in a unique way.

For example, one may have a class made up of students who, taken individually, seem to be fairly well adjusted, but who when in the group behave very badly. On the other hand, every teacher has had the experience of having a group that has had anything but a fine reputation in the school and, in spite of the anticipation of a bad school year, has found that the group works very well indeed. The feeling tone in the group, the unwritten code of behavior, the status that the

[1] Mildred Peters, *op. cit.*

[2] Leonard Zudick. "A Comparative Study of the Group Characteristics of Second, Fifth, and Eighth Grade Students, as Revealed by Social Choice Patterns" (unpublished doctoral dissertation, Wayne State University, 1953).

group affords, the willingness of the group to move toward the solution of their problems, all these nebulous factors seem hard to explain. Yet, we know that they differ from group to group and make up the unique character of the group. Cattell refers to them as "syntality factors." [3]

It is not enough to say that the group is unique or is a "hard group" or an "easy group" any more than it would be sufficient to pass such judgment on individuals. With the group, too, just as with the individual child, we need to ask, "What do they do?" To determine the answer we would need to collect data through observation to answer the following questions:

1. How do they respond to the absence of formal planning?
2. What do they do when left by themselves?
3. How do they respond to rules and regulations? To theirs? Yours? The school's?
4. Who talks and who listens?
5. What behavior will they tolerate and which do they reject from their own members?
6. What behavior will they tolerate from you and which do they reject?
7. How well do they work toward the solution of their group problems?
8. Do they help each other?
9. How do they respond under stress? To attack from without?
10. Do they make decisions on their own or do they wait for you to make decisions?

When we have collected anecdotal material to give us some general idea of what this group really does we can say that we have merely identified symptoms; symptoms of well being or unrest in the group. Just as with the study of the individual we are only now ready to say, "What is causing the behavior?" To understand the cause we will need to investigate some properties of this particular group.

The Teacher Finds That the Unique Structure of Each Group Affects Its Ways of Working

Structural properties of groups are those properties that one can determine with a fair degree of accuracy through the summarization of objective data on the group.[4] One structural property of a group is its homogeneity or heterogeneity. How many boys are in the group?

[3] Raymond B. Cattell, "New Concepts for Measuring Leadership in Terms of Group Syntality," in Dorwin Cartwright and Alvin Zander, editors, *Group Dynamics* (Evanston, Ill.: Row, Peterson and Co., 1953), pp. 14-27.

[4] Dorwin Cartwright and Alvin Zander, *op. cit.*

How many girls? What are the ages of the group members? What cul-tural, religious or other group affiliations do members have? What is the level of achievement? What is the physical size? What aptitudes are present? Some of these data may be collected through testing others through observation, and others through a plain counting process.

It can easily be seen that some factors related to homogeneity will affect the planning with the group. As was mentioned earlier in this chapter, wide variation in age will make a difference in the social behavior of any group. Any experienced teacher will tell you that a greater number of girls in a class will give you a more verbal class but there will be less noise from physical activity than there would be if you had a larger group of boys. Variations in ethnic, religious or racial background may or may not make for some tensions in the group, but on the other hand presence of such structure may mean that the teacher will have to consciously design some ways of working to promote better understanding to balance off outside pressures.

Another structural property of the group relates to the length of time the group has been together and the degree of knittedness in the group. The degree of knittedness of a group can be determined by sociometric techniques that will be explained in Chapter 10. The size of the sub-groups in a class, the number of isolated children, the tensions between sub-groups will all affect the learning situation and the gratification that group members receive. Classes that are broken up every semester, especially in the elementary years, have little chance to build knittedness. Boys and girls who have been together throughout the elementary years will tend in the beginning to form sub-groups in the junior high and will probably carry some of these sub-groups into the high school. As was shown in Chapter 8, the sub-groups in any class will give direction to the way in which we will organize ourselves for work.

A third area of structure relates to the group code. The code of any group or sub-groups will identify the limits of behavior. What agreed upon code of behavior or statement of goals is present in the group? To what degree does this code agree with that of the teacher? Is the stated code arrived at by teacher and students working together or is the teacher fooled into thinking that his statement of goals is all that is necessary? Determination of the group code is easier with young children but the farther up the developmental line our young people move the less easy it is to determine the whole code. However, teache who are not so busy focusing on their own codes, to the exclusion of the pupils', will soon learn through observation the major parts of the unstated code and knowing teachers have learned that stated codes and goals must be worked out with the class groups regardless of age. As children grow they can be given increased responsibility for the execution of their own code. All codes or stated goals need to be reviewed from time to time to make sure that they are still appropriate.

A fourth structural property of a group is the status connected with membership in the group. What past experiences of success or failure has this group had? How have they been perceived by others as a group? Are they referred to as those "awful kids in room 119"? Do other teachers say, "that nice seventh grade"? Status arrived at through such reputations, whether good or bad, is often hard bought and groups that have no other opportunities for status may have to hang on to the "game" that goes with the name given them.

What prestige is associated with being a member of this group? Perhaps it is related to the grade, such as being a senior group or "freshies," or perhaps it is pride associated with being in the homeroom of a generally beloved teacher. Fortunately the educational profession has moved a long way from the singing groups of "bluebirds" and "crows," but unfortunately divisions by intelligence quotients, academic grades and other such false divisions make it difficult for young people to find any prestige properties in some of their groups. All groups tend to develop symbols of identification for their groups. If these symbols are not badges, class songs, or of some material variety, they become verbal symbols such as club names, "Miss Johnson's class," "the seniors," or "our room." Groups that are denied prestige gratification in schools will have to set themselves off in some unique way even at the expense of their own learning and happiness of the school.

A fifth structural property of a group is the communication network. Referring to our earlier question of "Who talks and who listens?", we need to ask ourselves whether the lines of communication are truly open. If they are not, has the circuit been broken by the teacher or by some other dynamic factor in the group? A general atmosphere of, "You dare to ask me," and, "You are free to suggest," must be more than verbalized by the teacher. A check of our own anecdotal records will show whether we invite communication with us and among the class members.

It is hoped that none of us would fall into the dilemma of the poor substitute teacher who stated, "If you increase the size of the denominator you increase the size of the fraction," to the seventh grade math class. Jim put up his hand and said, "I think you mis-spoke. Don't you mean that if you increase the size of the numerator you increase the size of the fraction?" The teacher then turned to the class and said, "We'll take a vote on it. How many agree with me?" Permitting a vote in the class was not an opening of communication, but the fact that a student didn't dare to correct a teacher was sure evidence that communication was only permitted to flow one way.

Other structural properties that lie in the physical setting can also affect the group such as the size of the room for the number of students, the arrangement of the furniture, the lighting and the access to resource materials. Good classroom planning will give serious consideration to the structural properties present in any group. The very structure of the school itself, whether physical or through rules, will affect the climate within any classroom.

The Teacher Discovers That Individuals Have Unique Roles in the Group

Over and above the determination of leaders, or influence figures, rejects and isolates in groups, the teacher soon discovers that some individuals have continuing roles in the group and that these roles may change temporarily according to any given set of circumstances. For example, one student may continually play the role of the clown but the group seems to tolerate and use this clowning at one period of time and at another time may put a stop to the behavior or force the teacher to put a stop to it. The cause for the clowning would have to be determined by a study of the individual involved and does not necessarily reside within the group alone. The clown may not be finding any other way of getting status in the group; he may be overwhelmed by the difficulty of the work; he may have real need to bring the attention of the teacher to himself. The need resides within him but the way in which the group uses his need and the way in which he uses the group to gratify his own need may well reside within the group.

Supposing that the clown is the real influence figure in the class. In that case he may turn on the clowning just for the fun of it and yet if some other individual did the same thing the behavior would not be tolerated for a minute. If the clown is not the influence figure e may find that at times his behavior is not tolerated and that other mes it is reinforced. At the latter times we need to look for some other appenings in the group. Has the assigned leader miscalculated the ishes of the group and forced upon them an interpretation strictly accordance with his personal wishes? Perhaps the group is using the lowning as resistance and is trying to say something that they dare not y, except indirectly, because the lines of communication are not open.

One person may become the target for hostile group behavior. He ontinually becomes the ridiculed one, or is never allowed any high egree of participation by the group. Again, the need may reside ithin the individual. This may be a person who has such deep need or continual punishment that he unconsciously creates circumstances at call forth this response. This could only be determined through xtensive study of the individual. On the other hand, the cause may be uried in the group structure.

In a particular sixth grade Marian has really been suffering. Miss berly doesn't even seem to notice it. In the class there are three over-ge girls who are having trouble doing the school work. Each time ne of these girls passes Marian's desk she will either flip the book at Marian may be reading or flip one of her braids. When school is ismissed they often come up behind her and flip her hat over her yes. What is behind this behavior?

The three girls are one solid clique in the class. They are much

INDIVIDUALS HAVE UNIQUE ROLES.

older than the other students in the class and resent being with thes "babies." The teacher is actually afraid of these girls but presents a exterior of really "clamping down on them." However, she does no see the little things that this small group does to scapegoat Marian This clique has no status in the class either in ability or through thei age. They would not dare to use one of the teacher's particular "stars," so they pick a quiet youngster who they know will neither defen herself or report them to the teacher. They have discovered that it i safe to take their hostility toward the teacher out on Marian. On day that are particularly stressful for the rest of the class because Mis Eberly gets tense and demanding, other less sure students adopt th same behavior toward Marian, push her out of the way, or interrup her if she tries to talk with them.

Here is an example of a small group frustrated through lack o success, who cannot turn their hostility toward the teacher and hav to divert it toward an easy target. The adult leader in this group is s forbidding that even fairly well adjusted students adopt the behavio of the disliked group because in a sense they have identified with thei frustration. There is no means by which they can communicate thei feelings to the teacher so the pressure must go somewhere. It is take out on an individual who within his own need structure may invit some of this behavior, but not to this degree. The real pathology lie within the structure of the group and the attitude of the leader. In an other class with different structural properties, Marian may not be cas in this role at all. However, she would never be an influence figure Any extreme use of target, whether clown or any other role, is a cu to something behind the group resistance. One then looks to the degre of gratification the group is gaining from the learning situation an from membership in this group.

Roles emerging either from the need structure of the individual o from the group situation need not necessarily be negative in connota tion. Observation may show that certain individuals become the rea solidifying persons in the group. Others may rescue the group fron its own impulsivity. The error comes in misinterpretation of role in th group.

Mr. Spring's Social Problems class is made up of two majo cliques of seniors. The groups are social rivals in the school. At th beginning of the term they elected Fred as their class chairman. Fre was always a very vocal member of the class and Mr. Spring assume that he was a real leader in the group. When Fred chaired the grou ıd attempted to move them to action in deciding on their areas of udy and group divisions to carry out the work, much argument ısued. The argument would continue until Mr. Spring felt that he ould have to step in. Periodically Cary would speak up and say, Why don't we do it this way?" Even though Cary was not always ɔcal, the group seemed to accept his suggestion and peace would ign.

This was a case of the teacher's not realizing that Fred was not the al leader in spite of the election. He did not realize that by abandon-g any leadership himself he left the group in a position of not know-g where they were going, and they elected a boy that neither power oup cared for particularly and they had no intention of following im. Cary, who was the true influence figure, was acceptable to both oups. He allowed them to carry out their own impulsive behavior ut when the situation seemed to be getting out of hand he periodically scued them from their impulsivity. This was not done deliberately y Cary after calculating the state of affairs but rather as a natural ssumption of his leadership role.

Individuals do have unique roles in groups. The roles do not stem om the needs of the individual alone but also from the needs of the roup and the set of circumstances in which they find themselves.

Summary

Over and above the sub-group structure that exists in any classroom roup, the teacher will need to know who are the leaders, isolates, nd rejects. Even with this knowledge, if the teacher is to understand ıe behavior of any group and to help that group to the highest level f operation, he will need to recognize that groups, too, have develop-ıental characteristics. These developmental characteristics will help im to understand what type of behavior he may expect group-wise t any particular age.

In addition to the above factors the teacher will recognize that every roup is unique in its own make-up and if he is to understand that roup he will need to study the structural properties of the group. 'he structural properties of the group in turn will help him to under-:and some of the unique roles that individuals play in the group. Vorking with groups with these facets of structure in mind will assist ıe teacher in carrying out a higher level of pupil-teacher planning and vill help to create a healthier learning situation.

Selected Readings

Association For Supervision and Curriculum Development, *Fostering Mental Health in Our Schools*. Washington, D.C.: NEA, 1950.

Cartwright, Dorwin and Alvin Zander, editors, *Group Dynamics*. Evanston, Ill.: Row, Peterson and Co., 1953.

Cunningham, Ruth and others, *Understanding the Group Behavior of Boy and Girls*. New York: Teachers College, Columbia University Press 1951.

Redl, Fritz and William Wattenberg, *Mental Hygiene in Teaching*. New York: Harcourt, Brace and Co., 1951.

Wattenberg, William, *The Adolescent Years*. New York: Harcourt, Brac and Co., 1955.

Wittenberg, Rudolph, *So You Want to Help People*. New York: Associatio Press, 1947.

———, *How to Help People*. New York: Association Press, 1953.

HAPTER 10

The Teacher Uses Instruments for Group Study

The study of groups has been carried out for many years but most udies prior to 1940 were of a sociological nature, such as analyses school populations to determine their racial, religious, and ethnic ructure. Few studies of social relations were made up to that time. ne earliest published studies that have had some impact on school actices were those of Helen Jennings,[1] Ronald Lippitt and Ralph 'hite.[2] The Jennings study, made with girl groups in an institution, cused on an analysis of social relations in a group. The Lippitt and 'hite study was one of leader behavior with boys' groups and the fect of that behavior on the group. Since these studies, teachers have cused study more consistently on the group as well as on individual havior.

The commonest technique used to analyze a group is the socio-etric test. In the strictest sense this not a test of any skill. Rather, it a question to determine social choices in the group. It is, as its title iplies, a measure of social relations. As with any single measure this chnique has been much misused by people who have attempted to iange group or individual behavior on the basis of a single measure. his is not to imply that it is not a valuable tool when used with the ructural analyses mentioned in Chapter 9 and with observation of oup behavior.

---

1 Helen H. Jennings, *Leadership and Isolation, Second Edition* (N.Y.: Longmans, reen and Co., 1950).

2 Ronald Lippitt and Ralph White, "The Social Climate of Children's Groups," in *ild Behavior and Development,* edited by R. G. Barker, J. S. Kounin and H. F. right (N.Y.: McGraw-Hill, 1943).

The True Sociometric

The term sociometric should be applied only when the questio
given to a school group is for a social choice to fit a specific function
and a choice on which one expects to act. For example, if the teache
is going to give children the choice of seat-mates he might approac
the group with some such question as: "This year you are going t
have a chance to select those with whom you would like to sit. I canno
promise that all of you will get your first choices but I will try to giv
you some of your choices. Would you write down four people wit
whom you would like to sit?" The number selected would be in relatio
to the function to be carried out. For example, if the children wer
to sit in rows they would have four choices, one in front of them, on
in back, and one on either side. If seated at tables that accommodate
six students, then they would make five choices.

The Near-Sociometric

The near-sociometric question may be used alone or may be in
cluded in a questionnaire used to gather other information. For exam
ple, if the teacher is using a questionnaire to gather information abou
the hobbies and interests of the students, he might include such a que
tion as, "If you were giving a party, whom would you like to invit
from our class?" Such questions are awkward because we may ge
quite a list for the party and thereby make a great deal more wor
for ourselves in tabulating. On the other hand, if we limit the choice
we create a false situation because we would hardly invite just three o
four to a party. However, if the teacher would prefer not to use th
choices for a function in the classroom, then this kind of questio
may be used.

Those who prefer the true sociometric measure to the near-socio
metric contend that there is bound to be more emotional involve
ment invested in a social choice which one will have to live wit
after making the choice. However, one of the writers has used bot
near-sociometric and friendship scales with the same groups to whom
she administered a true sociometric question and has found that th
same constellations show up in all three types. Her objection is no
the same as those of other researchers in the field, but rather that th
true sociometric is a more natural way of working and not as likel
to raise suspicions in the minds of groups to whom the measure

administered. Students as well as adults are likely to suspect the motives of a teacher or anyone else who inquires about their friends or whom they would like to take on a party or picnic. Zudick[3] in his study used both a true sociometric and a near-sociometric and found that both showed just about the same constellations, except that there was more cross-choosing among boys and girls on the near-sociometric in the fifth and eighth grades.

What can we expect to elicit from the sociometric data? First, we can expect to determine the sub-groups in the larger group and some partial relations among those groups. We will see if there are any choices between groups. Next, we can expect to determine who are the highly chosen. Some writers refer to these people as the "leaders" or "influence figures." Next, we will know who is rejected by the group. Finally, we will know who the isolates are. However, we cannot differentiate between these latter two categories unless we use the negative question. In giving the negative question to groups it has been found that if we ask for a specific number of people, with whom the other person did not want to sit or work, some respondents tended not to use all of the choices. In some groups students reacted so strongly that they would not put down any names at all. It has been found that if the negative question is introduced in such a way as to reduce guilt feelings, the responses are more than adequate. For example, "We don't feel the same about all people. Everyone knows some people that they wouldn't particularly care to work (sit) with. If there are some people with whom you would rather not work (sit), would you put down their names?"

What is the difference between the isolates and the rejects? The isolates are those who receive no choices, positive or negative. They are the people whom others do not even notice. When they are absent from school, the class members do not miss them. The rejects, on the other hand, are very much in the awareness of the other students. These are the people who receive the negation from others. However, we must not jump to conclusions if a student receives one or two negative choices, or if one group sends negative choices to another group. The true rejects, which rarely number more than one or two, receive the great preponderance of negatives.

How do we summarize the data so that we bring meaning to them? First, we will prepare a data summarizing sheet in the following manner:

[3] Leonard Zudick, *op cit.*

	NAME	CHOOSES	CHOSEN BY	REJECTS	REJECTED BY
1					
2					
3					
4					
5					
6					
7					
8					
9					

FIGURE 3.

The number of lines needed will be equal to the number of students in the class. Next, we will arrange the papers in alphabetical order. One point that should be made here is that the results are usually better if we give a dittoed or mimeographed list of class members to the students. Their positive choices can then be underlined and the negative choices marked by an "x" or some other symbol. The reason that this is a more efficient way of working is that no student is omitted because of absence, and it does away with spelling errors that mislead the teacher when recording the data. It also avoids ambiguity arising out of having several children with the same first name. The response is not just "John," but rather an underlining of "John Smith," or "John Foley."

Next we list the members on our recording sheet. When this is complete we see that each student has a number. We are now ready to record the results from the children. In the column titled "Chooses," we will place the numbers of the children chosen by that child. See Figure 4. Next, in the column titled "Rejects," we will record the numbers of the children rejected by that particular child. We now no longer need the sheets on which the students recorded their choices.

We then turn to the "Chosen By" column. Here we will record the numbers of the children who chose this particular child. These can be determined from the "Chooses" column. For example, in the "Chosen By" column and next to their numbers we will put a number "1" for everyone chosen by number "1". If we refer to Figure 4, we will see that Joe chose Tony whose number is "5." We see that we put

	NAME	CHOOSES	CHOSEN BY	REJECTS	REJECTED BY
1	Joe	⑤⑨ ⑫	5, 6, 9, 12, 15	10	2
2	Susie	④, 11, 12	3, 4, 14	1, 13	9
3	Mary	⑧ 12, 2	8		
4	Sandra	②, ⑧, ⑬	2, 8, 11, 13, 14, 15		
5	Tony	①, ⑨, ⑫	1, 7, 9, 12	15, 10	
6	Jim	⑩, 12, 1	10	9, 15	
7	Frank	5, 9, 14		10	
8	Jane	③, ④, ⑬	3, 4, 11, 13	15, 10, 12	
9	Herman	①, ⑤, ⑫	1, 5, 7, 12	11, 2	6
10	Peter	⑥, 12, 14	6		1, 5, 7, 8, 12
11	Mabel	4, 8, ⑭	2, 13, 14		9
12	George	⑤, ①, ⑨	1, 2, 3, 5, 6, 9, 10	10, 15	8
13	Ruth	④, ⑧, 11	4, 8	15	2
14	Irene	4, 2, ⑪	7, 10, 11		
15	Bernice	1, 4, 8			5, 6, 8, 12, 13

FIGURE 4. SOCIOMETRIC TABULATION SHEET.

a number "1" in the "Chosen By" column following Tony's name. We see that Joe also chose Herman whose number is "9." In the "Chosen By" column we will put a number "1" after Herman's name because he was chosen by Joe whose number is "1." We continue with the rest of the numbers filling in all the "Chosen By" column. We will fill in the "Rejected By" column in the same way.

Next, we inspect the tabulations to find the mutual choices. We will look in the "Chooses" and the "Chosen By" columns to see if the same numbers are present in each column. If the number is the same in both columns, we will then *circle it in the "Chooses" column.* This will indicate a mutual choice, meaning that a student chose another and that the other student returned the choice. Referring to Figure 4 again, we see that next to Joe's name in the "Chooses" column, that numbers "5," "9," and "12" are circled. The *same numbers* are in both columns. We then carry out this procedure for the rest of the class. When this is complete we are ready to make the sociogram on graph paper. This will give us a graphic picture of the choices of the whole class.

First we will draw a diagonal line on the graph paper making sure that the line centers exactly in every box which it passes through. See Figure 5. Now we are ready for our selection of the first group. We will start with the student with the greatest number of mutual choices. Using our same illustration, look back to Figure 4. Here we see that several children have the same number of mutual choices. For convenience we will start with Joe. In the first box below the diagonal, we will put a number "1" to represent Joe. In the next box we will put a "5," then a "9" and finally a "12." These will represent all of Joe's

		1	5	9	12	4	2	8	13	3	6	10	11	14	7	15
Joe	1		⊕	⊕	⊕							−				
Tony	5	⊕		⊕	⊕							−				−
Herman	9	⊕	⊕		⊕		−						−			
George	12	⊕	⊕	⊕								−				−
Sandra	4						⊕	⊕	⊕							
Susie	2	−			+	⊕			−				+			
Jane	8				−	⊕			⊕	⊕		−				−
Ruth	13					⊕		⊕					+			−
Mary	3				+		+	⊕								
Jim	6	+		−	+							⊕				−
Peter	10				+						⊕			+		
Mabel	11					+		+						⊕		
Irene	14					+	+						⊕			
Frank	7		+	+								−		+		
Bernice	15	+				+		+								

SYMBOLS: ⊕ mutual choice + choice − reject

FIGURE 5. A SAMPLE SOCIOGRAM.

mutual choices. Next we turn to number "5" to see if he had any mutuals that are not already listed on our chart. We will need to do this because if Tony did have any mutuals not represented we would need to add that number because the student, whom the number represented, would be tied into this group through a mutual with Tony. We find that there is no such number. We then move to number "9" and check the same way, and finally to number "12." When we have exhausted all the mutuals in this way, we then list the same numbers across the top as we have down the side. Now we see the meaning of the diagonal line. This box is crossed out because it would represent the student's choice of himself. Now we are ready for a new group. Remember, *we are working only with mutuals.*

Going down the list we find that of the names left, both Sandra and

Jane have the same number of mutuals. We will record a number "4" for Sandra and then put down the numbers "2," "8," and "13." Then we check each number to see if any of these people have mutuals not represented. We find that "8" has a mutual with number "3" so we must add Mary's number because she is tied into this group through Jane. We now see that we have exhausted all the mutuals so we turn to the student with the next greatest number. We find that we have two pairs, Jim and Peter, and Mabel and Irene. We record their numbers and now we are left with two people who have no mutual choices. By inspection we pick the isolates and last of all, the rejects. If we had used a full sized class for a sample, we may have had some students who received positive choices but had no mutuals. If this were so, we would record their numbers before those who received no positive choices. We must make sure to have the same sequence of numbers across the top of the chart as we have down the side.

We will now place symbols on the chart to represent the choices made. We will use a plus sign with a circle around it for a mutual choice, a plain plus for a positive one-way choice, and a minus sign for a rejection. We will take our data from the "Chooses" and the "Rejects" columns only, because if we record the data from those columns we will have automatically recorded the data in the other columns. The graph will make a clearer picture if we box in each of the cliques and the pairs.

Sometimes we will see that we may have an overlap of cliques through a mutual choice. In that event, we would put the number of the person in the second clique immediately following the preceding clique. One can readily see that the sequence runs from the most closely knit clique, all the way out to the rejects at the edge of the chart. In respect to our sample, someone will say, "Yes, but Peter has just as many rejections as Bernice." We must answer this by saying that, "Peter does have one mutual choice so that puts him in a better social position." It is now obvious that Frank is the isolate and that Bernice is a reject, with Peter running her a close second.

When we examine the sociogram we find that we can see very quickly what choices any one student sent to the others in his class by reading the chart horizontally. If we wish to see how the class responded to any one of the students we will read the chart vertically. In other words, choices recorded across the chart are those of an individual and those recorded down the chart are those of the class. We see that George and Sandra are the highly chosen. We see that

Mabel and Irene would like to be in the girls' larger clique. That may be fairly easy to accomplish, because two clique members give positive choices to Mabel. However, we will proceed with caution and make further observations before we act. It well may be that clique members do not feel kindly toward Irene. Frank would like to be in the boys' clique, but there again we will proceed carefully on the basis of other knowledge that we may have.

This method of scoring was reported in Pflieger and Weston,[4] and was developed by staff members of the Detroit Citizenship Education Study. Two other methods of scoring were formulated earlier by Moreno [5] and Jennings,[6] and by Mary Northway.[7] They are presented in Figures 6 and 7. Figure 6 will clearly delineate the relationships between group members by the type of arrow indicated. In arranging the symbols that represent the students, clique members are clustered together. In Figure 7, the inner circle represents the highly chosen and each circle as we move out represents students in a lesser social position, until we end up with the isolates and rejects outside of the circle entirely. The teacher would decide arbitrarily on the placement within any one circle. For example we have put the students with the greatest number of positive choices in the inner circle, namely, numbers "4" and "12," because they each had six or more positive choices. In the next circle we placed those who had four to six positive choices, and so on until we ended with "7," the isolate, and "15," the reject, out of the circle entirely.

The method shown in Figure 5 is less cumbersome and includes the advantages of both of the other methods. It also has an additional advantage over other methods in that the relationships between cliques may be seen at a glance.

Using the Data

After we have summarized the sociometric data and charted it on the graph, we are ready to apply our findings to our classroom opera-

[4] Elmer Pflieger and Grace Weston, *Emotional Adjustment: A Key to Good Citizenship* (Detroit: Wayne University Press, 1953). See pp. 61-65 for the same method of scoring. (One of the present authors was a member of the staff that worked out this method of scoring.)

[5] Jacob Moreno, *Who Shall Survive?* (Washington, D.C.: Nervous and Mental Disease Publishing Co., 1934).

[6] Helen Jennings, *Leadership and Isolation,* Second Edition (N.Y.: Longmans, Green and Co., 1950).

[7] Mary L. Northway and Lindsay Weld, *Sociometric Testing,* (Toronto: University of Toronto Press, 1957).

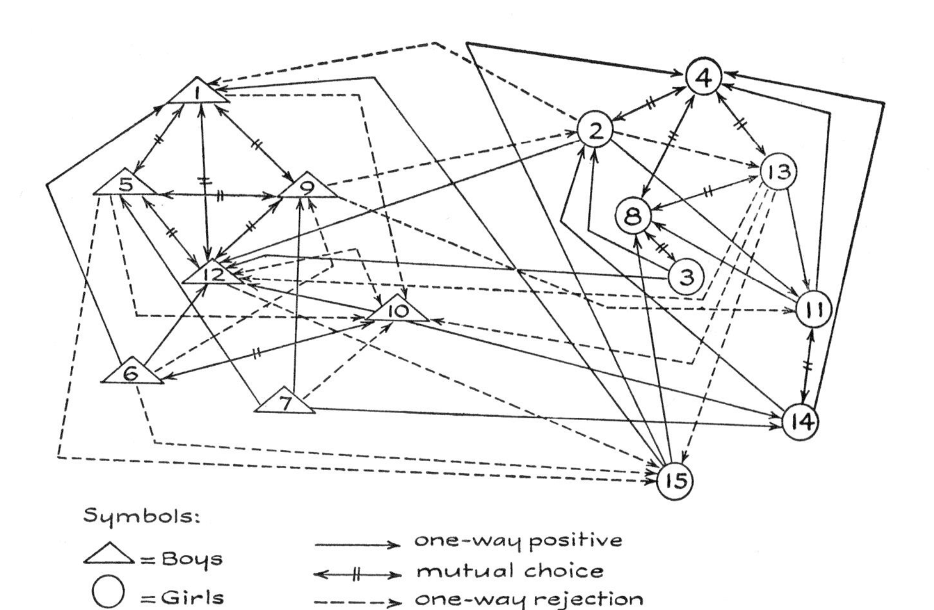

FIGURE 6. SOCIOGRAM BASED ON MORENO* AND JENNINGS† METHOD.

* Jacob Moreno, *Who Shall Survive* (Wash. D.C.: Nervous and Mental Disease Publishing Co., 1934).

† Helen Jennings, *Leadership and Isolation,* (N.Y.: Longmans, Green and Co., Second Edition, 1950).

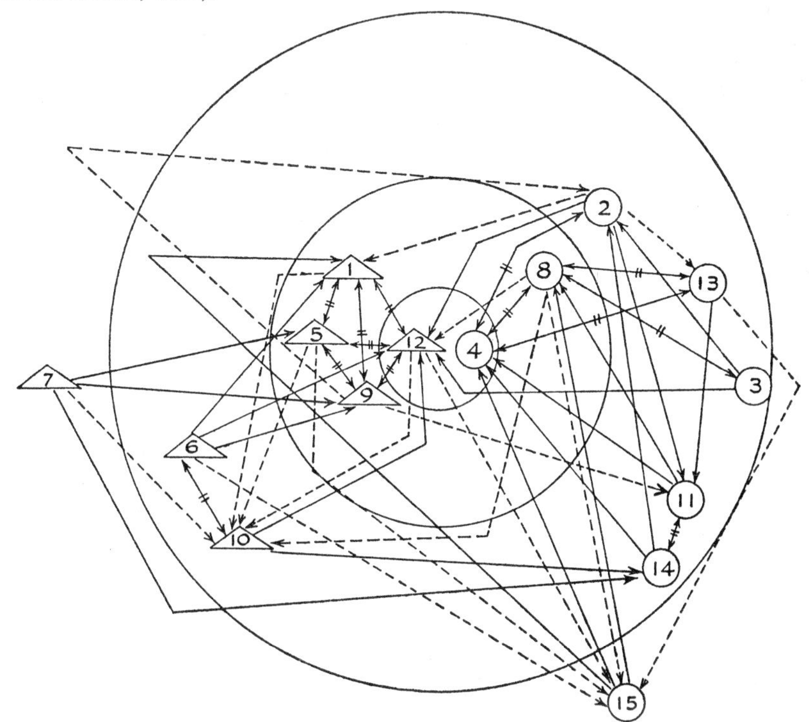

FIGURE 7. SOCIOGRAM BASED ON NORTHWAY* METHOD.

* Mary L. Northway, *A Primer of Sociometry* (Toronto: University of Toronto Press, 1952).

tion. If we have given the students a choice of seat or workmates, we must then carry through on our promises. Of course we may not be able to give the students all of their choices, but the only thing we need to avoid here is putting a child in a group with some others who have rejected him. Sometimes this will be difficult to avoid because some children, who have not rejected him, may have chosen and been chosen by others who did. The most important choices to us are the mutual choices. Our first organization will be built around these choices. We will try to put students together who chose each other mutually.

Immediately, teachers who have not used these techniques will raise objections. They will say, "If I put friends together they won't get any work done." Experience has shown quite the contrary. When people work with those whom they like, their work production improves. It would seem reasonable to expect that there would be a great deal more energy available for learning if one does not have to use up his emotional energy feeling angry or uncomfortable with someone else.

The real problem does not come with trying to place those who have been chosen by other students. It arises when either the rejects or the isolates have to be absorbed in a work group. Many times an isolate is harder to work into the group if the particular child is very withdrawn. The very thought of having to participate with others is frightening to these children. The teacher will need to study the particular case to determine what is causing the shyness and through observation try to determine how much contact the child can tolerate before he shows anxiety. There is an excellent film titled, "Shyness,"[8] that would be well worth seeing. It is the story of three different shy children in a class. When the causes are sought it is found that all three cases are quite different even though the surface symptom may appear to be the same. For example, a child who may be identified as an isolate, and is new to the group, at a later testing may be in a different position. Generally, however, research shows that the well chosen are immediately chosen. Working the shy child into the group will require tact and constant, but not obvious, observation. The most logical starting place is to give this type of child someone of his choice even though the choice was not reciprocated. Overtly aggressive children would be likely to be frightening to such a child.

[8] *Shyness*, 23 min. (McGraw-Hill, 1953). Produced by National Film Board, Canada.

A young boy named Don never participated in any of the games on the playground. The teacher noticed that when he approached the other fourth grade boys, one of the ring leaders would tell Don that he couldn't play with them. He would then walk away. When the sociometric test was administered it was shown that Don was a real isolate in the group. Further investigation showed that this boy was the middle child between two brothers, both of whom were much larger than he. His achievement was not up to grade level even though he scored in the superior intelligence range. His teacher did know, however, that he drew well. When she grouped the children, she put Don with some of the less threatening boys who also liked to draw. When they planned their work, she encouraged them to use illustration as part of it. This seemed to work well. On further study, however, she did find that Don's case was more serious than she thought, and she referred him to the school social worker. It was found that Don was so frightened of any hostility, his own as well as that of others, that he would not have been able to tolerate more aggressive children. This wise teacher, even without all of the data that she received later, did consider his position in his family and a skill that Don possessed, and with just those two factors made a good placement.

Some shy children may be more difficult to place than Don. Had he not had this special drawing skill the teacher may have been in a quandary. With children who show low tolerance for contact with others, the teacher may have to permit them to work on individual projects or, with just one other child, while he studies the cause of the shyness.

The most difficult of all to absorb into the group are the extreme rejects and the extremely shy. The rejects pose a special problem because they are often openly rejecting to the other children, argumentative, or highly critical. Children such as Cathy, whose case was discussed in Chapter 3, are not welcomed by others. Here, again, if the behavior is so extreme, the teacher may have to have this child work alone. However, this may be utilized with the child to help him to see that his own behavior does disadvantage him even though he cannot change it at this point of time.

One important step in the organization of the groups for action will be to utilize the natural leadership as much as possible. Even though we as teachers do not always perceive the highly chosen as people of influence, we will find more than a little trouble on our hands if we choose to ignore this natural leadership. These are the people that others seek out and, if we observe closely, we will find that these people can sway the group members readily. This was discussed more fully in Chapters 8 and 9.

The sociometric data will also show us some small sub-groups that do not seem to have any special relationships with others in the group. An illustration of this was found in a fifth grade where Miss Dean discovered that three boys, who chose each other mutually, were also students who had difficulty with their academic work. The difficulty seemed to reside in the fact that they all had reading disabilities. She permitted them to work out a project on fishing. They started by choosing to write a story about a fish. When they completed their story, they illustrated it and made it into a book to give to the second grade. It was an exciting child-like story that would interest younger children. From this they moved to types of fishing and then became absorbed in commercial fishing. Throughout the project, Miss Dean helped them with new words and the mechanics of the language. At the end of the semester, the least progress made was a year and one half in reading achievement, and one boy of the three progressed two and one half years. Here was a teacher who took her cue from the sociometric data and with some other knowledge of the boys, tried an experiment in learning that really paid.

Examination of the sociogram will show us how well knit our class is. The larger the sub-group, built on mutual choices, the more cohesive is the group.[9] Groups assembled for the first time will not have as large sub-groups as those who have been together for a long time. The size of the sub-groups will also be related to the degree of communication permitted. The age of the students will also dictate the size of the groups. Groups tend to enlarge as the children move up the chronological scale to puberty, then they decline somewhat, and stabilize in early adolescence. The negative choices decline continually as the children get older.[10] This is probably true because of the social conditioning that dictates that one does not express negation openly. Regardless of the decline of total negative choices, there are no fewer rejects proportionately in the older groups than in the younger.

Friendship Scales

Scales of this type differ from sociometric techniques in that they seek a rating of quality of choice. Instead of merely mentioning the

[9] Dorwin Cartwright and Alvin Zander, *op. cit.*
[10] Mildred Peters, *op. cit.*

names of those with whom he might work, the student rates all of the other students in the class. Examples of this type are the "Ohio Social Acceptance Scales." [11, 12] For this type of rating, the teacher supplies the student with a mimeographed or dittoed list of all the people in the class. Then the student is instructed to put a number in front of each name. The number should correspond to the description accompanying that number in the printed scale. For example, 1. "My very, very best friends;" 2. "My others friends;" 3. "Not friends, but okay;" 4. "Don't know them;" 5. "Don't care for them;" "6. Dislike them." Another of these scales is divided into five categories: 1. "Very, very best friends;" 2. "Good friends;" 3. "Not friends, but okay;" 4. "Don't know them;" 5. "Other people in the room."

In each case the student is instructed to put a number four in front of his own name so that all students will be rated and so that the ratings may be made anonymously. The first set of six categories was worked out for upper elementary classes and the second for grades seven through twelve. The second list would probably be less anxiety raising because the student is not invited to express his dislike openly. The "Other people in the room" category would bring forth the rejects and the "Don't know them" category would bring out the isolates. So that the meaning of the categories will not be ambiguous, each category is followed by a description of that category. Each description gives a little different gradation to the wish to have the person rated close to the rater or away from him, thus the title, "Social Distance Scale."

With this type of scale there is a fuller rating of each child by all of the other children. The disadvantage to such a rating is that it is so cumbersome to summarize. Some people, using such a scale, give a numerical weight to each category and convert the total received into a "social quotient." For example, on the five point scale, a numerical value of five would be given to the number ones, "Very, very best friends"; a four to the second category; a three to the third category; and so on. The totals then would give the teacher a range from the child with the highest score down to the lowest. However, with such a scale one cannot determine the relationships between the sub-groups. Helen Jennings does show a chart method for scoring gradations of

---

[11] *The Ohio Social Acceptance Scale for the Intermediate Grades,* issued by Ohio Scholarship Tests and the Division of Elementary Supervision, State Department of Education, Columbus, Ohio.

[12] *The Ohio Social Acceptance Scale for Grades Seven Through Twelve,* issued by The Bureau of Educational Research, Ohio State University, Columbus, Ohio.

ratings that might be used with this type of scale.[13] It would seem that for the data shown, the sociometric technique would be a more adequate one for the use of teachers. There may be some of the same dangers in using social quotients that there are in using intelligence or aptitude scores.

Guess-Who

This type of instrument is made up of questions such as, "Who gets along well with nearly everyone in the class?" "Who is willing to help other people or to share things with them?" "Who is cross, crabby and gets angry very easily?"; and "Who is very quiet and never has much to say?" As many items as wished may be included, but they should be worded in language that the group will understand. The children then write in the names of those to whom they think the question applies. The "Guess-Who" should contain a balance of positive, negative, and neutral items. No student is asked to sign his rating, thereby keeping his anonymity.

Although this type of instrument will reveal the highly chosen and rejected, it will not reveal any more than the sociometric, and the data are harder to process. The qualities that are brought out in the items can be observed in the behavior of the children anyway, and the level of generality does not tell us specifically what the group members really do, and how they relate to one another on a sub-group level.

Committee Selection

Some teachers prefer to have their students make choices in relation to committee work. The commonest ways of doing this are: 1. By having the students put their names under topics on the blackboard or, 2. To select committee members with whom they would like to work just as one would if he were making a sociometric choice. Some teachers feel that if committee work is a regular part of their class operation, this is a much more natural procedure and they prepare regular committee selection forms which the students fill out whenever they start on a new type of study. This would seem to be another simple way of making a social choice.

One final word on the making of social choices would be, that the

---

[13] Helen Jennings, *Sociometry in Group Relations,* (Washington, D. C.: American Council on Education, 1948).

sampling of choice should not be made so often that not enough time elapses between test and re-test.

Summary

Sociometric techniques can be very helpful to us as teachers in determining the sub-groups, the leaders, the isolates, and rejects in our classes. The graph method of scoring, built from mutual choices, is a clear way of showing the relationships among sub-groups and any individual and his class.

Some teachers prefer to use near-sociometric questions, friendship scales, "Guess-Who" techniques, or a committee selection plan, but data from these methods will not be of any greater help to the teacher than the natural sociometric choice for a situation where the choices will be acted upon.

Caution is required in the use of sociometrics just as in the use of any other type of data. Findings should never be used in isolation but put together with other data the teacher has collected on individuals or the group.

Selected Readings

Association for Supervision and Curriculum Development, *Fostering Mental Health in Our Schools*. Washington, D.C.: NEA, 1950.

Cartwright, Dorwin and Alvin Zander, editors, *Group Dynamics*. Evanston, Ill.: Row Peterson and Co., 1953.

Jennings, Helen, *Leadership and Isolation,* Second Edition. New York: Longmans, Green and Co., 1950.

——— *Sociometry in Group Relations*. Washington, D.C.: American Council on Education, 1948.

Northway, Mary, *A Primer of Sociometry*. Toronto: University of Toronto Press, 1952.

——— and Lindsay Weld, *Sociometric Testing*. Toronto: University of Toronto Press, 1957.

CHAPTER 11

The Teacher Relates Group Problems to the Curriculum

As was stated in Chapter 1, the major work of the teacher is to assist in the learning process. We do know that learning is a uniquely personal process and we are concerned with individual differences. However, we usually meet our students in groups; our classroom planning techniques are usually organized to be used in group settings; and our techniques for change in students in the classroom are generally carried out in a group situation. It would seem then that we would be wise to consider the make-up of the group as well as individual differences in planning curricular experiences.

The Teacher Takes Group Structure into Consideration in Classroom Planning

The importance of sub-groups and the structural properties of the whole group were brought out in Chapters 8 and 9. We found that no group is completely homogeneous. Even if all the students are within the same range of aptitude, we still have certain numbers of boys and girls, groups with varying interests, small groups bound to each other, and individuals who for some reason or other cannot relate themselves to others in the group. To create a good climate for learning, we will need to plan our work with all these factors in mind.

Miss Pastor's seventh grade social studies class was made up of children from many different ethnic groups. One large segment was of Mexican origin, another was of Maltese background, some had Greek parents, and others were the children of Chinese parents. The unit upon which the class was working was about city government. The students had read about the government of their own city, had visited some of the city offices, and had charted the structure of their city government. As they discussed the subject, some of the children raised the question about the kind of government in the cities from which their parents came. They decided to find out what they could from their own parents. They wrote to the consulates to inquire about the structure of city government in some of the cities where their parents had lived. They finally made up a small brochure about the government of their own city and the contrasts or likenesses to the governments of some of the cities that had been the former homes of their parents. These brochures they shared with their families. Here was a fine example of a teacher helping her students to understand something of the ethnic backgrounds of other students and to involve parents in the activity of the school. She had capitalized on the fact that the group was not completely homogeneous.

Variations in background may be taken care of in many different ways in the classroom. A variety of reading materials on different levels but on the same subjects will help to take care of the differences in skill. Although we have tried in recent years to move away from the stigma of ability groupings, small study groups such as in Miss Dean's class, cited in Chapter 10, can be handled well if the teacher takes some other factors into consideration. The interests of students should play a strong part in the choices we make.

A second grade was very interested in Indians. As they studied about the activities of American Indian life they learned about pottery making. Some of the students said that their parents were learning how to make pottery in the evening recreation program. The children decided that they wanted to try it themselves. Instead of using commercial clay they found that they could get clay from the local creek just as the Indians did. They cleaned the clay of grit and stones, made their pottery, and then fired it as the Indians did. They dug a pit, lined it with stones, and made an outdoor kiln with the aid of their special art teacher.

Many times the interests of boys and girls will be quite different and there is no reason why at some developmental levels we cannot have boy projects and girl projects. This was well demonstrated in a tenth grade geometry class. The students were working on the basis of the nature of proof. They were also learning the difference between inductive and deductive thinking. Instead of learning the theorems in their books by heart, and then applying them, they experimented and then arrived at generalizations of their own. A small group of boys that were interested in engineering worked out their own experiments, and a group of girls who were interested in design worked out principles that would need to be taken into consideration in lamp design. After the groups arrived at their generalizations they compared them with the theorems in the book and found that they knew how mathematicians arrived at some of the generalizations that they used. This teacher not only capitalized on interests but also on the fact that the boys and girls wanted to work separately on this project.

The sub-groups will need to be considered in our plans. Instead of dividing up friends, we will be wise to permit them to work together on their projects. The rejects and isolates can be permitted to work out some individual projects or to develop a partner relationship until their own and the class's tolerance has increased. The teacher will need to work with these students individually, to help them to see that a good adult is interested in them as individuals, before they can tolerate others. This is a necessary step even though we may have referral facilities available.

THE TEACHER UTILIZES THE NATURAL LEADERSHIP.

The Teacher Utilizes the Natural Leadership

Most adults, and especially teachers, are so used to making the decisions that they often forget that their ideas may not always be of interest to the students or that students are denied the experience of decision making. All people range in behavior from leaning on others to being the one to whom other people come when they have difficulties, but some are in the special position of being those to whom others repeatedly turn. These are the leaders or the highly chosen. In school groups, as has been pointed out, the teacher does not have exclusive rights to that position. All groups have their own highly chosen peers. What, then, does this mean for planning in the classroom?

It would be important, first of all, to ask ourselves how we stand as leaders in our classrooms. What is the reaction of certain individuals or cliques toward us? More particularly, how do the highly chosen react to us? What role or roles do we usually take with the group? Do we so jealously guard our leadership role that the emergence of the natural leadership is a threat to us? It is necessary for us to understand our own roles if we are to share them comfortably with the group members.

Mary is a member of an art class. Most of the class members are juniors in their particular high school. There is a small group of seniors in the class. Mary is not only a highly talented student but she is very well liked by the other students. She is the most highly chosen in the class, even by the seniors. Many times the students turn to her for suggestions or criticism. Her teacher, Mr. Henry, has found that she outdistances him in ability many times in spite of his extensive training. He could easily feel that his role is usurped in this class. He could feel that Mary is an affront to his own ego. He could appeal to the seniors, giving them the feeling that "just a junior" is outdistancing them. He does none of these things because he is secure as a teacher and as a person. Instead, he himself asks Mary's opinion many times and has put her in charge of many group projects. Yet he does not exploit her for his own aggrandizement or at the loss of time to herself to work on her own creative work. The arrangement is satisfactory to him, and to Mary, and the students feel comfortable with him because he recognizes their own leader and does not have to be the best himself.

Miss Joyce, a seventh grade teacher, was very disgusted with her class when they picked Eric for their chairman. She had worked out criteria for the selection of a chairman with them and she felt that Eric didn't fit any of the criteria. When he chaired the English class that was preparing to divide up into groups for putting on a play, Miss

Joyce kept making suggestions to him in front of the class or interrupting him when he made a suggestion. In a very short time the class seemed to be losing interest in the play although they had been highly enthusiastic about giving it. When Miss Joyce studied the situation she found that Eric was most uncomfortable as a chairman. He came to her and said, "I think you had better get a new chairman." She announced that Eric did not want to be chairman but the class did not want to elect another person. One boy said, "We're not getting anywhere. We better give up the idea of giving the play."

What had gone wrong? First, Miss Joyce had assumed that Eric would not be a good chairman and unconsciously had made it difficult for him to function in his job. Second, she had devaluated Eric in the eyes of the class who had high regard for this boy and they turned their resistance on to the teacher when she resisted his leadership. If Miss Joyce had been wise she would have helped Eric. If he needed to learn some of the techniques of organizing and chairing a group she could have helped him with suggestions when they were alone. It would be a very natural situation for the teacher to confer alone with the chosen chairman.

The success of our group management techniques will depend upon our utilization of the natural leaders and, in so doing, our role must be that of an assistant in goal setting. If we return the leadership and responsibility to the students and yet remain in the role of the mature adult who is ready to help; who is not disturbed when a student makes a mistake; who assists the group to evaluate their progress in relation to their own goals; the experiences will be more enjoyable for both the students and for ourselves.

3-

The Teacher Recognizes the Importance of Communication in a Group

As was pointed out in Chapter 9, the degree of knittedness in the group is dependent upon the degree of communication in the group. We cannot assume that the lines of communication are open. Let us go back to, "Who talks and who listens?" If we were to have a recording of a class session it probably would be shocking to many of us who think that we provide opportunity for students to communicate in our classes. Most recordings would show that the flow of communication is from teacher to student and return, with the greater emphasis on the former.

THE TEACHER RECOGNIZES THE IMPORTANCE OF COMMUNICATION.

A student council advisor received quite a shock. She had accompanied the president of her student council on a visit to the council meeting at another junior high. When they arrived they were met by the principal who introduced them to the president of the council they were visiting. After the introductions they proceeded to the council meeting. The discussion at the meeting related to a study of attitudes of the students at this school about the time of opening of school. Many students wanted their school to open earlier and close earlier. The council was surveying the situation and had sent out a questionnaire to parents and students. They had also sent another questionnaire to other student councils to inquire about the practices in the other schools. At this point the secretary asked for the floor and asked the visiting president why he hadn't answered their inquiry. Imagine the embarrassment of the sponsor when the boy said that he had not received their inquiry and the secretary said they had sent it in care of the sponsor. Communication in the first council had not been furthered by the sponsor. Withholding the communication was a lack of faith in the council to handle an ordinary item. Perhaps this sponsor was fearful that their council would want to conduct inquiries of their own.

We must keep in mind that communication does not take place through words alone. Miss Harrington included thorough discussion as a part of the regular procedures in her social studies class. The assistant principal, who was very well liked by the teachers in the school, had been invited by Miss Harrington to visit her class. The students were having a discussion on trade unions. Miss Harrington prided herself that she was accepting all kinds of comments, opinions, information, and ideas that the students presented. In all, it looked as if much different material was brought out and that there was a high degree of participation. Later when Miss Harrington talked with the assistant principal he said to her, "That was a very fine lesson you had today." As they talked further he said, "You didn't really approve of John's and Susan's contributions did you?" Miss Harrington looked surprised and then thought a minute. Then smiling, "I confess I don't approve of their strong pro-union viewpoints, but I didn't think it showed. How did you know?" He replied, "Well, when one of the students made a comment with which you agreed, you smiled and once in a while you would nod your head. When John and Susan made their contributions you would just say, 'I see,' and then go on to another person. We all do it but you do such a fine job with the children I thought you'd be glad to know." Miss Harrington laughed and said, "I guess I never realized that the way we feel is conveyed to others by our gestures as well as by our words."

Sincere belief in opening the lines of communication means more than being concerned with words and gestures. It means that we seek what the students think and what they already know about a subject. We don't assume we know, but rather we will try to develop a relationship with them that implies, "I am trying to understand how you see it and I want you to correct me if I am not getting a clear picture of what you think or know about it."

In starting a new phase of work, regardless of the subject, it is wise to ask students what they already know about it. We may find that they have many ideas already and then we can work together in enlarging conceptions and correcting misconceptions.

The same attitude applies to the setting of goals and planning for ways of working. Oftentimes we terminate the discussion of goals after the goals that we have in mind personally are stated, and we don't

SUBTLE REACTIONS CONVEY OUR FEELINGS TO OTHERS.

allow enough time for the students to verbalize other goals or wishes that they have about the practices and procedures. Utilizing our small groups for exploring a subject can be of great help in widening participation and opening communication to a greater degree. The attitude of being willing to receive suggestions and allowing enough time for exploration, either in the small groups or in the large group discussion, prepares the group for setting down specific plans. Just casually moving in the direction of the less verbal children and then turning to one of them and asking what he thinks may encourage him to enter the discussion.

Basically we are interested in helping groups to arrive at some decisions in relation to any subject, namely: 1. "What do we want to know about it?" 2. "How shall we go about finding out what we want to know?" and 3. "How shall we know whether we accomplished our goals?" The first question must be answered in broad areas and in specifics. The second will include the type of organization needed, who will do what, and suggestions as to resources, and finally, decisions as to time-lines and the ways in which information will be shared. The last question implies the means for evaluation, a process that can cut off communication or further it.

For evaluation, Mr. Seymour has several ways of working. First, he establishes with his group what kind of general knowledge they want from the experience, second, the kind of specific knowledge, and third, the kinds of skills they hope to gain. Then he asks his students to set down anything that they personally feel they want to accomplish that is unique for them. As the work progresses the group then works out ways that they can use to know that they have accomplished what they wanted. Finally he has individual conferences with the students on their self-ratings and a discussion of what they thought got in the way of their accomplishing what they set out to do. When his students enter a new unit of work they keep in mind the things that they did not gain in the last unit and the factors that interfered with their attaining their goals.

The climate of the whole school is improved when the communication is widened to include interaction between classes as well as within the class. We often think that this is easier to attain in the elementary school but it is also possible in the high school. Such a situation occurred in a large high school. Several students were in both the chemistry class and the art class. The school had acquired a new kiln for firing ceramics. Many of these older students were interested in the way in which the dried clay changed into pottery and, because they could not afford a wide variety of commercial glazes for their products, they thought they would like to experiment with making some glazes of their own. They approached Mr. Knox, the chemistry teacher and he said he would help them with their experiments. They took the experiment on as a part of both their chemistry and art classes. These students not only learned all about pyrometric cones to determine the level of firing but they also learned why clays and glazes fuse. In their experimentation they developed the formulae for several good glazes including a basic white and several colors. From then on they ground their own glazes to their own formulae and saved the school a great deal of expense. Mr. Knox felt that they had learned both chemistry and physics from the cooperative work. He also felt that the other students in the chemistry class had a greater respect for those who were interested in art because they had thought there was nothing scientific about the subject and that you didn't have to know very much to work in the art field.

Communication is the very heart of understanding, whether in the school or out of it. To understand someone else we have to communicate with him and in turn have to make some provision for him to communicate with us. We cannot leave this to chance but have to make sure that we plan specific ways of opening up the lines of communication between sub-groups, with us and with other parts of the school population.

Summary

If our curricular practices are to be successful, we must take into consideration the homogeneity and heterogeneity of our classes. We will be concerned with the appropriateness of our classroom work for the developmental level of the children and we will utilize the interests and knowledges that they have. The natural groupings in our classes will suggest ready-made work teams and we will devise ways to include the rejects and isolates in the group. This means that we must have great variety in ways of working and resources used.

As the teacher works with his group he will not be afraid to share his leadership with the natural leaders of the group. If these leaders need to learn some of the skills of working with groups he will help them to acquire those skills. He will involve both the group and their leaders in the goal setting, working plans, and the evaluative process.

Finally, as good teachers we will all be concerned that the lines of communication are open. We will make every effort to create the atmosphere that expresses, "I am interested in you. I want to understand what you think and feel and I hope you will correct me when I am wrong."

Selected Readings

Association for Supervision and Curriculum Development, *Guidance and the Curriculum.* Washington, D.C.: NEA, 1955.

——— *Fostering Mental Health in Our Schools.* Washington, D.C.: NEA, 1950.

Cunningham, Ruth and others, *Understanding the Group Behavior of Boys and Girls.* New York: Teachers College, Columbia University Press, 1951.

Faunce, Roland and Nelson Bossing, *Developing the Core Curriculum.* Englewood Cliffs, N.J.: Prentice-Hall, Inc., 1952.

Kelley, Janet, *Guidance and the Curriculum.* Englewood Cliffs, N.J.: Prentice-Hall, Inc., 1955.

Willey, Roy DeVerl and W. Melvin Strong, *Group Procedures in Guidance.* New York: Harper and Brothers, 1957.

PART IV

THE TEACHER WORKS IN A TEAM

CHAPTER 12

The Teacher Works with Other School Personnel

The Teacher Recognizes That He Cannot Work Alone

The classroom teacher is without doubt the key figure in the guidance structure. He is instrumental in developing the daily environmental experience for each child. He is often the only guidance person that the average student sees with any degree of regularity. However, the teacher who views his guidance role with a broad perspective soon realizes that he cannot do an effective job by working alone. He cannot be all things to all children. Thus, the first prerequisite for a successful team approach to guidance is the teacher's recognition that there may be times when he will need to work with others.

Figure 8 illustrates the varied professional contacts which are possible in a school setting. The ability to work cooperatively for the mutual benefit of the student seems simple enough on the surface. In practice, the inter-relationships among the staff may actually operate in such a way as to disadvantage the student. Getting people to work together is one of the most difficult tasks to accomplish, not only in professional matters but in any area of human relations. A functioning, effective team approach doesn't happen by accident; it has to be worked at continuously. It is a slow and sometimes painful process, but we have evidence that school people are learning effective methods of cooperative teamwork.[1]

The Teacher Works with the Administrator

The teacher-administrator relationship is, next to the teacher-pupil relationship, the most important one in the school. Administrators,

[1] G. Robert Koopman, "Teamwork and Social Change," *Educational Leadership* (Washington, D.C.: A.S.C.D., March 1957), XIV:6, p. 356.

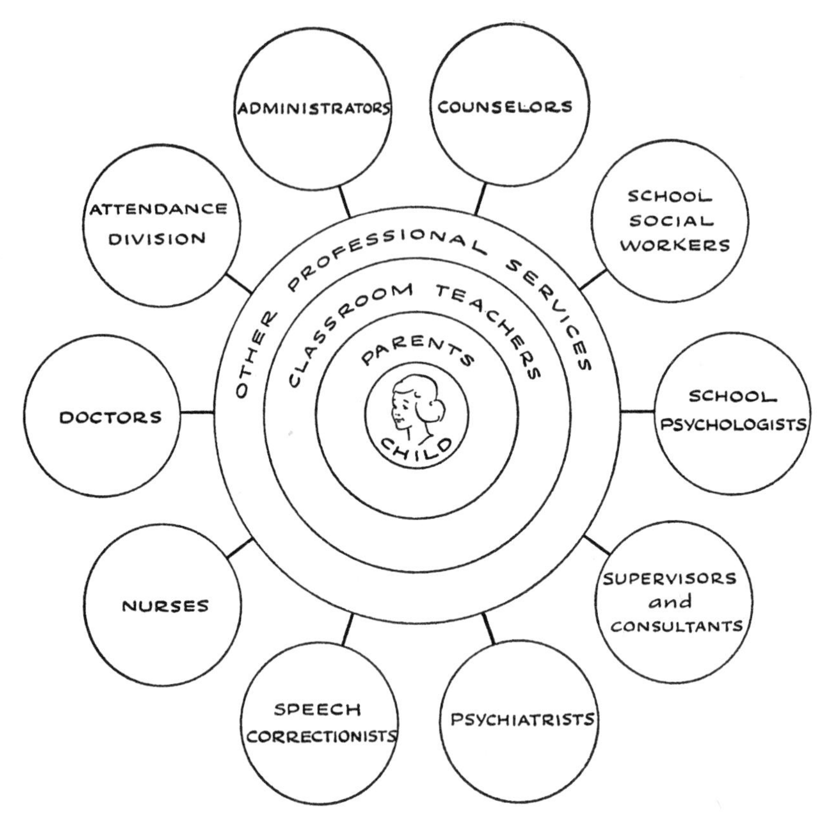

FIGURE 8. THE SCHOOL SERVES EACH CHILD.

This figure depicts the child as the center of the educational universe. Next to the parents, the classroom teachers represent the most important persons in the educational life of each child. The teachers may work with any of the school people listed in the small circles in order to help the child.

because of their status and power roles, need to lend their active support to any cooperative guidance project. Concern over support has too often prevented teachers from making their maximum contribution to the entire educational process. This timidity, this hesitation may extend not just to an unwillingness to initiate action but even to an avoidance of proposing ideas. Administrative support is, of course, not the whole story. The teacher's perception of himself both personally and professionally may have greater significance for his relationship with the administrator than the matter of support.

If we have a situation where both the teacher and the principal have sufficient inner security in themselves and their roles, the teacher will be in a position to help the administration by proposing ways in

THE TEACHER WORKS WITH THE ADMINISTRATOR.

which the guidance needs within the school can be assessed and met. In addition, the teacher will be able to render immediate service toward the process of coordinating and integrating staff efforts by cooperating through serving on those faculty groups, study groups, or guidance committees in which he is interested.

An effective total school approach to guidance is difficult to achieve unless leadership is identified. This means that someone needs to be designated as coordinator of guidance. The person the administrator selects should have an adequate background in guidance and *be able to work well with teachers.* A good illustration of how an administrator functioned as a guidance consultant and coordinator is presented near the end of this chapter.

The Teacher Works with Other Classroom Teachers

One of the basic functions of a guidance program is to provide for acceptance and recognition of each student in the school as an individual worthy of respect as a human being. It is easy to see then why it is important for a classroom teacher to do everything he can to get this idea to permeate the entire school. Of major concern is the manner in which he strives to lead his colleagues to embrace this concept.

Many teachers have come to recognize and accept the right of their students to think differently—to be individuals. However, when the teacher works with his professional peer group, he may find himself unable to apply the concept of individual differences to them. He may be unwilling to give them any of the rights he grants his students.

Throughout this book we have written about the teacher's study of the individual and the group. This is not something that can be done in isolation. Teachers need to share their perceptions and understandings of pupils. The school's guidance program can be only as good as the relationships among the people who are parties to it. One of the major concerns therefore is the process by which teachers work together, since it may go a long way toward determining the quality of the relationships. The heart of this process often lies in the extent to which each group member can be involved without feeling threatened personally or professionally.

In more and more schools teachers are being involved in curriculum and guidance planning committees. This usually means that they are studying problems that they have in common. In a guidance committee, each teacher would probably perceive the needs of the school and the children a little differently than others do. If the process of sharing these ideas is successful, each teacher will very likely emerge with greater insight into the needs of the total guidance program.

A teacher's need to share with other teachers the problems of his pupils will exist to some degree at all grade levels. However, it is readily apparent that the degree to which this need exists will vary considerably as a school progresses from a less to a more departmentalized program. If we look at three teachers at different grade levels, we may get a clearer picture of this.

> Mr. Fischer is a fifth grade teacher who has 30 students in his class. He has them from nine a.m. until three p.m. with a few exceptions. Occasionally during a physical education period he sends his girls to Miss Taylor, the other fifth grade teacher, who sends her boys to him. Once a week his pupils meet with Miss Clay, the school librarian, who does a wonderful job of story-telling and then helps each pupil, regardless of reading ability, find a book that he would enjoy reading. One afternoon a week Mr. Fischer is on lunchroom or playground duty.

This brief glimpse of Mr. Fischer's situation would seem sufficient to indicate that, except for three instances, he may not have a pressing need to work closely with other teachers regarding specific pupils. There would be times when he would probably want to discuss his students with Miss Taylor and Miss Clay, and there might be reason to meet with the other teachers concerning the lunchroom and playground problems of the students.

> Mr. Simpson is an eighth grade teacher in a block-of-time program. He teaches math and science to one class for two hours from 9 to 11. Then he has a ninth grade algebra class from 11 to 12. He meets his last class, a math and science class, from 1 to 3. Since Mr. Simpson averages 30 students to a class, this means he works with 90 students each day. His students all have another teacher for a two hour period in English and social studies. Each one is also required to be in a class in physical education. In addition the students select another class based upon their interest in art, music, or shop.

If Mr. Simpson really wants to understand his students, he is going to have to arrange to share his observations and ideas with the English and social studies teacher, the gym teacher, and some of the art, music, and shop teachers.

> Mr. Evans teaches in the Senior High School. He meets five separate classes each day: three American history classes, and two American government classes. He meets approximately 150 students a day. His students scatter in all directions to a variety of classes which, outside of English, they elect for different reasons.

Mr. Evans recognizes a need to consult with other teachers but feels frustrated at the prospect. He seldom has time for anything except an occasional chat with teachers whom he meets in the faculty room. His is a solitary journey through the educational labyrinth of the secondary school.

Assuming that Mr. Fischer, Mr. Simpson, and Mr. Evans are all three equally interested in the necessity for making guidance inseparable from instruction, we can easily see that the difficulties increase rapidly from elementary to senior high. Not only does it become more difficult to share with other teachers, but the fact is that five or six teachers may be working at cross purposes. Opportunities to reinforce what has been taught by other teachers are lost, and at times the efforts are even negated.

Although it is not possible to sit down with a total faculty to share the needs of all students, at least two real possibilities for cooperative sharing do exist: first, to inform one another of objectives, and second, to pool information about particular pupils.

In any departmentalized system the teachers of each subject matter area should make known to all other teachers those of their purposes which can be accomplished only if other members of the faculty are aware of, accept, and seek to facilitate these purposes. In developing a list of objectives teachers do not have to be asked to list all their objectives; only those among their instructional goals which can be achieved if the teachers of other subjects are also mindful of them.

A number of possibilities exist for the pooling of information among teachers. As mentioned earlier in Chapter 6, teachers could utilize an instrument such as the Mooney Problem Check List or the S.R.A. Youth Inventory to survey the problems that students feel they have at a particular time. These findings, while not applicable directly toward individualizing the instructional program, will do much to provide the teachers with a better understanding of their pupils and will certainly offer suggestions for curriculum revision.

Another way in which many teachers pool information is through informal gatherings at the faculty lunch table, the faculty rest room, and in other unplanned contacts. This kind of informational exchange is well known to almost all experienced teachers. Unfortunately this may fail not only because of its irregular nature, but also due to lack of objectivity.

An outstanding example of sharing among teachers is described in the book, *Helping Teachers Understand Children,* a publication of the American Council on Education. This book demonstrates how individual teachers worked together to deepen their understanding of the causes that underlie the conduct of children, and how they increased their skill in identifying such causes in the case of particular children and groups.[2]

In many school systems, local curriculum and guidance planning groups have managed to make their sessions a part of university courses offered off campus. These sessions are conducted within the school and enable in-service education and graduate study to become more meaningful.

Not many schools are fortunate enough to be able to develop teacher study groups along those lines. In most instances teachers are asked to involve themselves in professional study groups which meet on their own time. These groups are usually formed under headings such as Guidance Committee, Child Study Committee, or any topic related to professional education. These groups offer the teacher interested in guidance an opportunity to explore new possibilities, to share ideas, to evaluate what is now happening, and to recommend changes.

---

[2] American Council on Education, *Helping Teachers Understand Children* (Washington, D.C.: American Council on Education, 1944).

THE TEACHER WORKS WITH OTHERS IN CASE CONFERENCES.

There is at least one other important method by which teachers may cooperate in their efforts. This is through the staff or case conference. This may emerge as a function of a faculty guidance committee, or may come about through the efforts of teachers or counselors recognizing the need and taking the matter up with the person in the school identified as the leader or coordinator of guidance services. Some personnel workers like to make a slight distinction between the staff and the case conference. In the staff conference all the personnel within the school who are concerned meet to discuss the problems of a given student or group of students. In a case conference all available workers both from within and outside the school who are concerned with the case are included. This might involve workers who are not school personnel.

The conference, regardless of the name we attach to it, furnishes an excellent opportunity to pool information, to interpret test results, and in general to relate various types of available data about a pupil in such a manner that those who are concerned have a better understanding of his developmental growth and behavior. In addition teachers become increasingly skillful in observing pupil behavior and interpreting it, and in assessing the significance of all the data in a particular case.

The Teacher Works with Special Teachers Within the School

There are many special teachers to whom the classroom teacher can turn for assistance. Some of these might be the librarian, the physical education teacher, the art teacher, the music teacher, the home-making teacher, the shop and vocational teacher, and the special education teacher. The size of the school, the level—elementary, junior high, or senior high—and the kind of personnel available are primary factors in determining the assistance a classroom teacher could expect from this group. The teacher's first need however is to recognize that other teachers represent a tremendous potential for guidance resources.

The library, the shop, the gym, the playfield, and special classrooms provide different learning atmospheres and diversified opportunities for boys and girls. The type of activity often conditions the response. Some classes lend themselves to freer activities which enable children to express themselves more completely. A child who is withdrawn in a verbal setting may be able to express himself in a different medium. The school environment—particularly the elementary school—is unfortunately oriented primarily to ways of living which are more acceptable to a woman's world than to a man's. A boy who presents a pattern of aggressive behavior in one teacher's room may be able to maintain controls when participating in a different activity. When teachers are in a position to observe different aspects of expression and the meaning these have for children, the need to bring these teachers together increases.

The Teacher Utilizes Special Resources Within the School

As long as the teacher maintains responsibility for supervising the curricular experiences of students, he has to be recognized as the professional person who is in the position to exert the major influence on the student. However, there are other people in the school who are vital to the success of the educational program. Without their assistance the learning process may be totally inadequate for certain pupils.

Many of the problems that students have can be resolved with the help of competent teachers. This is probably as true in the twelfth grade as it is in kindergarten. The kinds of problems students have at different levels change because of cultural and developmental differences. However, the ability of a teacher to help students is not necessarily lessened because of age or grade level. It is true, of course, that there are certain developmental stages such as in early adolescence which require what might appear to be a supreme taxing of a teacher's patience and understanding. Additionally, we ought to realize that some teachers are more relaxed and function more effectively with children in certain age ranges.

Most important of all we should recognize that there will be students with whom teachers cannot establish good relationships; there will be students who have problems for which teachers lack time, knowledge, or ability; there will be students who need to be referred to counselors or school social workers.

The Teacher Works with the Counselor

No school is effectively staffed guidance-wise when there isn't someone in the school who can function as a counselor and handle the kinds of cases which are referred by classroom teachers. The guidance movement has witnessed a curious phenomenon in the public schools. The importance of the teacher's role in guidance probably received its main impetus at the elementary school level. The necessity for employing counselors, dating from its beginning emphasis in vocational guidance, had its roots in secondary education. Two trends seem to be apparent now. There is a definite recognition moving from the elementary into the high school of the importance of the teacher in guidance. There is also a definite movement from the secondary school into the elementary school recognizing the importance of having someone able to work with students who are referred by teachers.

The guidance relationships between teachers and counselors often lie in a kind of no man's land. This is especially true when the counselor seems to be neither fish nor fowl, neither teacher nor administrator. The most desirable designation for good relationships would seem to be to have the counselor viewed as a regular member of the teaching faculty. As Esther Lloyd Jones has so ably put it, *counseling is deeper teaching.*

Regardless of the organization of the school's program, if the guidance functions are going to be implemented successfully, we need to look at a pressing problem in the area of teacher-counselor relationships, namely a clarification of responsibilities. When does a teacher refer a child to the counselor? What kind of help does the counselor expect from the teacher? Does the counselor have responsibilities to teachers as well as to students? In what ways can the teacher and counselor facilitate each other's functions?

The latter question is probably the most crucial one. It implies an awareness of each other's guidance functions and a desire to cooperate. The specific functions for teachers and counselors can be answered only in terms of real school situations. In general, however, we might view the teacher's main function as one that promotes the total growth of students through the learning process. Following this we can perceive the counselor as having two primary functions. The first is to help those students who, for one reason or another, have important needs which aren't being met and which block the student's progress in the total learning process. His responsibility is to concentrate personal attention upon the student who has unusual problems with which to contend, and to help him smooth out his difficulties.

The second of the counselor's two main functions is to serve as consultant. The student who is working with the counselor still spends most of his daily school life within the atmosphere of his regular classes. The counselor's responsibility to the student cannot cease when the student leaves the counseling office. The counselor and the teacher ought to be closer together than ever. They both seek the same goal, a healthy personality and an educable one.

If then the counselor is working with the boy primarily in an individual setting, and the teacher works with the boy primarily in a group setting, their interactions complement each other. The teacher who believes strongly in a guidance point of view, and who has security in himself as a teacher, will be able to consult with the counselor and plan the kind of learning situation that is best for the student. The counselor's possibilities as a consultant include helping the teacher not only with students who have been referred, but also with those students whom the teacher can help provided he has the occasional assistance of the counselor.

The authors recognize that there is still a great deal of confusion and uncertainty over the respective guidance roles of the teacher and the counselor. It is to be hoped that, as agreement begins to emerge, it would point in the direction of recognizing counseling as a service which facilitates learning. This should mean, not less guidance by teachers, but better guidance.

The Teacher Works with the School Social Worker

The school social worker, sometimes known as the visiting teacher, has emerged relatively recently on the educational scene. Ordinarily, the school social worker is someone who has had training in social work and education. He is usually assigned to a number of schools, and is thus limited to periodic visits to particular schools. Students are referred to the school social worker when their problems are of such a nature that the regular guidance services of teachers and counselors

THE TEACHER WORKS WITH THE SCHOOL SOCIAL WORKER.

are inadequate to give the child the help he needs. School social workers often work with pupils on a fairly intensive basis in that they attempt to provide continuing relationships which may require a series of interviews with the child over a long period of time.

When a child is referred to a school social worker, the teacher has a natural expectation that the referral might result in some kind of improvement by the child in the classroom setting, whether it be academic, social, or emotional. One of the major problems in establishing effective relationships here is that of communication. The teacher is bound to be curious. What is happening to his student? What has the school social worker discovered? Will the worker think that the child's difficulty is aggravated by the teacher? Too often, the teacher does not have any direct channel to the school social worker, and yet the child continues to show up in the teacher's class each day, perhaps still exhibiting many of the symptoms that occasioned the referral. Unfortunately this lack of communication is not necessarily the fault of either the teacher or the school social worker. The administration may be unable to provide time for this kind of conference; the school social worker may be overburdened with a heavy case load; teachers may be reluctant to work closely with someone who has a psychological orientation which they do not understand; school social workers may not understand the realities of classroom teaching. There will never be the good relationships which are essential to this phase of guidance until some provision is made to bring teachers and social workers together regularly.

There are many others who might be listed as special resources within the school; the nurse, the school psychologist, the speech correctionist, remedial instruction specialists, and at times even the school custodian. Each of these persons can be valuable resource people for the classroom teacher. Relationships between teachers and other school personnel will improve only as each faculty recognizes this need to work more closely together, and devotes time and attention to the relationship.

The situations which follow illustrate how some teachers have succeeded in working cooperatively with other people to improve their teaching and guidance functions.

Teachers, Assistant Principal, Nurse, and the School Social Worker

Several teachers in an elementary school discovered that they had a common problem in their classrooms. Their problem appeared to be how to handle instances of children masturbating in class. Mr. Hall, the assistant principal with whom the teachers had discussed their cases individually, arranged a noon meeting and invited in the school nurse and the school social worker.

Mrs. Best, the school nurse, presented a brief summary of the normal development of sexual activities from infancy up to adolescence. Mr. Hand, the school social worker, summarized the psychosexual development of children. With this background the discussion then focused on masturbation, with Mrs. Best emphasizing the possible psychological reasons. Each teacher then had the opportunity to discuss the particular case with which she was concerned and received some insight regarding ways of handling the situation. Provision was made for further consultation individually if desired.

Teachers and the School Librarian

What can a teacher do when he takes a job teaching at a grade level that is completely new to him? Mr. Bree, a former high school teacher who took a job as a fifth grade teacher, was confronted with this problem. He soon discovered that teaching a group of youngsters all day long called for skills and understandings quite different than those needed for teaching in a high school. His most pressing problem was lack of familiarity with instructional materials.

Two teachers contributed to his security and eventual success on the job, the fourth grade teacher and the school librarian. The fourth grade teacher was a tremendous resource person. She helped him plan to meet a variety of needs in his class, ranging from teaching arithmetic skills to planning social studies units that would allow his pupils to explore their own interests in the curriculum.

It was with the development of the social studies unit that he came to appreciate the school librarian. With a class of thirty students ranging in reading ability from one non-reader to students who could read material at the tenth grade level, he recognized the need to provide resource material that could sustain interest. In turning to the school librarian he found a teacher who was acquainted with almost every one of his pupils. By consulting with her he was provided both the material he needed and an excellent resource person to whom he often referred his pupils.

A Teacher and a Counselor

Ted was a seventeen year old in the sixth semester of high school. Anyone who knew him in his early days in the school would have doubted his ability to remain in school long. Besides being several years behind his grade level in reading ability, Ted had earned a reputation as "a troublemaker." Mr. Burns, the counselor, to whom he was referred whenever he was in trouble was unable to reach him.

In Ted's second semester at school his English teacher, Mr. Pauling, succeeded in establishing a good relationship with Ted. Several conferences after school enabled Mr. Pauling to discover that Ted had interests that might be explored more fully if his program were revised. Mr. Pauling consulted with the counselor who called Ted in and arranged a different program. In addition, a job in the school cafeteria was provided. Ted's new relationship with Mr. Burns, the counselor, and his continued relationship with Mr. Pauling seemed to be important factors in helping him function adequately in school, both academically and emotionally. They may well have been the main factors in helping him adjust to a broken home situation which occurred during Ted's fourth semester in school and which resulted in his placement in a foster home.

Teachers and a Counselor

Mr. Roberts observed that Ray, a tenth grade student in one of his biology classes, had extraordinary skill in reproducing textbook drawings. Although not an exceptional student otherwise, Ray appeared to have superior ability in this area of art. Mr. Roberts conferred with Ray's counselor and discovered that Ray, who had a poor academic record in his school subjects, had never been in an art class. It was late in the semester, but after consulting with Ray and everyone else concerned, the counselor allowed Ray to drop R.O.T.C. and enroll in an art class.

The art teacher found that Ray had a great deal of artistic talent, and hoped to encourage him to continue his art studies following graduation from high school. In the meantime Ray's achievement in all his subjects improved noticeably.

Teachers and Mental Hygiene Workers

There are times when teachers work with specialists who are not employees of the school system. This was true in the situation which occurred in Rochester, Michigan.[3]

The Haven Sanitarium, a private mental institution, placed some of its children, who were still in treatment, in the Rochester Public Schools. The sanitarium appreciated the school's generosity in accepting the children and volunteered the services of a staff psychiatrist to work in the school mental-health program. The Rochester Public Schools made funds available for additional part-time personnel, and a full clinical team, consisting of a psychiatrist, a psychologist, and a psychiatric social worker, began to work in the schools on a one-day-per-week basis. The Rochester Plan for Mental Health emerged from this cooperative relationship.

One of the specific aspects of the Rochester Plan was a program of conferences between teacher and mental hygiene worker designed to secure teacher support and understanding of the entire project. The evaluation by the mental hygiene workers of their relationships with classroom teachers indicated that each group learned from the conference experiences.

---

[3] M. L. Falick, Mildred Peters, Morton Levitt, and Ben O. Rubenstein, "Observations on the Psychological Education of Teachers in a School-Based Mental-Hygiene Program," *Mental Hygiene,* Vol. XXXVIII, No. 3, July 1954, pp. 374-386.

One of the important learnings for the mental hygienists was to distinguish their role from the teacher's role. Mental hygiene workers who are seeking to aid children with emotional problems have a therapeutic goal. The teacher goal is an educative one. Therefore the mental hygiene workers discovered that teachers needed help in dealing with emotional problems from the standpoint of sound instructional techniques.

It was found that teachers who identified with the permissive role of the therapist became confused by their attempts to synthesize teaching and treatment at one and the same time in the same personality. The effects of this confusion were varied. Some teachers became resistant and would no longer cooperate with the program. Others, after further work with the mental hygienists, gained increased insight and worked cooperatively with the therapist. The mental hygiene workers, as a result of their re-orientation to the teacher's role, helped the teachers to see that understanding behavior does not mean unquestioning acceptance of that behavior. One of the conclusions resulting from the Rochester Plan was that the success or failure of the program rested upon the ability of the therapeutic team to accept and support the teacher in the role of the teacher. The teachers were helped when they were assisted in becoming more effective teachers, not part-time therapists.

Summary

The teacher's need to view himself as the key guidance worker should not cloud his recognition that other school personnel have their guidance roles also. What seems to be a crucial need in all guidance programs is to eliminate the ineffective procedures whereby different school personnel who are concerned with the same student are unable to pool their understandings. Counselors in addition to working with students individually need to be viewed by teachers as consultants, and as participants in curriculum planning. The primary focus of each member of the education family is the same: the development of healthy and educable personalities.

Selected Readings

American Council on Education, *Helping Teachers Understand Children.* Washington, D.C.: American Council on Education, 1944.

Association for Supervision and Curriculum Development, *Guidance in the Curriculum.* Washington, D.C.: National Education Association, 1955.

Falick, M. L., Mildred Peters, Morton Levitt, and Ben O. Rubenstein, "Observations on the Psychological Education of Teachers in a School-Based Mental-Hygiene Program", *Mental Hygiene,* Vol. XXXVIII, No. 3, July 1954.

Kelley, Janet A., *Guidance and Curriculum.* Englewood Cliffs, N.J.: Prentice-Hall, Inc., 1955.

Martinson, Ruth and Harry Smallenburg, *Guidance in Elementary Schools.* Englewood Cliffs, N.J.: Prentice-Hall, Inc., 1958.

McDaniel, Henry B. and G. A. Shaftel, *Guidance in the Modern School.* New York: The Dryden Press, Inc., 1956.

CHAPTER 13

The Teacher Works with Parents

The Teacher Understands the Importance of Home-School Relationships

For approximately nine months of the year millions of parents relinquish to the schools—whether they wish to or not—their most precious possessions, their children. Should we be startled then when parents are concerned with what happens to their youngsters? The wonder is that we don't have more parental pressure than we do. The relationship between parents and teachers arises out of a common concern for the child. When parents understand what teachers are trying to do in school, and teachers understand what parents are trying to do in the home, they can find ways of working together cooperatively.

Many schools have recognized the value of reaching parents even prior to the child's entrance into the school. Programs have started in the nursery school on the basis of an orientation to and an understanding of the public school. Since most schools do not have access to parents through nursery schools, the beginnings of good home-school relationships usually take place in the kindergarten and first grade. The school personnel with whom parents first come in contact play a major part in helping parents understand the role of education in a democratic society and in laying the groundwork for future relations between home and school. At the elementary school level there have been many successful experiences in promoting effective working relationships with parents.

When we turn to the junior and senior high schools, the picture changes dramatically. The apparent collapse of good home-school relationships in the secondary schools is really unfortunate, because it is during adolescence that students meet new problems and face dilemmas of evaluation and decision. Young people have urgent need of parental support and understanding; family planning is often required. Educational programs and vocational objectives may not be realistically planned without the close collaboration and support of parents.

The Teacher Reviews the Factors Affecting Home-School Relationships

It would be unrealistic of school people not to be aware of the factors which underlie and influence the possibilities of parent cooperation. A reasonable place to start an inquiry is within the school itself.

Does the school through the administration and the teachers impart a feeling of belonging? Children and parents who have backgrounds different from those of the teachers because of race, nationality, social status, or other factors often feel deeply rejected by our entire educational system. Teachers need to understand the values and customs of the parents and children and allow their understandings to influence the school's total program.

Does the school encourage parental participation and cooperation? Is there a comfortable place in the school where teachers and parents can get together individually and in small groups for private and uninterrupted conversations? Are the teachers provided with time for conferences?

The organizational structure has a lot to do with the kind of program that is possible. The less departmentalization a school has, the greater is the likelihood for effective teacher-parent meetings. This is evidenced by the fact that the schools which have reported a good deal of success in setting up parent-teacher programs are primarily elementary schools and those secondary schools which have core or block-time programs.

In addition to taking a look at the conditions which prevail in the school, teachers should be aware of home conditions. Some of those which affect home-school relations are broken home problems; parents too poor to dress "properly" to go to school; parents not ready emotionally to meet parental responsibilities; parents preoccupied with everyday problems of living; parents afraid of or hostile to school; parents who have had unhappy school experiences themselves.

Perhaps the most important of all are parental attitudes and feelings toward education and teachers. Each parent carries with him attitudes which will have a direct bearing on the child's educational

TEACHERS SHOULD BE AWARE OF HOME CONDITIONS.

process. The parent may have strong positive or negative feelings about worthwhileness of school or at least certain school activities. He may have had educational experiences which left him with a feeling of fondness for the good old school days, or he may recall feelings of hostility, anger, or fear. Previous perceptions may be hard to change. Research on drop-outs has rather conclusively demonstrated that thousands of able students leave school primarily because of attitudes which they and their parents have toward education.

Very often tensions develop between teachers and parents as a result of social and economic conditions. This can be witnessed in the problems of adjustment confronting communities where integration has recently occurred or is likely to take place; where neighborhoods are changing rapidly in urban and suburban areas; where pressure groups create cleavages between homes and schools in an effort to change the philosophy, curriculum, and methods of the school, and to limit the financial backing of public education.

There are psychological factors within the family which hinder continuous home-school relationships. These factors occur to a considerable extent as a result of the developmental changes in the parent-child relationship. Most children in the early elementary grades want their parents to visit the school and their teachers, whereas many boys and girls in junior and senior high school will do everything in their power to keep their parents away from school. Teachers and parents should understand that this may be more than a drive for independence or a result of poor relations between parents and child. As boys and girls mature they explore new ways of negotiating their adjustments and relationships to their fathers and mothers. For many adolescents the safest and easiest way to accomplish this adjustment is to put both psychological and physical distance between their parents and themselves.

In the past decade both parents and teachers have been constant targets for criticisms for alleged incompetence in raising children and in teaching them. Teachers and parents should be working together to meet children's common needs, instead of criticizing and trying to fix blame. This aspect of separateness needs to be overcome. Schools ought to provide more opportunities for parents and teachers to discuss and come to some agreement about the purpose and goals of education. These opportunities should also include discussing together what each is trying to do for and with children. Chapter 14 explores in greater detail ways in which teachers utilize parents and others in the community, as resources in the instructional process, and as consultants in curriculum planning.

The Teacher Meets with Parents

Teachers have had a one-way communication system with parents directly and indirectly for years. The most direct form has been the report card which is sent home at regular intervals. The primary purpose of such an instrument is to communicate the child's progress to the parents. In the opinion of almost all educators a satisfactory written report card has yet to be developed. However, Strang has noted these favorable trends in reporting to parents:

1. The trend away from subject-centered reports and toward pupil-centered reports.
2. The trend toward using more descriptive and anecdotal material and interpretive comments to supplement the quantitative data.
3. The trend toward reporting on character and personality development as well as on academic achievement.
4. The trend away from mere judgment passing and toward analysis of difficulties and concrete suggestions for improvement.
5. The trend toward emphasizing the individual pupil's progress rather than comparing it with the achievement of fellow pupils.
6. The trend toward fewer and more significant reports sent when necessary or desirable instead of routine reports sent at frequent, specified intervals.

7. The trend toward the use of letters or conferences with parents as substitutes for report cards or supplements to them.[1]

The teacher's indirect communication with parents has always been and continues to be the verbal reports children carry home with them. The child's likes and dislikes in school have often given parents distorted and limited pictures of the teacher as a personality, and of the curriculum and teaching methods.

If report cards and children's impressions were to continue to be the primary means of communication between teachers and parents, the school might lose not only the opportunity to provide the best kind of educational program for individual students but also the confidence of the parents who are the staunchest advocates of education for all American youth.

Many schools in the past invited parents into the school on just three occasions; when the child entered school; when the child was in trouble; and when the child graduated. Although this situation still exists in many schools, the trend across the country is a positive one. Schools at all levels have increased group and individual parent-teacher meetings.

Group Meetings

From kindergarten through the twelfth grade, group meetings involving teachers and parents are usually held for one or more of these reasons:

1. To interpret the school's program to the parents.
2. To help the parents understand what the curriculum and teaching methods will be.
3. To acquaint the parents with the teacher.
4. To acquaint the teacher with the parents.
5. To provide an understanding of developmental growth in general.
6. To discuss problems that students have in common.
7. To discuss common problems and concerns of parents.
8. To enable parents to observe students and curriculum.
9. To develop cooperative relationships between school and home.
10. To structure future meetings with parents.

The first meeting of the parent, the child, and the school is extremely important. It may serve to reinforce or modify previous ideas about school. As mentioned earlier in this chapter, kindergarten and first grade teachers probably play a major role in orienting both parent

[1] Ruth Strang, *Reporting to Parents* (New York: Bureau of Publications, Teachers College, Columbia University, 1947), p. 8.

and child to school. The effectiveness of these teachers may determine to a large extent the parental attitudes which teachers in later grades will encounter.

It would be foolish for a school to stand or fall on an initial meeting. The need to get together with parents exists as long as the child attends school. Every grade level, every teacher means new experiences not just for the child but also for the parent. Parents seldom lose interest in their children, but the school may lose the cooperation and support of the parents if it is unable or unwilling to develop a program which includes parent involvement.

PTA

One kind of group meeting deserves special attention. This is the Parent-Teacher Association meeting. Since there are more than 42,000 local school PTA's, the majority of teacher-parent group meetings probably emerge from this background. These should constitute the best means for achieving an effective home-school partnership. The key to the operation of a successful Parent-Teacher Association can usually be found in the leadership and support which school administrators and teachers provide, and in the willingness of school people to explore educational matters with parents.

Whether or not a teacher lives in the community where he teaches, he has a professional obligation to participate in school community activities such as the PTA. Unfortunately the obligation can not guarantee that teachers will actively cooperate. In too many communities teachers function as a part of PTA only to the degree that "their arms are twisted" by the administration.

The PTA can appeal to parents on a continuing basis only if school people are willing to concede parents their rightful place in making important educational decisions. Parent involvement means more than coming to hear Susan sing in the glee club. It means parent participation in such matters as curriculum revision. It takes a good deal of planning to have a successful PTA meeting or any other kind of group meeting. Many schools have found that in organizing a group meeting the planning group should include teacher and parent representatives; whenever feasible, it should also include students.

The following examples illustrate some of the group meetings that teachers at different grade levels have found effective.

I

Fifth Grade Teacher and Parents

Mr. Adrian taught in an elementary school which had recently adopted the policy of inviting the parents to meet with their child's classroom teacher early in the school year. The policy included released time in the middle of each semester for a parent-teacher conference.

In preparing for his group meeting Mr. Adrian wrote a brief letter which he then mailed to the parents of each student in his class. The letter stated that he would like to meet with the parents so that they could get acquainted with each other. He added that he particularly wanted to discuss with them the kinds of activities that would be going on in his classroom during the school year.

The students were not left out. At the time the letter went home Mr. Adrian discussed with the students the purposes of the group meeting with the parents. He sought and received suggestions of things to be sure to take up with the parents. Each child was then asked to make name tags for his parents on 3 by 5 cards furnished by the teacher.

Mr. Adrian's Summary of the Meeting:

I began by introducing myself, telling a little about my birthplace and where I had spent my childhood and youth. Then I described briefly my educational background and related some of my previous professional experiences. Following this I asked each parent to tell us a little about his background and his occupation.

When the introductions had been completed, I read the letter which had been sent to each parent and elaborated on the purposes in holding this meeting. I stressed that it was not intended to consider individual problems at this time.

I launched into my presentation by first apologizing to those parents who may have had children in the fifth grade previously and who undoubtedly knew a great deal about the points I would mention. Then I proceeded to discuss the fifth grade curriculum, first in terms of general objectives, and then in specifics. My major points were that as their children's teacher I was concerned with the same things they were, namely the ability of their children to learn and to continue to learn everything needed to make them happy individuals and useful citizens. This led to an enumeration of the areas which we as teachers and they as parents recognize as important learnings—academic, physical, social, and emotional. I stated that the academic learnings were the focal point of most of our activities; that the fundamentals were essential as the skills needed in order to grow intellectually; that in a sense we were always working on fundamentals but that there would be times when the skills would emerge by exploring areas in which the children were interested. I discussed the general nature of the units which we would be studying. I gave examples showing how interests might be utilized in a future unit on the Westward Movement to encourage reading, map-making, writing letters, dramatizations, spelling, arithmetic, and music.

After my presentation the parents were encouraged to ask questions. Most of their concerns had to do with what I would do with the children "who were slow learners" or "whose teachers hadn't taught them very much before this," and "how about the bright ones?" I explained my own procedures for working with students in small groups in so far as it was feasible in the skill areas. In addition I mentioned that I hoped to enrich the studies of the brighter students by capitalizing on their specific interests in encouraging more creative projects. I concluded with the point that I hoped to develop the kind of classroom atmosphere where boys and girls would feel free to question, to create, to work as individuals when they desired, and to be able to work effectively with others when this was appropriate.

My last remark to the parents was to the effect that time would be available for individual conferences in the middle of each semester, but that special conferences could be arranged after school from 3:15 to 4:00 on Mondays, Wednesdays, or Fridays. I added that I would be attending classes at the college on Tuesdays and Thursdays.

II

Twelfth Grade Teacher and Parents

The second PTA meeting of the year at the Senior High was set aside as an open house. The business meeting began at 8:00 p.m. and at 8:30 the parents were invited to visit in the different classrooms.

Mr. Bruce had decided to use this open house as an opportunity to discuss a future course for seniors called "Senior Problems." Prior to the open house he had sent a letter to the parents of each senior whose son or daughter might be in one of the two classes in senior problems. He explained in the letter that he would appreciate an opportunity to talk with the parents about this course that would be offered for the first time the following semester.

Mr. Bruce's Summary of the Meeting:

After introducing myself I described briefly how, throughout the United States, high schools were offering courses for seniors similar to the one we were going to start teaching. This decision was made upon the recommendation of a faculty committee which had explored the need for this type of course in our high school. It would be a course which attempts to meet the immediate problems facing the seniors as well as endeavoring to provide an intelligent basis for future decisions. I described some of the units which we were going to study indicating that the amount of time we devoted to a particular unit might vary according to the specific desires of the seniors. The course would begin by getting the seniors to list the kinds of problems about which they were concerned. Previous experience indicated that the problems fell into two large categories: first, what to do following graduation, and second, personal problems.

I encouraged the parents to ask questions. Most of the questions had to do with college planning. I told how those students considering college would be able to use the course as a means of studying procedures in selecting a college and applying for admission. I added that this included consulting with one's parents.

One parent asked what kinds of personal problems would be studied. I replied that ordinarily the students wanted to talk about dating, going steady, and even the problem of learning to live with one's parents. A negative comment came from one father who said that he didn't see any need for discussing personal problems or even teaching this course. I explained that, in as much as many of the students would be on their own on jobs or in college in a short time, these became very important issues. Except for the one parent, the entire discussion brought forth positive reactions. After my closing comment that I would be happy to see any of them during my preparation period between 9:45 and 10:45 any morning, or after school any afternoon, many of the parents came up to me and congratulated the school and me for introducing this kind of course.

When all the parents had drifted out, one mother returned for a few seconds. It was the wife of the man who had made the negative comment. She said: "Mr. Bruce, I just wanted to tell you that I'm so happy about this course. You see, although my husband doesn't think it is important, I want our son to take it. I'm worried about him. You know, he's never had much responsibility, and next year he'll be going to college away from home. He'll be on his own for the first time, and he has never dated a girl. So I hope you'll be able to help get him ready for some of life's real problems."

Individual Meetings

Group meetings serve many useful purposes, but they must not be the sole means of teacher-parent communication. There is no substitute for the individual conference between parent and teacher. All of the reasons given for holding a group meeting may be present in an individual conference, but there is one extremely important addition, namely, to permit the teacher and parents to focus on a specific child.

However, the teacher must bear in mind that the child is an extension of the parent. Any discussion about the child is bound to affect the feelings of the parent and to involve the parent's self concept. Some teachers focus too often on what is wrong with the child. The teacher should first concern himself with how the parent perceives the child. The goal is to arrive at agreement as to how teacher and parents can work together for the benefit of the child.

For some teachers the interview with a parent or parents may be an awkward or painful experience. To keep these kinds of experiences to a minimum we should strive to meet the following prerequisites to successful teacher-parent interviews. First, the teacher needs to be a relatively mature person psychologically; second, the teacher needs to feel secure professionally; third, the teacher needs to believe that parent conferences have value; and fourth, the teacher needs either in-service training or previous study in understanding the process of interviewing.

The first two points are interrelated. Questions or criticism may be taken as personal indictments by many teachers who are unable to give even temporary acceptance to the feelings of others. When a teacher does not feel comfortable with his own performance as a teacher, he will not be relaxed at the prospect of conferring with many different parents some of whom may question his goals and methods. Feelings of personal and/or professional inadequacy place real limits on the possible effectiveness of the interviews.

The third point, belief in the value of the interviews, may be the easiest to achieve. Teachers are likely to attribute value to parent-teacher conferences *after* they have been held. Feelings of rapport with the home, and greater insight into the developmental behavior of the child are just two of the more prominent reasons why teachers may begin to see the desirability of putting time and effort into conferences.

Training in interviewing, the fourth prerequisite, is essential if teachers wish to view their relationships with parents as those of professional people. The most feasible approach would seem to be an in-service program geared to the kinds of interviews ordinarily

IN-SERVICE TRAINING IN THE TECHNIQUES OF INTERVIEWING IS IMPORTANT.

held by teachers. Some of the techniques which have been used successfully in training programs include socio-drama, tape-recordings, and written records of actual interviews for discussion purposes. Any in-service program should consider more than interviewing techniques. Discussion should also include a consideration of the philosophy underlying parent-teacher conferences, reasons for holding these conferences, and plans for evaluating them.

The records of the following conferences suggest some of the reasons for which teacher-parent conferences can be called, and indicate possible outcomes as well as ways of handling specific situations.

I

First Grade Teacher and Mother

The teacher scheduled the interview with the mother in an attempt to get her consent to have her son take a series of psychological tests. Prior to the interview the speech correctionist who suggested the testing communicated with the mother. The mother, quite emotional, and very firm in her refusal to acknowledge any unusual characteristics in the boy, stated that the son was "as normal" as any other child, and that she saw no reason for referring him to the psychologist. She added that she would not permit anyone to test her child.

T: Good morning Mrs. Burns. I'm so glad that you were able to come in this morning. The youngsters are in the auditorium until 10:30 today, so this will give us a good chance to talk without any interruptions.

P: Well, I've been wanting to come over to see you—to talk to you about Jimmy, but—well, I don't know—there's always so much to do.

T: Well, it was good of you to come today. I know how busy you must be, but there are a few things which I would like to discuss with you and I feel that they are important enough to warrant your immediate attention.

P: I know you want to talk to me about Jimmy. He sure thinks a lot of you, and I've never seen such a change in him since he's been in your room.

T: Jimmy is a fine little boy, and during the short time I've known him he has been apparently a very happy child in our room. However, there are a few incidents which have occurred, and a few things which I have observed which lead me to believe that Jimmy does have problems, problems which are standing in the way of his progress and complete and satisfactory adjustment in our grade group. So I felt that by asking you to come in we could discuss this situation, and with your help, we may be able to work out a plan by which we can help Jimmy to face his problems, and eventually overcome them, and help him to adjust better to his own group.

[A pretty long statement by the teacher, and perhaps it is too quick a jump into "her boy has problems." However, she makes good use of the idea that the teacher and parent—we—can work together.]

P: He loves school. I never have trouble about his not wanting to come to school, but he's always so tired it seems.

T: Would you like to tell me about him? What does he like to do? What do you mean by being tired?

P: Well, his father and I try to work with him—you know—reading and writing and that, and he always acts tired. Have you noticed that in school?

T: I have noticed that he is a very pale child. He appears very restless at times. Have you had him checked by a medical doctor?

P: Just before school started I took him to the doctor and he said there was nothing wrong with him. So it made me mad when the speech teacher told me that Jimmy needed to be tested by the psychologist. There's nothing wrong with my boy. It's just my family and everyone who makes fun of him, just because he can't talk like the other children. (Tears, overflowing.)

T: Tell me about it. You say your family and everyone makes fun of Jimmy?

P: Yes, ever since he was little. He didn't talk till he was four. And he was slow in walking too. Then when he did talk, it never got any better. It got so nobody could understand him. Then everyone made a lot of fuss over at his cousins. Even my own mother used to make fun of Jimmy.

T: And now?

P: Well, now I don't take him over there any more, because he just clams up.

T: When he is with you, at home, how does he act?

P: Oh, he's fine with me.

T: But around anyone else he clams up?

P: Well—Yes, I guess so. I just don't know what to do. He's such a good boy. It just makes me feel so bad (crying).

T: You see, Mrs. Burns I want to help Jimmy, but I must have your help also. I have noticed that Jimmy is very listless, and unusually preoccupied. There are entire periods during the day when he seems far away from the classroom. He doesn't hear a thing that is being said, he exhibits no interest in those around him, or in any activity in the room. Frequently he sits slouched in his chair, staring straight ahead of him, as if his thoughts were far away.
(A long pause followed and I didn't know what was going to happen. It seemed as if she were going to burst into tears. Then, very slowly, almost as if she were talking to herself, she answered.)

P: It has been such a long time since anyone asked me for my help. It's always been someone telling me what to do. I should do this for Jimmy.

I ought to do that, always somebody telling me what to do. And I know nobody really wanted to help him or me either.

T: I would like to help you, but you and I will have to work together.

P: What do you think I should do? I want the best for Jimmy and I've tried everything I know. He is just like you say, listless. Sometimes I don't think he even knows I'm there with him. He seems to be thinking of something else, or something—(she began to cry softly). I just don't know what to do anymore. I didn't want to let anyone else know he's like that with us, too.
(Pause)
Jimmy thinks the world of you, and I really feel for the first time that someone really does want to help him. Whatever you think is best for Jimmy, I'll go along with.

T: How do you think your husband will feel about this?

P: Oh Jimmy's dad is so good to us, and he wants Jimmy to have a good education, so I know whatever you say will be all right with both of us.

T: I'm glad to hear you say that because now you can have some help through the facilities of the school system. Other people have had various problems with their children and have asked us to help them. You would be surprised at the large number of good results that usually follow work given by the psychologist. His main job is to try and determine the causes of the unusual behavior. I feel that he should be given an opportunity to work with Jimmy and see if he can suggest steps to be taken to help your son. I'll phone him and arrange a testing date this week.

P: Thank you so much for all you've done. I sure do appreciate it.

T: I'm glad you've come in to talk over this problem. I will phone you within the next few days regarding the date of your appointment with Mr. Whitney.

P: All right, that will be fine. I feel kind of relieved now.

T: Good. Now, I'd like very much to have you stay for a while this morning, if you can, to hear Jimmy read. We are also working on a very interesting project in numbers, which you might find most interesting, and I know Jimmy would feel so proud to have you sit in on some of his classes.

P: Well, thank you. I don't want to be in the way, but I would like to stay for a little while.

T: Fine. The children will be coming back in about five minutes, so you just make yourself comfortable and if you'll excuse me, I'll go down to see if they are ready.

[The teacher has been able to establish a good relationship with this parent and to have her change her mind about sending her child to the psychological clinic. This was accomplished in spite of a tendency to talk too much and to use other techniques that might not be regarded as good counseling. The only concern here is that the parent may now have overly optimistic expectations about the ability of the psychologist to solve all of Jimmy's problems.]

II

Seventh Grade Teacher and Father

This father had spoken casually with the teacher at an open house some months before. His concern at that time was that the teacher should have found it necessary to reprimand his son. The implication was that his son had been taught to expect to conform and work during school hours, and should not have acted in such a way as to demand correction by the teacher.

On this day, the school secretary phoned to ask the teacher to see the father, who was waiting to see his son's teachers. Since the teacher was familiar with the father's cooperative attitude, the appointment was made for the teacher's lunch hour.

T: Mr. Sires? I'm Mrs. Rigg. It's good to see you again.
(They shake hands.)

P: How are you, Mrs. Rigg?

T: Shall we go down to my room? It's a bit busy in the office at this hour.

P: Yes. I understand I'm interrupting your lunch hour. I didn't mean to do that.

T: (Smiling) I'll be glad to talk with you. I know you are busy, too. (They are walking through the corridor to the science room which the teacher unlocks and they walk in.)

P: I'm working afternoons. I'll have to be getting to my job, too. But we were shocked about Tom's card. I am very concerned about it.

T: Won't you sit down? (They seat themselves on opposite sides of the classroom table.)

P: I can't understand how Tom is going downward in everything. (The father's manner is quiet and shy.)

T: In everything?

P: Yes. He went down in music, science, math.

T: He went downward in all his subjects?

P: Yes, in everything. Now in music, I can see why he might not like that or do so well in it. He is not interested.
(He pauses, seemingly embarrassed.)

T: I know how it is with seventh graders in music education. My own seventh grade daughter has a long background of training in music, but she says she has trouble being interested.

[The teacher may be giving reassurance which is of doubtful necessity at this time.]

P: (Nodding in agreement.) But in science. He likes science. It's always been something he could get his teeth into. And now he's fallen down in it too.

T: Tom and I had some conversation about this the other day. The class did notebooks for our last unit. Much of the work was from reference books, so it was necessary to record it along with material from movies. Many of the students did large volumes, because they understood this mark would be on a sort of competitive basis. Tom turned in a few sheets in a piece of folded construction paper.

P: (Shakes his head and says sadly) I can't understand it.

T: Tom has a lot of ability. I like his attitude. When I said, "Tom, what's with this notebook?", he immediately replied, "I know. I've really fallen down." We talked a bit about ups and downs and the fact that at his age one down-spell was not bad if it didn't become a habit. He appeared very understanding and agreeable.

P: (Still shaking head.) I know he likes science. Anything you could do— We've talked about college. He knows he has to work if he wants to go.

T: Yes. His class is a good class. We talked one day about the closing college doors. One of the university professors had mentioned the fact that students with less than a B− average might be denied admission. The class was very interested.

P: (Mr. Sires looks very interested at mention of college entrance requirements.) Tom wants to go. We've talked about it. I know he can do it.

T: Yes, I'm sure he can.

P: Anything you can do to make him. He might have to be forced.

T: Uh-huh. But at Tom's age, boys are wanting to become responsible for themselves. If we force him, this will not make him want to do good work.

P: I suppose not.

T: Actually, I suppose our concern is to create good study habits for the future as much as it is to get him through seventh grade.

P: (Speaking almost in a whisper.) But I never thought I'd see my boy bring home an E.

T: An E?

P: Yes, an E. He had an E in Math.

T: (Trying to conceal her surprise since Tom has a high scholastic aptitude test score.) His math teacher is Mr. Smith?

P: Yes. Mr. Smith. (He looks down at the table.)

T: You are going to talk with Mr. Smith?

P: Yes. But I can't understand why—(Stops talking, silence.)

T: I know that Tom can do seventh grade math.

P: I know too. (He glances at report card in his hand.) But he's going down in everything. Especially science. I know he's good in science. He likes science.

T: Is there a particular suggestion you have about his science?

P: No. But anything, anything you can do will be appreciated.

T: He sits next to Ralph. Is he a particular friend of Tom's?

P: No. I don't know him.

T: How about Jerry Evans?

P: Is he a big kid?

T: No, he's average and has red hair.

P: No, I don't know him.

T: These boys are all pretty peppy. I do have a couple who prefer to sit alone.

P: Maybe that would be good for Tom. He tries to be such a great guy all the time. But, do anything at all to make him work. He can do it, I know.

T: Yes. I'll talk again with Tom. He seemed very willing to work on his problem.

P: Well, thank you. I won't take up your time. I'll go on to see Mr. Smith about the math.

T: Yes, we're all very glad to help.

P: I'm sorry to take up your time, but thanks again.

T: You're very welcome. If you see something that I can do at any time, just phone the office. They'll make an appointment. I'll be glad to talk with you again.
(Teacher smiles and walks to the door with the parent.)

[Although no solution was found for his boy's problem, the father had talked out his feelings with an understanding teacher. At the moment the problem may be more the father's than the son's. However, the teacher does plan on talking with the boy.]

5 The Teacher Clarifies His Individual Relationship with Parents

One of the real problems which confronts teachers in their work with parents is that of delimiting their function. When a teacher and parent get together, the primary focus is on a third party, the child, and what is best for him. The teacher who tries to be therapist, parent, social case worker, policeman, and judge may create psychological problems more severe than the ones he may have undertaken to help solve. Among the matters that do not lie within the teacher's province are marital difficulties, situations that reveal deeply rooted problems, and physical health problems.

The teacher's relationship with a parent may approach a counseling relationship. If it were to be a true counseling situation, the primary focus of the interview would be on the parent, his feelings, his concerns, his personal growth. In many instances the teacher will have to venture into those areas. However, the teacher should not forget that the binding factor in the entire relationship is the child.

Even when the child's ability to learn effectively appears to be hampered unless the parent can be helped, this is seldom a legitimate function for school teachers or counselors who usually have neither the time nor the training to work with parents who are emotionally disturbed. In most communities there will be some kind of family service agency, clinic, or other community agency to which a referral can be made. A teacher is justified in attempting to counsel parents only if there is no possible referral service available, and if the teacher is the most qualified professional person in the community.

This is not to minimize the need for someone to work closely with parents. Indeed every school system in America should invest one classroom teacher's salary for a staff person whose full-time concern is reaching parents.

Summary

In recent years the schools have moved in the direction of removing the barriers which have served to isolate the home from the school. Educators have recognized their responsibility to improve home-school relationships, and the trend at all educational levels is to welcome the parents into the schools. The program in most schools involves setting up group meetings and individual conferences between teachers and parents. The primary purposes of this movement are to provide a general understanding of education in a democratic society, and to promote cooperative relationships so that both the school and the home may make their maximum contribution to each child's growth and development.

Selected Readings

Association for Supervision and Curriculum Development, *Guidance in the Curriculum,* 1955 Yearbook. Washington, D.C.: Association for Supervision and Curriculum Development, 1955.

Brown, Muriel W., *Partners in Education,* Bulletin No. 85. Washington, D.C.: Association for Childhood Education International, 1950.

D'Evelyn, Kathryn, *Individual Parent-Teacher Conferences.* New York: Bureau of Publications, Teachers College, Columbia University, 1945.

Langdon, Grace and Irving W. Stout, *Teacher-Parent Interviews.* Englewood Cliffs, N.J.: Prentice-Hall, Inc., 1954.

Leonard, Edith M., Dorothy D. Van Deman, and Lillian E. Miles, *Counseling with Parents.* New York: The Macmillan Co., 1954.

National Elementary Principal, *Parents and the Schools,* 36th Yearbook, Bulletin of the Department of Elementary School Principals, Vol. XXXVII, No. 1. Washington, D.C.: National Education Association, Sept. 1957.

CHAPTER 14

The Teacher Works with the Community

Does the community influence what goes on in a school? Is the classroom affected when the community composition changes on a religious, racial, or nationality basis? What happens within the classroom when community insecurities are present in the form of poor housing, illness, unemployment, transiency? The observant teacher sees daily evidence of the indirect influence which the community has exerted upon the total learning process of his students.

In addition, there is the direct influence. No other country in the world operates schools under a plan of local control comparable to ours. Local communities have tremendous freedom and authority to determine the kind of program they want and are willing to support. The role of public education, the quality of the educational program, and in a sense, the role of the classroom teacher rest in the hands of the citizens of the community. These are community facts of life which every teacher should face.

The community which is labeled as "transient" or "underprivileged" is usually one of the most difficult and challenging places in which to teach. The majority of teachers represent people with middle class backgrounds. They carry into the classroom their own standards, values, and morals. In urban centers throughout the United States the problem of teaching children in communities which are overcrowded and transient is multiplied by the fact that the teachers are so often dealing with people and situations which they do not understand or accept.

One of the authors of this book had the opportunity to work as a consultant in the Citizenship Education Study in Detroit. A good deal of her work centered around a school in an industrially drab and fairly poverty stricken neighborhood. One of the outstanding faculty groups in the school was the Community Relations Committee.

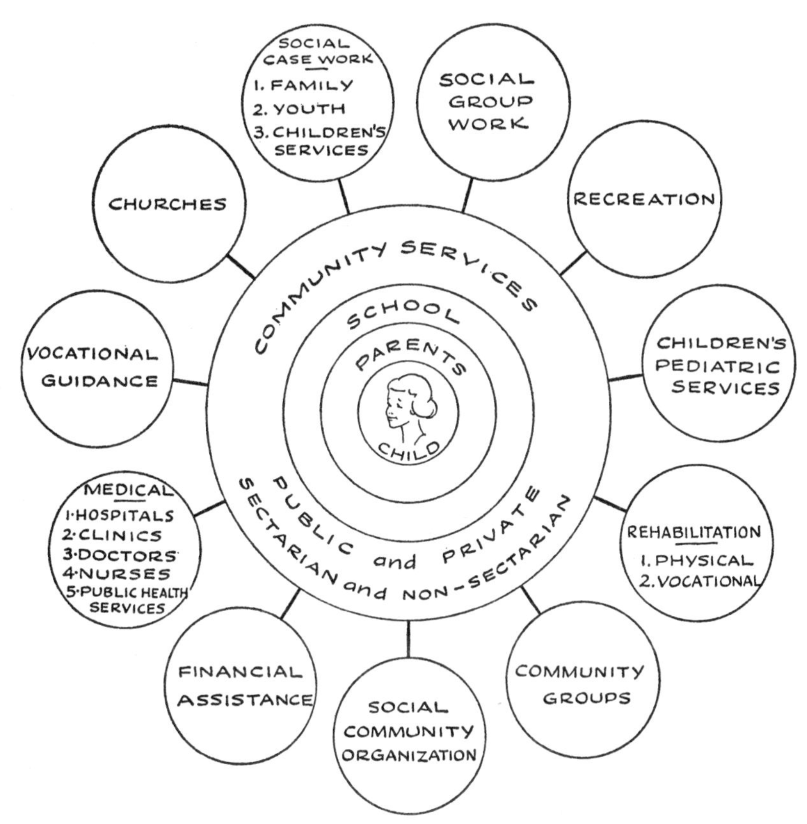

FIGURE 9. THE SCHOOL AND COMMUNITY SERVE EACH CHILD.

The child is the focal point for school and community. The parents are the most important figures in the child's life. The school serves each child and has access to many community services. It is to the child's advantage to have school and community services work together.

It was instrumental in organizing a Community Council which encompassed all the leading agencies of the community.

The first year of the Council was devoted to neighborhood problems including recreation, cultural patterns, health, and juvenile delinquency. Perhaps the major project undertaken was a Housing Survey designed to give pertinent information relevant to solving some of the vital problems of the community. Data covered by the survey included such items as housing (rooms, type, etc.); demography (race, age, sex); home living; recreation; and health. This survey revealed the conditions of homes and the attitude of residents toward the problem of housing as well as family patterns and affiliations.

This was just one of the many community activities which had its inception with the teachers. They demonstrated both in their school and community efforts that teaching in an "underprivileged" community can be rewarding when the school is able to understand, accept and involve the students, parents, and organizations of the community.

It can readily be seen that the teacher who has accepted the philosophy underlying the importance of the teacher's role in guidance has committed himself to an approach that makes teaching not only more exciting but also more exacting. As witnessed in Chapters 12 and 13, he has committed himself to cooperating with other school personnel and with parents. This chapter represents further recognition on the part of the teacher that his classroom cannot be an academic island.

The Teacher Studies the Community

It is fairly easy for any teacher to get a quick, over-all picture of the socio-economic background of the community. A trip to the library and a study of the United States Census Reports will provide a wealth of information. Additional data can be procured by looking through the classified section of the telephone directory. Books are not the only resources available. A walk through the community can

THE TEACHER STUDIES THE COMMUNITY.

be of great value, particularly for the teacher who does not live in the community in which he teaches. Visiting local industries, talking with long time residents, and attending various group meetings in the community will breathe life into the data obtained from books.

To expect every teacher to go off on his own to conduct a community study would be unrealistic. Teachers, working together, can accomplish a good deal more. One of the best examples of this kind of cooperative endeavor has taken place in Baltimore, Maryland.

"The community study program in Baltimore is a voluntary activity and allows teachers to enroll for as little as one year's activity or as much as four years of participation. Each year's schedule consists of fifteen after-school sessions, on alternate Tuesdays or alternate Thursdays, each lasting two hours. Some participants are permitted to take the first and second year programs concurrently. This is possible since the two programs meet on different alternate Tuesdays and Thursdays. Moreover, it is even advisable for a few teachers who come into the program with some previous background, and are thus able to take the first year work, which is largely orientation, along with the second year program which brings the participant into a specialized problem area. No participant may take the third year program until he has fully completed the second year work, nor may he take the seminar unless he has fully completed the third year program.

"The minimum time to complete the full program is three years with many participants also taking the fourth year seminar. At no time, however, are participants made to feel that they must stay with the program for the four years. While each year is integrated with the others, it also has unity in its own right and teachers are permitted to drop out of the program after one or more years. A few do drop out along the way. More than eighty-five per cent, however, stay for three or four years and only a few drop out after one year.

AIMS OF THE PROGRAM. The program underscores three C's in its goals:

Child acculturation—understanding the environmental and cultural influences that affect the child in his relation to the school and to learning.

Curriculum revision—working with students, community leaders, parents and others to bring about learning that has meaning and purpose in terms of the child's developmental tasks and his societal needs.

Community action—working with community agencies for the improvement of the child's environment and toward better community living.

"The planning committee of the community study workshop spelled out these three goals in ten concrete aims:

1. To create awareness of the community, its historic, economic, sociological and industrial aspects and problems.

2. To make use of community resources for learning purposes at all educational levels.

3. To carry on a continuous program of curriculum revision in the light of available resources and community needs and problems.

4. To be aware of the total environment in which the child lives in order to know the child.

5. To understand the tensions and problems of the community and to have the school contribute, together with other agencies, toward their solution.

6. To understand the techniques of group cooperation for the purpose of fulfilling local needs.

7. To encourage teacher-growth in understanding the role of the schools in community life.

8. To encourage participation on the part of the educational staff in significant community activities.

9. To create better intergroup relationships.

10. To help create public consciousness of the community needs and problems, and raise the level of general civic participation."[1]

Studying the Community Within the Classroom

The curriculum in the early elementary grades usually involves some study of the community. Too often the rest of the grades ignore the community in preference to studying the state, the nation, and the world. This is not to suggest that the other areas are not worthwhile. To the contrary we need a more thoughtful approach to understanding people, places, and events. However, the heart of the learning process lies in the realm of the daily experiences which the student has. We ought to try to teach so that students can bridge the necessary relationships between their life involvement in the community and the rest of the world. This should be done at every grade level.

In a sixth grade class the students embarked upon a study of world geography. To accomplish their objectives the students had planned a trip around the world. An itinerary was prepared and the students selected places which they would study and describe to the rest of the class. The project was quite successful. After four weeks of preparation each student presented his findings regarding geographical and industrial features, social customs, and famous landmarks. The reports were presented in the form of pictures, maps, graphs, and talks.

[1] Harry Bard, *Teachers and the Community* (New York: National Conference of Christians and Jews, 1953), pp. 14-16.

In the class evaluation of the project the students felt they had learned a great deal about many famous places. As a last question the students were asked, "If you were to start this project over, what would you like to change or add?" A boy who had recently entered the class after this project had started stated that he would like to know as much about the town in which he now lived as he did about some of these famous places. The class began to react to this statement. A few of the students said that they had lived in this area a long time but they, too, would like to know more. With this discussion as a starting point, a new unit was allowed to emerge by the teacher. People as well as books were consulted and the students ended up exploring their own community even more thoroughly than they had other cities in their unit on world travel.

A twelfth grade class in Senior Problems in a rural high school was in the midst of a discussion on the general topic of occupational selection when one of the students said that he was worried about not being able to get a job following graduation. This turned out to be the concern of a good many of the seniors. A planning committee was formed to explore ways in which they could meet their need for finding jobs. This committee reported back to the class that there were three things which needed to be done. First, the students should find out what jobs were available. Second, they ought to study those things they needed to know in order to get the jobs. Third, they should try to decide whether they wanted the job to be temporary or permanent, and what differences this would make.

Following up the first point, the teacher discussed with the class how to proceed with a community occupational survey. The class decided that the best way to obtain the desired information was to develop a questionnaire and conduct personal interviews. They enlisted the support of the principal who mailed letters to every business establishment in the surrounding county. The letters explained the purpose of the survey.

In the classroom the students conducted role-playing sessions in order to get experience in interviewing techniques. Then the class was divided into teams of two students each, and they were allowed to leave school to obtain their assigned interviews.

The survey did more than uncover a listing of the number and kinds of jobs that would be available to the seniors. The results were quite significant for the community as well as for the school. Employment opportunities for young people were declining. This meant that the community would not be able to retain its youth in any significant numbers. It also meant that the high school might want to conduct follow-up studies of its graduates in order to determine possible curriculum re-organization in the light of the experiences of its alumni.

THE TEACHER COOPERATES WITH COMMUNITY AGENCIES.

The Teacher Cooperates with Community Agencies

In Chapter 12, *The Teacher Works with Other School Personnel,* it was pointed out that the teacher could not work alone if every child was to be helped. Similarly, the school is not the only agency concerned with the children in the community. As the figure at the beginning of the chapter indicated, the school is the one institution outside of the family which permeates the life of every child. There are many other institutions and agencies which function to promote the education and welfare of children. One of the real problems of modern society is to coordinate the helping efforts of various individuals and groups.

For the school this means improving guidance relationships with the community. These questions have to be answered: Who needs help? What facilities are available to provide the help? Who shall make the referral?

The problem of determining who needs help has been pretty well covered in previous chapters. It usually starts with the classroom teacher as the person who recognizes the student in need of help.

Community facilities are seldom used to maximum advantage by school people. Teachers and counselors need information on the nature of community services and the way in which community agency people function. One way to be sure of this information is to develop a card file of community resources available to the school. For each agency the following information could be recorded on a card:

1. The nature of the service provided.
2. The name and telephone number of the person to be contacted in using the service.
3. The names of school staff members who used the service.
4. Suggestions for using the service in the future.[2]

One of the problems confronting community agencies is that of the unreachables, the parents who are reluctant or unwilling to accept help for their child. Many times the schools are in a better position to reach the parents than the agency is. The teacher's direct relationship with the child leads to meetings with parents out of which referrals often can be made. In fact, a family service agency located in or next to a school is one of the most important services to help the "hard to reach" parents.

This leads to the question, who shall make the referral? The direct referral probably should be handled by the person who has the best relationship with the child and parent. However, in order to avoid duplication of referrals or confusion about the referral process, one specific person should be the key figure, the coordinator, in maintaining continuous communication with the agencies. In the elementary school it might be one of the administrators or teachers. In the secondary school it could logically reside with one of the counselors. In any case the parent would not have to be involved with more than one person in the school. If the classroom teacher is the contact person, he would then get in touch with the school representative assigned to make the referral. In small communities and in some elementary schools it might be more feasible to have each teacher handle his own direct referrals to agencies.

Very often teachers or counselors who have made referrals to agencies never hear from the agency. A school person has both a right

[2] Merle M. Ohlsen, *Guidance, an Introduction* (New York: Harcourt, Brace & Co., 1955), p. 387.

and a responsibility to call a social agency regarding a case which he has referred. At the same time we should recognize the agency's obligation to withhold confidential information which has no bearing on the educational problems of the child.

Several problems arise in this matter of providing more effective services to children through school referrals. One is to make sure that, when we combine the school's efforts with those of other agencies, we do not subvert the concept of teamwork to mean "ganging up" on a child. Another problem is not to oversell one's services, not to take on more responsibility than can be handled. School and community people need to do a better job of awakening the public to its needs and the lack of existing facilities to meet those needs. Above all, the community must be made aware that the real needs are those of the community, not the school's or the agency's needs.

The Teacher Utilizes Community Resources

In working with the total community, teachers will find people who can function as consultants in curriculum and as resources in the instructional process. One outstanding example of school-community cooperation in curriculum planning occurred in Ferndale, Michigan.

Prior to the opening of the Jackson elementary school, a school community committee was formed. The committee's original purpose was to assist in planning the new school building. The enthusiasm of the committee led to the School Board's invitation to work out a series of statements which would describe in advance the kind of school they wanted for their children. Three months and twelve meetings went by before the committee presented to the board a list of fifteen "We-Believe" statements. The Board of Education in a regular meeting accepted and endorsed the following list of statements:

Statement to the Board of Education and Superintendent of Schools from the Andrew Jackson School Community

School District of the City of Ferndale

1. We believe that children should learn the tool subjects (3 R's) by the best available methods, utilizing their interests whenever possible.
2. We believe the children's learning experiences should be related to their physical, mental, social and emotional development.
3. We believe there should be a close relationship between home and school so each can reinforce the learnings fostered by the other.

4. We believe maximum use should be made of new-type learning aids and materials—radio, movies, etc.
5. We believe the school should provide many opportunities for creative expression.
6. We believe the school should provide for the continuing development of pupil self-direction and self-control.
7. We believe that more attention should be given toward establishing better human relations.
8. We believe the school should seek ways to foster in each child a feeling of security, satisfaction, and a sense of belonging in the group.
9. We believe there should be freedom in program planning on the part of the teacher and class group.
10. We recommend that the teacher-parent conference method of reporting be used for at least one year, with a re-evaluation of this method at the end of such period.
11. We recommend that the teacher and children work together for at least a year, and as much more as the school staff may decide is necessary to gain a long time view of the children's growth and development.
12. We believe parents can help in the school program and activities through teacher-parent conferences, PTA and room meetings; and by helping with trips, hobby groups, child organizations, and the like.
13. We recommend a twelve-months' program—ten months' regular school, and two months' supervised recreation.
14. We believe that the school should be a community center.
15. We believe that these, and other characteristics the Board and school staff will think of, will, if achieved, make the Andrew Jackson School a good school for our children.[3]

The school community committee's work did not end at this point. When the school opened, the Andrew Jackson Curriculum Planning Committee was formed.

There are literally hundreds of possibilities whereby teachers can utilize the community to enrich the curriculum. For example, the business establishments of a community provide an active laboratory for the study of business economics, consumer economics, and principles of business management. Unions may also be involved in the process. When businessmen, labor officials and school people are on good relations, this laboratory is available to the schools through excursions and the exchange of speakers and demonstrators.

Teachers often find that there are parents and others in the com-

[3] Statement accepted and endorsed by the Ferndale Board of Education in its regular meeting of May 22, 1950.

THE TEACHER UTILIZES COMMUNITY RESOURCES.

munity who can make excellent resource people. Sometimes the school is in the convenient position of being able to draw upon resources which lie outside the immediate community. The Winship elementary school in Detroit has made extensive use of such resources.

Winship Teachers Use Community Resources

Winship elementary school has imported individuals from the school neighborhood and from as far away as Europe and South America to enrich the lessons taught pupils in the classes.

Recently, a French army officer, Monsieur Renee Robert, gave a brief talk to Helen Lord's homeroom classes about France and its culture.

Two law students from Wayne State University were brought in to discuss the Little Rock situation before Paul Stolarsky's sixth grade language class. The students discussed the legal aspects of the integration problem pro and con as a part of a project in language arts.

Member of the Detroit Astronomical Society, Gerard Raths, visited the science workshop and talked to the members about his specialty—telescopes and lens grinding.

A local physician and father of a Winship pupil discussed the human heart with the science pupils during a study on blood circulation. He informed the class about the latest findings in the field of medicine pertaining to the human body's circulatory system.

There were foreign visitors from Mexico City who supplemented the third grade Spanish class.

Members of another class were treated to a slide lecture on medieval

> life and times presented by William McGonagle, Detroit Institute of Arts education department.[4]

The Lamar elementary school in Amarillo, Texas, found that it had a wide range of occupations, interests, and special skills represented by the parents of the children in the school.

> During the opening weeks of the school year in a new elementary building, teachers and principal were impressed with the wide range of occupations, interests, and special skills represented by the parents of the children in the school. At the organizational meeting of the parents' group early in the fall, plans were set in motion to find out just what talents and hobbies were available for use in the classrooms of the school. A committee, consisting of two parents, a teacher, and the principal, was organized to look into the possibilities.
>
> One of the committee members, a mother of two children in the school, was chosen to act as school-community co-ordinator for the project. She had the responsibility of preparing for the approval of the committee, a questionnaire that could be sent to every parent in the community. A copy of the school's curriculum guide was used as an aid in selecting main points to be incorporated. Within a short time 240 of the 342 questionnaires sent out had been returned.
>
> The school-community co-ordinator summarized the information and set up a filing system under four large headings: collections, hobbies, occupations, and talents. Under "collections" were such items as foreign travels, rocks, stamps, plants, tropical fish, model airplanes, coins, records, and Indian relics. Hobbies which were listed included woodworking, photography, ceramics, weaving, leather and metalcraft, magic, puppet-making, radio, and Indian lore. A variety of special talents was represented—painting, dramatics, travel-talks, playing musical instruments, speaking foreign languages. Among the parents in the school were geologists, ministers, teachers, lawyers, doctors, psychologists, and many more.
>
> The resource file was placed in the office for use by teachers and others who had need of it. Original questionnaires were filed alphabetically in a central place for use by teachers and other school personnel. Records are kept up to date by the secretary. Newcomers to the school and community constantly add to the file.
>
> As a result of the activity, many people have had and continue to have the experience of participation in a school-community project. Parents enjoy coming to the school to share their particular resources with children. Boys and girls profit greatly from their visits. Teachers, in turn, learn to know the community better and have a deeper understanding of the youngsters they teach and the homes from which they come. Parents seem to feel the school belongs to them, and an increasing number of civic groups are using the school auditorium. As a result

[4] *Detroit Schools,* May 1958, p. 8.

> of the participation of so many individuals in the program, parents are eager to have teachers use the vast resources at hand to provide a richer learning experience for children.[5]

Vocational guidance offers one of the most obvious means for developing cooperative relationships with the community. Career days and cooperative work experience programs are an increasingly important part of a school's total guidance program. Teachers can take advantage of the community's interest in vocational guidance by inviting local organizations to make personnel available to the classrooms. In one junior high school, potential drop-outs were identified and put together in one class. Students helped organize their own curriculum. As part of their planning, resource people were brought in to give information about job opportunities. This process helped to cut down the number of drop-outs.

Occasionally a school finds itself in need of equipment with no provision in the school budget for securing the items in the near future. Such was the case of the Will Rogers School in Pontiac, Michigan. Here was a brand new school surrounded by a playground with nothing on it but sandy soil. At a PTA meeting a planning committee was formed. Plans were developed which included ideas submitted by the students in the classrooms. The entire community was called into action. Labor and materials were volunteered. This project eventually provided a play area with all the regular playground equipment plus a railroad track; a picnic area with tables, grills and grates; an obstacle course; a miniature golf range; and topsoil, trees, grass and shrubs. The school was soon surrounded not only by a playground and grass, but also by a community which had invested itself in the school and had become a part of it.

The Teacher Participates in Community Organizations

Almost everything that has been written previously has dealt with the teacher's professional role. No one should expect or want a teacher to live his job 24 hours a day. However, teachers have personal responsibilities to their communities which cannot be overlooked. This is a perplexing issue because we know that as the size of a community increases it becomes more difficult to retain the teachers in the imme-

---

[5] National Society for the Study of Education, *Citizen Cooperation for Better Schools* (Chicago: University of Chicago Press, 1954) 53rd Yearbook, N.S.S.E., Part I, pp. 87-88.

diate community as residents. The resultant dichotomy presents itself in the form of trying to maintain an active professional interest in the community which employs, plus an active personal role in the community wherein one resides.

Education is the institution which probably binds a community closer together than any other. Occasionally the church may attempt this, but it brings together only those of a specific faith. As communities grow and develop in complexity, the school becomes more and more a focal point, a meeting place, for people to come together to resolve their problems.

Teachers are in an excellent position to help the school shoulder its share of the responsibility. Community action requires active citizen leadership. Teachers can involve themselves in this role. They can put to use their professional knowledge so that all the citizens are made aware of and understand the problems of the community.

Schools, through teachers, need to take leadership roles in stimulating community organization, in organizing planning committees or councils which coordinate and stimulate community activities. Above all we need to create community climates of opinion which will support significant cooperative adventures. To accomplish this we need to use all the modern media of communication—press, radio, television, movies, and stage. We need to do a much more skillful job than we have in the past "in dramatizing and disseminating information about education; about schools; about the needs of teachers, parents, children; about human rights and responsibilities. Only in this way can we reach, in ever larger numbers, the individuals and families who are not members of cooperating organizations but are an integral part of community life." [6]

Summary

The community exerts too great an influence on the school for teachers to attempt to function without regard to the existing community conditions. Teachers need to study the environment and culture at least in so far as they affect the educational program. As teachers broaden their outlook and gain new perceptions of the community, they are able to make use of newly found resources. Parents and others in the community can be involved as resources in the instruc-

[6] Muriel W. Brown, *Partners in Education,* Bulletin No. 85 of the Association for Childhood Education International (1200 Fifteenth St., N. W., Washington, D.C.: A.C.E.I., 1950), p. 36. Reprinted by permission of the Association.

tional process, and as consultants in curriculum planning. Lastly, teachers have two roles, a professional one and a personal one. Leadership needs to be exerted through both roles if the community is to become responsive to all its needs.

Selected Readings

Association for Supervision and Curriculum Development, *Guidance In The Curriculum,* 1955 Yearbook. Washington, D.C.: The A.S.C.D., a department of the National Education Association, 1951.

Bard, Harry, *Teachers and the Community.* New York: National Conference of Christians and Jews, 1953.

Brown, Muriel W., *Partners In Education,* Bulletin No. 85 of the Association for Childhood Education International. Washington, D.C.: Association Childhood Education, 1950.

Hymes, James L., *Effective Home Relations.* Englewood Cliffs, N.J.: Prentice-Hall, Inc., 1954.

Menge, J. Wilmer and Roland C. Faunce, *Working Together For Better Schools.* New York: American Book Co., 1953.

National Society for the Study of Education, *Citizen Cooperation for Better Schools,* 53rd Yearbook, N.S.S.E., Part I. Chicago: University of Chicago Press, 1954.

Olson, Edward G., and others, *School and Community Programs.* Englewood Cliffs, N.J.: Prentice-Hall, Inc., 1949.

Stearns, Harry L., *Community Relations and the Public Schools.* Englewood Cliffs, N.J.: Prentice-Hall, Inc., 1955.

PART V

THE TEACHER EVALUATES HIS ROLE

CHAPTER 15

The Teacher Evaluates His Contribution to Pupil Growth

The Teacher Sees His Role as Promoting Growth

As indicated in the beginning of this volume, we believe that the primary responsibility of the teacher is promoting learning and that the importance of his function as a guidance worker lies in the necessity of appropriate guidance if effective learning is to take place. It may help to look a little more closely at what we mean by "learning." There are many different kinds of learning which take place in the school as well as outside. Actually the most significant learnings, both in number and in importance, take place before the child ever enters school! Some kinds of learning are desirable and others undesirable (a statement which demands close scrutiny of our criteria of "desirability"). As pointed out in Chapter 2, individuals learn at different rates and the same individual finds some kinds of learning more difficult than others. Conditions, both external and internal, affect the readiness of the child—or adult—to learn. Any way we look at it, learning is a complicated process.

For the purpose of this discussion we shall consider learning as *the modification of behavior through experiences of the learner.* It is an active, not a passive, process. The changes in behavior result from the interaction of the self with the environment. Moreover it is sequential; each learning experience has changed the individual. As Ulysses says in Tennyson's poem, "I am a part of all that I have met." From this point of view, learning is synonymous with growth, and desirable learning experiences are those which stimulate the learner to grow in the direction of self realization and effective participation in the culture of which he is a part.

Traditionally, in school, we have taken a narrow and limited view of the scope of learning experiences. We have overemphasized knowledge, which is important but only as it is put to use, and a relatively limited variety of skills. We have underemphasized attitudes, values, meanings, and those kinds of behavior through which the individual learns to adjust to factors in the environment. Knowledge, to be significant, must be translated into action; skills must be incorporated into competence in important activities of living; attitudes must be developed which respect alike the right of the individual to be himself and the orderly demands of the social groups to which he belongs. In all of this we need to be aware of the condition of the individual learner—his developmental level, his past learnings, his goals and desires, the factors in his background which have conditioned his present readiness or unreadiness for new learning. As the teacher appraises the learning experiences he provides, he will find it profitable to view them in terms of pupil growth. Those experiences are most valid which help each pupil to develop his capacities progressively toward full and responsible adulthood.

The Teacher Recognizes That Evaluation Is More Than Measurement

We have been inclined to base our appraisals of pupils to a large extent on the results of tests, either standardized tests or those the teacher constructs for specific uses. As pointed out in Chapter 6, tests have an important place in guidance as well as in instruction. Tests, however, need to be used with caution. We need to be sure that those we use are appropriate for the purposes we have in mind. We also need to recognize that some outcomes of learning are not easily measured by paper-and-pencil tests. Test makers have been inclined to measure those learning outcomes that are easy to measure, not necessarily those most significant.

A modern definition of evaluation indicates the broader scope comprised in the term. According to Wrightstone, evaluation is: "the measurement and appraisal of a comprehensive range of objectives, defined in terms of pupil behavior, through the use of a variety of techniques."[1] In the volume from which this definition is taken, the authors discuss nine "major evaluation techniques," (of which only

[1] J. Wayne Wrightstone, Joseph Justman, and Irving Robbins, *Evaluation in Modern Education* (New York: American Book Company, 1956), p. 462.

two are types of tests), and ten "major objectives and situations" about which the school will wish to gather evidence. The latter include: achievement in language arts and mathematics, achievement in selected courses (social studies, natural sciences, music and art, foreign languages, industrial arts, business education), interests, aptitudes, personal-social adjustment, attitudes and values, thinking and problem solving, health and physical development, socio-economic status, and school and teaching practices.

It is not to be expected of a teacher that he be an expert in all of the evaluative techniques listed, or that he evaluate for every pupil all the outcomes indicated. It is reasonable, however, to expect that the teacher be concerned with what is significant and not simply what is easy to measure. To this end it is essential that he have clear objectives in mind, that the objectives be defined in terms of behavior which will be exhibited by pupils showing growth toward those objectives, and that situations be identified in which learning (i.e., growth) can be observed. Whatever evaluative instruments the teacher uses should be selected with these criteria in mind.

Two further points about evaluation should be stressed. In the first place, effective evaluation is continuous. It is an on-going process integrally related to instruction. Its function is not judgment of the pupil, but diagnosis that future planning may be effective. The second point is closely related. Students need to be involved in the evaluation as well as in the planning. Guidance-minded teachers are concerned to see that the young people with whom they work develop independence of judgment. Such judgment, like any other learning, comes only through practice. As pointed out by the writers of the yearbook, *Guidance in the Curriculum,*

> The effectiveness of the teacher in guiding the pupil is measured by the degree to which he is able progressively to make himself *less* necessary to the youngster.
>
> *A teacher who effectively integrates guidance with his classroom teaching is able to accept diversity 'in stride' and to retain perspective in spite of confusing variations in pupil behavior.*[2]

Evaluation need not be a burden, if it is conceived as a part of the teaching-guiding function. It is rather an essential means to a more effective job of promoting pupil growth. For a school or a teacher the program of evaluation should be planned in terms of time and re-

[2] *Guidance in the Curriculum,* 1955 Yearbook, Association for Supervision and Curriculum Development (Washington: National Education Association, 1955), p. 23.

sources available and should operate on a comfortable level of comprehensiveness.

3 The Teacher Evaluates the Growth of Individual Students

Students learn as individuals. We may—appropriately—measure the progress of a class toward the attainment of worthwhile objectives. In doing so, however, we are really determining the progress of the individuals who make up the class. In every class there are important variations in pupil growth. (Even the most "homogeneous group" isn't homogeneous in all characteristics and doesn't maintain its level of homogeneity.)

As the teacher evaluates his role in furthering individual pupil growth, he will ask himself some critical questions.

AREAS ARE IDENTIFIED IN WHICH INDIVIDUAL PUPILS HAVE DIFFICULTY.

1. *Has he taken full cognizance of the range of abilities represented?* The range in pupil capacities calls for use of instructional materials of different levels of difficulty and with varied appeal. A single textbook and undifferentiated assignments will not meet this criterion.

As instructional materials must be varied to suit individual needs, so must the methods employed in the classroom if all pupils are to be helped to achieve optimal growth. Only procedures which make it possible for the teacher to work with individuals, and to adapt learning situations to the level of readiness discovered in his guidance work with pupils make an affirmative answer to this question possible.

2. *Has he identified areas in which individual pupils have difficulty and given them personal help?* A classroom where he is expected to do work which he doesn't understand and in which he faces successive experiences of failure can be a very frustrating situation for a child. Under such circumstances desirable learning will not result. As the teacher knows more about individual pupils he will discover who needs help in improving his reading ability, who is prevented from learning by emotional problems, who needs encouragement to try new tasks.

3. *Has he located special abilities and given stimulus to their development?* Concern for individual differences extends to the more able as well as to the student with learning difficulties. As Malcolm McLean has said, "Teachers need to be talent scouts as well as trouble shooters." We are sure that McLean would provide for a broad definition of "talent" and not interpret it in terms of "high IQ" alone. Some recent proposals for reorganization of American education have focused on the intellectually gifted (especially in science and mathematics) to the neglect of the abilities and needs of all youth. Some have looked nostalgically at the European pattern of special educational opportunity for a selected few. Others would set rigid academic standards for the secondary school and expect all students to achieve them.

It is probable that the sober second thought of the American people will refuse to abandon the unique American pattern of education adapted to the needs of all and will find within that pattern adequate opportunity to challenge those with special talents in any field of human endeavor. Many good schools and many devoted teachers are doing just that. More concern for identifying and encouraging students of superior ability will doubtless emerge from the present public interest in education. The guidance minded teacher will be on the lookout to find such students and to give them encouragement.[3]

4. *Has he understood what the individual pupils in his classes think? Know? Want?* The more the teacher comes to understand pupils as individuals the more sensitive he is to *their* feelings and desires. We sometimes assume that students don't know anything about a subject introduced, with the result that the materials we present will appear to pupils monotonous, redundant, and boring. We may be surprised at what they know already if we attempt to discover this and use it as a starting point for individual learning. Only as the factors of pupil feelings, knowledge, and wishes are taken into account is the situation a fruitful one for learning.

5. *Has he fully utilized the resources available to him for understanding individual children?* These resources—both within the school and in the community—have been discussed in Chapters 12 and 14. The professionally alert teacher will have explored the possibilities available for advice and

[3] Sound proposals for education of pupils with superior ability are to be found in a recent yearbook: National Society for the Study of Education, *Education for the Gifted*, 57th Yearbook, Part II (Chicago: University of Chicago Press, 1957).

referral and will have established contact with those likely to be of most assistance to him.

6. *Has he involved the student in his own evaluation?* Evaluation should be a learning activity, not a judgmental one. The student who has set goals for himself will be anxious to appraise his own progress toward them. The sensitive teacher will recognize this fact. He will help the pupil to select worthwhile goals which are appropriate for him and to play an active part in judging the degree of success in attaining them.

7. *Has he enlisted the cooperation of parents in evaluating their children's growth?* Too often, in the traditional school, communication has been a one-way affair and limited to the conventional report card. Parent conferences represent a new and desirable approach to parent-teacher contact. Whether through such conferences or in other ways, the teacher will wish to interpret the school program to parents in terms of pupil growth and to secure their active participation in appraisal.

HAS HE INVOLVED THE STUDENT IN HIS OWN EVALUATION?

The Teacher Evaluates Group Progress

In Part III of this volume we have considered the significance of group structure, some of the instruments teachers may use to study groups, and ways the teacher can use his increased understanding of the group in planning instruction. As he reviews his success as group leader, the teacher will ask himself:

1. *Have goals been planned with the group?* In any guidance situation the goals desired are of paramount significance. This applies to groups as well as to individuals. As teachers we are concerned with guiding groups and individual students toward desirable goals. In fact the modification of goals is the only effective way to change behavior. An essential first step in

this is to identify the present goals of the group. It will be particularly worthwhile to identify conflicts of goals within the group and between the group and society as represented by the school. Of special significance is the conflict of teenage and adult codes. Customs change and peer group values are modified in each succeeding generation. As Lewis Mumford says, "The commonest axiom of history is that every generation revolts against its fathers and makes friends with its grandfathers."[4] We must know and respect group goals if we desire to change them. The significance in pupil-teacher planning lies, to a large extent, in the teacher's identifying himself with the goal setting of the group and joining with them in the progressive refinement and development of goals.

2. *Has the group helped to determine ways of working?* Pupil-teacher planning involves real partnership in determining the pattern of activity, the projects undertaken, and the organization of sub-groups to work on particular phases of a class project. The extent to which a group can assume responsibility for its own activities will depend on the level of maturity of the pupils, the degree of "knittedness" in the group and previous experiences in group planning. In any case, when group planning is undertaken, the sharing of responsibility by the teacher must be real. It is easy for a teacher to deceive himself into thinking that he is carrying out group work when class officers are chosen and small groups set up. The test of genuineness is the extent to which responsibility for decisions is shared. Do students play an active part in this? Are their suggestions welcomed and encouraged?—or brushed aside when they do not meet the teacher's preconceived notions of what is suitable? The teacher who is committed to group planning as an effective way of learning and who has confidence in the ability of young people to make intelligent and responsible decisions will see his role as consultant and guide. He and the group will determine cooperatively the most effective ways of working to achieve the goals they have set for themselves.

3. *Has he formulated evaluative procedures with the group?* In discussing evaluation, we pointed out the importance of pupil involvement. This is particularly important in assessing the progress and development of groups. Often members of the groups do not, themselves, realize the reasons for their group reactions or the results for individuals or the group. Development of effective group living is likely to come only as pupils think about their own group behavior. What do we want for our group? What are the obstacles to achieving our aims? How do we operate in group relations? What can we do to improve our group? As many teachers who have worked in group activities can testify, students welcome the opportunity to study themselves and show a surprising degree of maturity and objectivity in their appraisals. Such evaluations are regularly a part of group planning in activity-oriented elementary schools, and of "core programs" at the secondary school level, as well as in "problems" courses, "life adjustment" classes, and other courses based on pupil identification of problems. There

[4] Lewis Mumford, *The Brown Decades* (New York: Brace and Company, 1931), p. 3.

is no reason why they should not be a part of the appraisal function in any course.

A good illustration of group evaluation in the core program is presented by Faunce and Bossing. Discussing pupil-teacher evaluation of group functioning in the program, they suggest the following questions:

> What have been the best features of our work together? In what ways are we becoming more effective in our work as a group? In what ways have we failed in our objective? How could we improve our ways of working together? How can we make more effective use of each other, and of other resources? [5]

HOW DOES EVALUATION TAKE PLACE?

Another list of suggestions for pupil evaluation of group activity illustrates procedures adapted to any class where group planning is involved:

> *How does evaluation take place?*
>
> A. At the close of each session the chairman brings his whole committee together to determine what has been accomplished that day and where the group intends to start at the next session.

[5] Roland C. Faunce and Nelson L. Bossing, *Developing the Core Curriculum* (Englewood Cliffs, N.J.: Prentice-Hall, Inc., 1951), p. 271.

B. Throughout the daily work the teacher acts as a guide who aids the committees in a kind of evaluation during the committee process.

C. Periodically the teacher, at his own discretion, brings all the committees together to review progress to date.

D. From time to time the teacher will remind committees of approaching due dates. (This is a more necessary step in the early stages in the learning of the unit process).

E. At the close of the unit, part of the evaluation may be a write-up of resources, materials or results that may be used as a resource unit for other classes.

F. The group evaluates the kinds of experiences that they have had in this unit. (These may include reading, writing, dramatizing, visiting, constructing, etc.)

G. For future units the group determines what kinds of experiences they will need to spend more time on, e.g., if certain individuals or committees have had rich reading experiences but very few opportunities to write or to build, then those people must work toward a balancing of their needs in future units.[6]

Summary

Learning is most effectively interpreted as growth and appraised in terms of observed behavior. Evaluation is a much broader term than measurement, although it includes the latter. Evaluation involves consideration of the objectives to be achieved and determination by a variety of means of the extent to which the desired objectives have been reached. The teacher will recognize the effects of group interaction on learning and will provide for appraisal of group, as well as individual, progress.

Selected Readings

Association for Supervision and Curriculum Development, *Guidance in the Curriculum*. Washington, D.C.: National Education Association, 1955.

Hatch, Raymond N. and Buford Steffire, *Administration of Guidance Services*. Englewood Cliffs, N.J.: Prentice-Hall, Inc., 1958.

Lefever, D. Welty, Archie M. Turrell, and Henry I. Weitzel, *Principles and Techniques of Guidance,* Revised Edition. New York: The Ronald Press Company, 1950.

Martinson, Ruth A. and Harry Smallenberg, *Guidance in Elementary Schools,* Englewood Cliffs, N.J.: Prentice-Hall, Inc., 1958.

[6] *Carrying Out Group Planning* (Unpublished bulletin, Department of Guidance and Counseling, Wayne State University, 1952).

Remmers, H. H. and N. L. Gage, *Educational Measurement and Evaluation,* Revised Edition. New York: Harper and Brothers, 1955.

Traxler, Arthur E., *Techniques of Guidance,* Revised Edition. New York: Harper and Brothers, 1957.

Willey, Roy DeVerl, and Dean C. Andrew, *Modern Methods and Techniques of Guidance.* New York: Harper and Brothers, 1955.

Wrightstone, J. Wayne, Joseph Justman, and Irving Robbins, *Evaluation in Modern Education.* New York: American Book Company, 1956.

CHAPTER 16

The Teacher Evaluates His Own Growth

The Teacher Looks at His Own Participation in the School Guidance Program

The story is told of a teen age youngster who stopped at a drug store and asked permission to use the telephone. The druggist overheard the following conversation: "Is this Mr. Brown, the lawyer?" "Do you need a boy to work after school, running errands and cleaning up the office?" "Oh, you have a boy now? Well, is his work satisfactory?" "It is? Well, thank you very much." Impressed by the boy's initiative, the druggist said, "I chanced to overhear your inquiry about a job. I could use a boy around here to run errands after school. Since that other place was filled, maybe you would like to work for me." The boy replied, "Oh, I don't need a job, thank you. I have one. You see I'm that boy I was asking about. I was just checking up on myself."

The professionally minded teacher, too, will wish to "check up on himself." He will be concerned not merely with the growth of pupils, but with his own growth. In particular he will wish to assess his increasing competence in the process of "guiding as he teaches." In our judgment, that increase in competence will come most dependably from self evaluation rather than from "merit rating" or "close supervision." There is no question of the contribution to teacher growth which can be made by a sensitive, informed, and democratic supervisor or of the value of imaginative programs of in-service education. Such programs, to be effective, however, must enlist the support, the understanding, and the participation of teachers. A new and growing movement views supervision as a group-centered process concerned with releasing the full capabilities of the participating staff, in which the leader (administrator, supervisor) sees his role as a facilitating one.[1] Teachers, like pupils, grow as individuals, and the most effective stimulus to growth comes from within.

Has the teacher developed increased skill and confidence in studying pupils? Is he familiar with the various techniques of child study described in previous chapters? Above all, has he acquired that skill through actual application of suggested procedures to students in his own classes? Learning *about* anecdotal records or case studies or sociograms is one thing; learning to use them to improve the quality of school experience for young people is something very different. Many teachers accept intellectually the facts of individual differences revealed by research, but this acceptance makes no difference in classroom practice. The learning has not become a part of them, as it will only through experiment and application.

Has he developed greater skill in adapting instruction to the needs of individual pupils? Does he see the integral relationship of guidance and curriculum? The skillful teacher will not neglect opportunities for students with special talents, or expect the slower maturing to meet standards inappropriate for them. Increasingly he uses the knowledge he has gained of individual pupils to adapt the experiences of the classroom to assure to each his optimum growth. Such a teacher is ingenious in locating and using a variety of resources for individual and group projects. He is not content to rely on a single textbook or fixed assignments as the basis for learning for an entire class. As he grows in competence to use guidance information in his teaching, he will build up a store of ideas and materials for adaptation of learning experiences. He will canvas the library, sources of free and inexpensive teaching aids, visual materials, community resources, and suggestions of pupils.

Does he understand group relationships better? Is he more skillful in using group processes to promote learning? As pointed out in Chapter 11, the teacher who has developed competence in working with groups comes to realize the added richness group interaction brings to the learning situation. He learns to sense conditions which interfere with group morale and to utilize the resources of the group itself to correct them. He is increasingly conscious of the interplay of the

[1] This point of view is particularly well expressed in writings by Harold Spears, e.g., *Improving the Supervision of Instruction* (Englewood Cliffs, N. J.: Prentice-Hall, Inc., 1953), and Kimball Wiles, *Supervision for Better Schools* (Englewood Cliffs, N. J.: Prentice-Hall, Inc., 1950).

individual and the group, and recognizes that both group and individual needs must be met if a healthy climate for learning is to result.

Is the teacher learning to use more effectively the resources of parent interest in their children and the school? Do parents feel free to discuss problems they face in dealing with their children, without being put on the defensive? Does the teacher feel increasingly at ease in talking with parents, viewing the parent as partner in the rewarding enterprise of helping children grow? Increasingly schools are recognizing home-school contacts as a two-way street. The traditional report card is being replaced, in many instances, by parent-teacher conferences. The teacher may profit from these as much as the parent. Certainly the guidance-minded teacher is aware of the value to be gained from working with parents, and plans consistently to increase his understanding and skill in parent relationships.

The Teacher Looks at the Quality of His Team Membership

A school visitor, on successive days, spent some time in each of two neighboring schools. The areas served by the schools were similar, the socio-economic levels, comparable. Teachers of the two schools were of equal competence in terms of academic preparation, degrees held, and length of experience. Yet the visitor sensed at once a contrast in "climate"—in the atmosphere of the schools.

The pupils in School A seemed tense and on edge. At lunch in the cafeteria, Miss Evans complained of the lack of preparation of the students of her class because "Miss Jones doesn't teach them anything." Miss Jones, later in the day, expressed resentment at the lack of cooperation of some other teachers (no names mentioned, but Miss Jones had seen the visitor at lunch with Miss Evans) "who haven't had a new idea since 1900." Mr. Williams, the physical education teacher, commented on the lack of team spirit in the staff and said, "If my football team were split into as many factions as this bunch of teachers, we'd be in the cellar for sure."

In School B, by contrast, there was an evident lack of tension in classrooms and halls. There appeared to be a spirit of friendliness among pupils and teachers. The visitor was invited to an impromptu coffee hour with a group of teachers who had free periods at the same time. The conversation was pleasantly social, but touched on professional activities when one of the other teachers asked Mr. Harris about an experiment he was carrying on with his ninth grade science class. Comments, questions, and suggestions flew back and forth, but in a general spirit of interest and helpfulness. Throughout the day, the visitor noted in classes and in the faculty group a pride in "our" school and generosity in giving credit to the contribution others were making.

What explains the contrast? It was evidently a difference in that indefinable but significant characteristic called "morale." There may have been—probably was—a variation in the quality of administrative leadership. In any case, there was an unmistakable distinction between Schools A and B in the acceptance by teachers of each other and in the quality of teamwork displayed.

Chapter 12 directed attention toward ways in which the teacher can increase his effectiveness as he works with other staff members—in committees assigned responsibility for guidance and curriculum planning, in informal relationships with other classroom teachers, and in utilizing the resources of administrators, special teachers, counselors, and other guidance workers. An appraisal of his effectiveness in these relationships will provide the teacher a measure of his growth as a team member.

A school staff, like a class, is most effective as it utilizes to the full the resources of all its members. This calls for skill in analyzing problems cooperatively and arriving at group decisions for their solution. It also calls for group self-discipline based on the acceptance of common purposes. Increasingly schools make use of committees, faculty councils, workshops, and other types of group organization to plan and carry out responsibilities for the staff as a whole. This kind of activity is not "busy work" but an essential part of every teacher's function if the educational program of the school is to achieve success. Developing skill in group process is an important measure of teacher growth.

We may not see eye to eye. Learning to respect the points of view of those with whom we differ does not demand the sacrifice of our own convictions. Most of us, at some time or other, have been members of a group where, at first, there was restraint and distrust but where, as participants came to know and accept each other, defenses were relaxed and members were free to be themselves. It then became possible to accept ideas of others, to admit mistakes or inadequancies, and to arrive at a compromise solution which was acceptable to all. Usually the process was made possible because of the warmth and obvious respect for others exhibited by some members of the group. This receptiveness was contagious and released unexpected capacities in others. The teacher who is growing in maturity as a team member will increasingly reveal this kind of receptiveness.

The Teacher Becomes Aware of His New Insights

As with pupils, so with teachers; some of the most significant growth is not in added knowledge or polished skills, but in new ways of looking at familiar objects, people, or activities. We have all had the experience of looking at a well-known picture or listening to a musical composition and suddenly finding in it something we never saw or heard before. Our whole conception of the work is changed. It isn't the same landscape or the same symphony ever again. The same thing can happen to us professionally and, when it does, it represents an important kind of growth.

The guidance-minded teacher will ask himself, "In what way do I see pupils differently, as I improve my guidance skills?" "Is there a change in my concept of the teacher's role?" "Do I see my relation to the whole school program in a different light?" One of the most helpful statements of new insights which come to the teacher who is concerned to see pupils as individuals is presented in a volume to which we have had occasion to make frequent reference. *Helping Teachers Understand Children* presents what many teachers have found the best single statement of "what it means to understand a child." The writers outline six characteristics of the understanding teacher and summarize as follows:

> To sum up, our definition of understanding a child includes contrasting subjective and objective elements. On the one hand, it calls for the subjective acceptance and valuing of individual boys and girls —emotionally and philosophically rooted and serving to reassure and afford security to all children, even when they misbehave. On the other hand, it also implies objectivity in the use of sound procedures and knowledge to interpret the causes of a child's acts, to appraise his adjustment problems and personal needs, and to work out practical ways of helping him master his developmental tasks.[2]

One desirable outcome, then, is a new way of looking at students.

As teachers study their pupils, they gain a broadened concept of the teaching role and a new standard of professional competence. It

---

[2] American Council on Education, *Helping Teachers Understand Children* (Washington, D.C.: American Council on Education, 1945), p. 12.

is important to recognize that a concern for pupil growth does not mean neglect of knowledge or skills. Intellectual growth is still a major concern of teacher and school. It is, however, set in a larger framework which includes social and emotional learnings as well.

As he works with pupils, individually and in groups, in the light of his growing understanding of the factors involved in human growth and development, the teacher recognizes that learning takes place best in an atmosphere of security and freedom. Children who feel threatened, who are burdened with personal problems, or who experience a sense of futility as a result of repeated failure are not in a favorable condition to learn. A pupil must be able to accept himself if he is to make the most of his own abilities and to work cooperatively with others. The atmosphere of the classroom can do much to foster self-acceptance or to hinder its development.

One important insight is the recognition by the teacher that, in his relations with pupils, he may be satisfying his own needs—to feel loved, to achieve recognition, to exert power over others. All of these are important and legitimate motivations of human beings, when exhibited in moderation and kept in balance. We are the product of our own past experiences. The teacher has the same emotional needs as those we have earlier identified in children. As the teacher comes to understand his own motivations better, he will recognize those drives which are concerned with satisfying his own needs and will find acceptable ways to their realization. As a professional person he will feel the obligation to avoid building his own security at the expense of pupils.

The teacher needs to understand—and to accept—himself. Cantor has developed this point exceptionally well. Pointing out the "polarity of the self," he indicates that each individual has ambivalent drives—toward security and toward adventure, for recognition and acceptance and for individual creativity, toward dependence and toward independence.[3] Applying this concept to the professional function of the teacher, he says:

> The teacher is placed in a position which by its nature carries prestige and authority so far as the pupils are involved. The temptation to use the prestige and authority of the position for one's personal needs is ever present. And the temptation is strengthened by the difference in age between teacher and pupils. Furthermore, in any

[3] From *The Teaching-Learning Process* by Nathaniel Cantor. Copyright 1953 by The Dryden Press. Reprinted by permission of the publishers.

THE TEACHER NEEDS TO UNDERSTAND AND TO ACCEPT HIMSELF.

> contest or clash of wills, the teacher realizes she cannot lose. The structure of the classroom is thus an ideal setting for the teacher to work out personal tensions. It closely parallels the home, where parents are similarly tempted to use their children as targets for their needs.
>
> To struggle against and gradually overcome this temptation requires an unquestioned conviction on the part of the teacher that her job is to help pupils, not to be helped by them. Her function is to aid the development of children through her specific skills. She offers a professional service in a professional manner.[4]

Only the teacher who feels secure himself is free to provide a nonthreatening atmosphere for pupils. To recognize one's limitations without self-depreciation and to appraise one's strengths objectively are marks of psychological maturity. These characteristics are essential for the teacher who sees his role as creating a favorable climate for pupil growth.

These are some of the kinds of new insight the teacher may find himself acquiring as he recognizes the significance of his guidance role. This list does not exhaust the changes in outlook the teacher may experience. In the development of insight, too, there are individual differences, and the new attitudes will depend on the past experiences,

---

[4] *Ibid.,* p. 271.

the circumstances of the teaching setting, and the creative imagination of the individual teacher. Basically, they will add up to the recognition of his professional role as one of facilitating growth.

THE TEACHER SETS NEW GOALS FOR CONTINUED GROWTH.

The Teacher Sets New Goals for Continued Growth as a Guidance Worker

For a book on adult education, Dorothy Canfield Fisher uses the intriguing title, *"Why Stop Learning?"* This question is of particular significance for the professionally minded teacher. Unless the teacher continues to glimpse new horizons of professional achievement and to move toward them, stagnation is inevitable. The lines such growth may take have been suggested in the preceding sections of this chapter. Essentially the new goals the teacher sets for himself will lie in the areas of enlarged vision, increasing competence in his present activities as a guidance worker, and experimentation with promising procedures he has observed in other schools, has read about, or has devised. Some effective ways of promoting continued professional growth are suggested below.

1. *Action research.* This means the attempt to solve problems of immediate concern to the teacher or his school through trying out what seem likely hypotheses for their solution and keeping a systematic record of what happens—what Corey calls "research for practitioners." Action research is most effective as it is a cooperative study of school problems. It can, however, be carried on by an interested and competent teacher as an individual project. Action research is particularly appropriate in guidance, where the teacher is concerned to improve conditions for learning through use of carefully considered instruments and procedures.[5]

2. *Participation in professional organizations.* The teacher desiring to grow in professional competence will find many opportunities for active participation in local, state, or national organizations devoted to improvement of the educational program. The American Personnel and Guidance Association, the Association for Supervision and Curriculum Development, the National Education Association, the American Federation of Teachers and their state and local affiliates are among the professional groups which welcome teacher interest and support. In these and similar organizations, there is always demand for ideas and leadership. The interested teacher will find many opportunities to work on projects or committees concerned with phases of guidance.

3. *Writing and Publication.* Descriptions of guidance activities written by classroom teachers are few. There is a dearth, in guidance literature, of such first hand reports from the field. Your experiences will interest and profit other teachers. Furthermore, writing an account of an experiment conducted with your pupils or discussing guidance proposals in the light of your experience will clarify ideas in your own mind.

4. *Professional reading.* To keep abreast of developments in any professional field calls for familiarity with significant current publications. To no field is this more applicable than to teaching. Ours is a complicated profession which draws on new knowledge from many fields. Particularly in relation to the guidance aspects of his role, the teacher will need to familiarize himself with the newer findings of research in psychology and child development, guidance practices, and school-community relationships.

It should be stressed that professional reading is not limited to books on education! Sociology, anthropology, and other disciplines are rich in suggestions leading to understanding the child, his family relationships, and the community of which he is a part. The humanities, too, have a contribution to make. The intuitive insights of the poet or novelist may broaden understanding of individual motivations and deepen faith in human potential.

Some schools make recent significant books and professional magazines available to the staff. In other cases, teachers pool their funds for magazine subscriptions and purchase of books and operate through a library committee. Many teachers consider a personal professional library an essential

---

[5] For an excellent discussion of the character and possibilities of action research see: Stephen M. Corey, *Action Research to Improve School Practices,* (New York: Bureau of Publications, Teachers College, Columbia University, 1953).

tool of their trade. In any case, the teacher concerned with professional growth will continue to be a student of his field.

5. *Advanced professional courses.* Professional growth is not measured by credits earned or degrees held. As previously suggested, the teacher may plan his own regimen of professional study. At the same time, he will find that the guidance provided by an organized program of course work, and the stimulus of an informed teacher and a group of other students concerned with comparable problems will broaden horizons and enhance learning. Such study is most fruitful when focused on practical problems faced in the classroom and directed toward areas in which the teacher sees need of additional knowledge and understanding. The movement for cooperative study of local problems with college or university leadership has gained ground in recent years and represents a functional type of in-service education.

The workshop type of course is especially appropriate for improvement of guidance programs and showing the interrelated function of guidance and curriculum. Significant in the workshop approach are the selection of problems by members of the group, attack on the selected problems by small groups interested in the specific problems, the service of staff members as consultants rather than instructors, and the continual appraisal of progress by the participants. An excellent analysis of workshop techniques with illustrations drawn from more than ten years' experience in conducting workshops for elementary and secondary school teachers is presented by Kelley.[6]

Teachers concerned to improve their skills as guidance workers will find profit in electing courses in those areas suggested as desirable in the preparation of counselors and other personnel workers. This will not only help the teacher to carry out his present teaching-guiding role more effectively, but will serve as basic orientation for those interested in eventual appointment to more specialized positions in guidance. The most promising recruiting ground for the counselors and personnel workers so urgently needed in schools is the classroom. Among the areas which will help the teacher in furthering preparation for his guidance role are: the psychology of child development, mental hygiene, sociology and cultural anthropology, educational philosophy, curriculum development, evaluation and measurement, case study techniques, the counseling process, group methods in guidance, occupational trends, family and community relationships, community resources, and supervised practice in counseling. Specific proposals for counselor preparation have been made by a number of state and national committees.[7]

---

[6] Earl C. Kelley, *The Workshop Way of Learning* (New York: Harper and Brothers, 1952).

[7] A detailed description of several such proposals will be found in H. B. McDaniel, *Guidance in the Modern School* (New York: The Dryden Press, 1956), pp. 443-55. A stimulating discussion of the qualities desired in counselors is presented by C. G. Wrenn, "The Status and Role of the School Counselor," *The Personnel and Guidance Journal*, XXXVI, pp. 175-83, November, 1957.

Summary

The teacher will continually appraise his growth in effectiveness as a guidance worker. He will evaluate the contribution he makes to the guidance program of the school through his day-to-day contacts with pupils in his classes. He will see guidance as an activity involving the cooperative activities of all members of the staff and will appraise the extent to which he is growing in perceptiveness and effectiveness as a 'team member." New insights, new ways of looking at pupils and at his function as a teacher-guide will represent an important measure of growth. Finally, the teacher will look ahead and will set new goals for continued growth. Some of the activities which may contribute to that growth are action research, participation in professional organizations, writing and publication, professional reading, and advanced professional course work in colleges or universities.

Selected Readings

American Council on Education, *Helping Teachers Understand Children.* Washington, D. C.: American Council on Education, 1945.

Cantor, Nathaniel, *The Teaching-Learning Process.* New York: The Dryden Press, 1953.

Corey, Stephen M., *Action Research to Improve School Practices.* New York: Bureau of Publications, Teachers College, Columbia University, 1953.

Gordon, Ira J., *The Teacher as a Guidance Worker.* New York: Harper and Brothers, 1956.

Association for Supervision and Curriculum Development, *Guidance in the Curriculum.* Washington, D. C.: National Education Association, 1955.

McDaniel, H. B., *Guidance in the Modern School,* Chapters 17, 18. New York: The Dryden Press, 1956.

Redl, Fritz, and William W. Wattenberg, *Mental Hygiene in Teaching.* New York: Harcourt Brace and Company, 1951.

ANNOTATED BIBLIOGRAPHY

Part I. Philosophy and Structure of the Guidance Program

Johnston, Edgar G., *Administering the Guidance Program.* Minneapolis: Educational Publishers, 1942 • A handbook for school administrators. Part I presents a guidance viewpoint which enhances the teacher's role.

McDaniel, Henry B., and G. A. Shaftel, *Guidance in the Modern School.* New York: The Dryden Press, 1956 • Four major aspects of guidance are considered: organization of the school for identifying and serving pupil needs, systematic study of the individual, informational program, and principles and practices of counseling. The functional guidance program is shown to be eclectic in nature and to involve the whole school: teacher, administrator, specialist, and parent. Unsolved problems are discussed and areas needing further study considered.

Mathewson, Robert H., *Guidance Policy and Practice,* Revised Edition. New York: Harper and Brothers, 1955 • Presents philosophical and psychological principles applicable to a guidance program and procedures in implementation of guidance policy. A final section is devoted to trends and prospects in guidance.

Ohlsen, Merle M., *Guidance, An Introduction.* New York: Harcourt, Brace and Company, 1955 • This book is an overall view of guidance and counseling, including an educational philosophy supplemented by procedures, case studies, and techniques for students new to the field of guidance.

Smith, Glenn, *Principles and Practices of the Guidance Program.* New York: Macmillan Company, 1951 • The varied phases of a guidance program are discussed. The functions of the specific groups performing on each guidance level are outlined. The principles delineated are discussed with case stories providing practical demonstrations. Descriptions of the means by which schools and communities may cooperate in realizing the objectives of education pertaining to the all around development of each individual are presented.

Strang, Ruth, *The Role of the Teacher in Personnel Work,* Fourth Edition. New York: Bureau of Publications, Teachers College, Columbia University, 1953 • Professor Strang draws on a rich background of experience and authorship in the guidance field. Part III, "Technics of Personnel Work," gives extended consideration to teacher's observations, daily schedules and other personal documents, developmental records, and case studies.

Warters, Jane, *High School Personnel Work Today,* Second Edition. New York: McGraw-Hill Book Company, Inc., 1956 • A broad approach to student personnel work, giving consideration to its relationship to curriculum and to administration. The major emphasis is on counseling and the book will be most useful to those officially assigned to guidance functions. At the same time the interested teacher will find many suggestions he can apply in his own guidance activities.

Part II. Study of the Individual

American Council on Education, *Helping Teachers Understand Children.* Washington, D.C.: American Council on Education, 1945 • Procedures for studying child behavior in a school setting as described by teachers participating in an in-service training program. Many detailed observations and engaging case studies. Chapter 2 describes different types of anecdotal records and gives examples. Chapters 9 and 10 offer good illustrations of uses and limitations of sociometry.

Arbuckle, Dugald S., *Guidance and Counseling in the Classroom.* Boston: Allyn and Bacon, Inc., 1957 • An enlightened view of the teacher's role in guidance. Emphasis is on the teacher's functioning as a counselor with many illustrations of teacher interviews.

Blos, Peter, *The Adolescent Personality.* New York: Appleton-Century-Crofts, Inc., 1941 • Through intensive case studies of four adolescents, Dr. Blos and his collaborators laid the basis for a psychology of adolescence. The latter, in turn, is made real and practical by illustrations from the case material. The case histories can be read profitably without reference to the theoretical material.

Cantor, Nathaniel, *The Teaching-Learning Process.* New York: The Dryden Press, 1951 • Within the limitations imposed by his professional position, a teacher should create a permissive but challenging atmosphere. All learning, the result of self-discipline and self-motivation, should be "reality-centered" in the classroom. Fear offers the greatest obstacle to learning. Under the title, "Toward a New Teacher," Cantor presents helpful suggestions for professional growth based on self-understanding.

Cronbach, Lee J., *Essentials of Psychological Testing.* New York: Harper and Brothers, 1949 • An analysis of psychological tests of ability and aptitude with implications for their use in studying individuals. A basic reference.

D'Evelyn, Kathryn E., *Meeting Children's Emotional Needs.* Englewood Cliffs, N. J.: Prentice-Hall, Inc., 1957 • Demonstrates how needs of both normal and deviate children can be met within the school. Especially helpful for teachers.

Freud, Anna, *Ego and Mechanisms of Defense.* New York: The International Universities Press, 1946 • Shows how the defenses develop and the function of the ego in personality development.

———, *Psychoanalysis for Teachers and Parents.* New York: Emerson Books, Inc., 1935 • A series of talks to parents and teachers on the psycho-sexual development of children.

Gordon, Ira, *The Teacher as a Guidance Worker.* New York: Harper and Brothers, 1956 • No longer assigned to any single group of specialists, effective guidance for the maximum number of students depends upon the teacher as guidance worker. He uses all his knowledge of human development and community forces to deal with students and parents as group worker, individual counselor, and action researcher.

Hamrin, Shirley A. and Blanche B. Paulson, *Counseling Adolescents*. Chicago: Science Research Associates, Inc., 1950 • After discussing and evaluating both directive and non-directive techniques of counseling, the authors advocate an eclectic approach which draws on the most workable features of each. They illustrate their ideas with recorded interviews and case summaries.

Hartman, Heinz, Ernest Kris, and Rudolph Lowenstein, "Comments on the Formation of Psychic Structure" in *The Psychoanalytic Study of the Child, Volume II*. New York: The International Universities Press, 1946 • Shows the psychodynamic process of personality development and the conditions essential for learning. Environmental, as well as maturational, influences on psychological development are considered.

Havighurst, R. J., *Human Development and Education*. New York: Longmans, Green, and Company, Inc., 1953 • The author analyzes the developmental tasks for the various age levels of our society. He shows the implications for educational philosophies and curricula in handling these situations so as to promote optimum adjustment of each individual. Scales for rating each area of growth are presented.

Hymes, James L., Jr., *A Child Development Point of View*. Englewood Cliffs, N. J.: Prentice-Hall, Inc., 1955 • Principles derived from child development research are applied to typical problems in teacher-teacher relationships, the curriculum, and classroom organization and management. The author studies the totality of a child's life and brings to light generalizations that have been uncovered in child development that can strengthen one's sensitivity and sharpen one's goal in teaching boys and girls.

Olson, Willard C., *Child Development*. Boston: D. C. Heath & Company, 1949 • A systematic review of the development of the child with special emphasis on the school years. Sound application of growth principles to education and training of the child. In addition, the book serves as a basic source of detailed data on the special aspects of the subject (such as physical growth, motor development, and the like).

Prescott, Daniel, *The Child in the Educative Process*. New York: McGraw-Hill Book Company, Inc., 1957 • What the teacher needs to know about children's emotions in order to work successfully with them. Presents examples of what some schools are doing.

Rasey, Marie I. and J. W. Menge, *What We Learn From Children*. New York: Harper and Brothers, 1956 • The authors present a re-examination of assumptions about how children learn and grow in light of their responses and behavior. Case studies of children in a home for the exceptional child illustrate this behavior. Help in overcoming their difficulties is afforded by understanding, patient observation, and treatment based on the children's own needs and ways of reacting to experiences.

Redl, Fritz, and William W. Wattenberg, *Mental Hygiene in Teaching.* New York: Harcourt, Brace and Company, 1951 • General discussion of this problem area. Presents useful "influence techniques" such as "signal interference," "humor," "ignoring," "proximity control," etc., which the teacher can employ in specific kinds of situations to support or help the child control his behavior when his own ego seems unequal to the task.

Traxler, Arthur E., *Techniques of Guidance,* Revised Edition. New York: Harper and Brothers, 1957 • A comprehensive and well documented discussion of guidance procedures. Chapters 4 to 8 discuss a variety of informal methods of studying individuals.

Wattenberg, William W., *The Adolescent Years.* New York: Harcourt, Brace and Company, 1955 • This book attempts to preserve the essential wholeness or integrity of growth by presenting its contents under four broad patterns of adolescent experience and behavior. The first of these provides a general overview of late childhood, adolescence, and youth in western culture as they appear to adults, to observers representing various scientific disciplines, and to the individual himself. The second pattern illustrates cultural, social, educational, and physical influences which act upon the adolescent and their interrelationships. The third presentation includes sexual, social, emotional, and vocational problems which typically beset the adolescent. The fourth part discusses adults' reactions to and problems with adolescents. Suggestions are made for adjustive or remedial action in the home, classroom, and counseling clinic, and for the recreation leader, clergyman, and civic or community leader.

Part III. Study of the Group

Association for Supervision and Curriculum Development, *Fostering Mental Health in Our Schools.* Washington, D. C.: National Education Association, 1950 • This yearbook discusses problems faced in the course of every normal child's development. It is sectioned into factors which may determine development and behavior, motivations within the child, and ways in which both teacher and school can better know and help the child.

Cartwright, Darwin and Alvin Zander, editors, *Group Dynamics.* Evanston, Illinois: Row Peterson & Company, 1953 • To provide a collection of the more significant articles which describe the methods and findings of research on group dynamics and systematically summarize their results, the editors have chosen six theoretically defined problems and grouped literature in these areas. Group cohesiveness, pressures and standards, goals and locomotion, structural properties, and leadership are discussed.

Cunningham, Ruth and others, *Understanding the Group Behavior of Boys and Girls.* New York: Teachers College, Columbia University Press, 1951 • Report by a team of Denver teachers on what they learned when they paid special attention to group adjustment in school situations at the first, fourth, and eighth grade levels. Sociometric, group self-analytical approach is presented in semi-narrative style.

Jennings, Helen, *Leadership and Isolation,* Second Edition. New York: Longmans, Green and Company, 1950 • An analysis of the significance of the "choice process" to human personality. Included are the results of a study of 450 individuals showing the relationship between their mutual approvals and rejections and the personality traits of the participants. The study also shows the differences in behavior between those that were underchosen and overchosen. Valuable to social psychologists, social workers, youth group leaders, and professional workers in related fields.

Jennings, Helen, *Sociometry in Group Relations.* Washington, D.C.: American Council on Education, 1948 • Presents techniques for sociometric analysis of groups with illustrations from school practice.

Northway, Mary L. and Lindsay Weld, *Sociometric Testing.* Toronto: University of Toronto Press, 1957 • Sociometric tests are used to study relationships among children (and adults) in groups. Study of the structure of groups and the sociometric status of its members is explained. Setting up and giving a sociometric test, compiling, interpreting, and using the results are illustrated. This book is intended as a guide for teachers, but is suitable for use by others as well.

Strang, Ruth, *Group Work in Education.* New York: Harper and Brothers, 1958 • A re-writing rather than a revision of an earlier work by Strang, this volume presents a comprehensive study of group activities at the high school and at the college level. It includes consideration of the theoretical basis of group activities, principles in group dynamics, and the role of leadership.

Thelen, Herbert A., *Dynamics of Groups at Work.* Chicago: University of Chicago Press, 1954 • A basic text concerned with group action which reports the work of the Human Dynamics Laboratory at the University of Chicago. The first part of the book presents concrete illustrations and specific suggestions for the organizer, leader, and member of groups. Successful practice in six fields is described and analyzed: citizen participation, classroom teaching, in-service professional training, administration and management, human relations training, and public meetings. The second section develops basic concepts drawn from all the relevant social sciences and common to all areas of social action.

Wittenberg, Rudolph M., *So You Want to Help People.* New York: Association Press, 1947 • In the first part of the book, relationships between the professional social worker and the group are discussed. The second part is devoted to those matters of discipline which often result in the complete disillusionment of the worker. One chapter under the caption, "Boy Meets Girl," discusses that important phase in the development of the adolescent in which he attempts to enter into relationships with the other sex. The suggestion is made that, as a part of the education of boys and girls, the establishment of the sexual life be made the subject of group discussion. The final section deals with some of the typical settings in which leaders operate.

Wittenberg, Rudolph M., *How To Help People.* New York: Association Press, 1953 • This handbook establishes principles for group leaders to use in structuring the group process while helping the individual to adjust. Specific problems, as well as relationship of leader to group and individual to individual, are discussed.

Part IV. Curriculum

Association for Supervision and Curriculum Development, *Guidance in the Curriculum.* Washington, D.C.: National Education Association, 1955 • A provocative volume which presents the point of view that guidance and instruction are integrally related. The implications of this viewpoint are well developed. Appropriate for teachers of all grade levels.

Cottingham, Harold D., *Guidance in Elementary Schools.* Bloomington, Illinois: McKnight, 1956 • An introduction describing guidance as a point of view, a process, and a service is followed by a discussion of administration and specific guidance techniques. The conclusion presents basic principles underlying guidance in the elementary school.

Department of Elementary School Principals, *Guidance for Today's Children* (33rd Yearbook). Washington, D.C.: National Education Association, 1954 • Guidance in the elementary school is defined by reporting numerous activities and programs now being carried on in the schools of the nation. Ruth Strang, in an opening chapter, emphasizes that guidance is for all children, and that it is inherent in all the experiences of the child for which the school is responsible. Grouped in chapters to emphasize significant phases of a guidance program are case studies, illustrative stories, and outlines of programs.

Faunce, Roland C. and Nelson L. Bossing, *Developing the Core Curriculum.* Englewood Cliffs, N. J.: Prentice-Hall, 1952 • In their introductory chapter the authors describe the "core" or "common learnings" curriculum as a course consisting of learning exeperiences which every pupil needs to have, regardless of what occupation he may expect to follow or where he may happen to live. In the following chapters they examine the widespread criticisms being made in the United States of educational practice, the history and philosophy of the core curriculum, the core curriculum in relation to the learning process, the core class in action, the planning of teaching for a core class, the use of resources, the role of the teacher and the administrator, teacher training, and evaluating progress in a core class. The guidance responsibility of the core teacher is stressed.

Kelley, Janet A., *Guidance and Curriculum.* Englewood Cliffs, N. J.: Prentice-Hall, Inc., 1955 • The concept of the teacher as the pivot of the guidance function in the integration of guidance, instruction and curriculum is shown to broaden the role of guidance personnel. Dr. Kelley indicates need for a different perspective of the extracurricular program and inclusion of it in the above integration process.

Martinson, Ruth A. and Harry Smallenberg, *Guidance in Elementary Schools.* Englewood Cliffs, N. J.: Prentice-Hall, Inc., 1958 • Presents a variety of techniques which can be used by the classroom teacher, as well as a consideration of the roles of other school personnel. Guidance is presented as a day-to-day function of the classroom teacher.

Part V. Working with Others

Brown, Muriel W., *Partners in Education,* Bulletin No. 85. Washington, D.C.: Association for Childhood Education, 1950 • A report of the sub-committee on Home-School Relations of the National Conference on Family Life, this bulletin presents practical suggestions for effective cooperation in childhood education. The suggestions are based on discussions of a series of representative groups of parents and teachers, focused on four questions: What are the values and goals in home-school cooperation? What are the conditions in schools and communities which particularly affect home-school relations? What are some of the psychological factors in the relationships between parents, children, and teachers which affect success of the partnership? How can parents, teachers, and children learn to work more effectively together?

D'Evelyn, Kathryn, *Individual Parent-Teacher Conferences.* New York: Bureau of Publications, Teachers College, Columbia University, 1945 • This volume points out the significance of good working relationships between parents and teachers for the development of children, presents a number of case studies of parent-teacher interviews, and provides suggestions for making such interviews more effective.

Hymes, James L., Jr., *Effective Home-School Relations.* Englewood Cliffs, N. J.: Prentice-Hall, Inc., 1953 • The background of home-school relations, psychology of parent-teacher relationships, social setting of schools, and problems of parents and teachers are identified and discussed. Constructive ideas and techniques for building better home-school relations are given.

Langdon, Grace and Irving Stout, *Teacher-Parent Interviews.* Englewood Cliffs, N. J.: Prentice-Hall, Inc., 1954 • A presentation of all of the considerations to be taken into account in conducting the individual conference with the parent. The material is divided into four main categories, each dealing with a practical phase of the problem: (1) an introduction pointing up the values and the simplicity with which interviews may be held; (2) an analysis of the individual perspectives with which each of the participants enters the activity—the child, parent, teacher, and administrator; (3) the content of interviews, and (4) the administrative considerations, such as time, place, and length.

Leonard, Edith, Dorothy Van Demon, and Lillian Miles, *Counseling with Parents in Early Childhood Education.* New York: MacMillan Company, 1954 • The authors approach the problem of parent-teacher relations with a concern for parent group meetings as well as the personal contact. It personalizes the presentation through the eyes of a hypothetical Jane LeRoy, thus giving the reader the feeling that the activities described can be practiced by any good teacher. The book has a wealth of practical aids, such as types of reports to use and forms which may be helpful in keeping records of activities.

Menge, J. W. and Roland C. Faunce, *Working Together for Better Schools.* New York: American Book Company, 1954 • The authors take the point of view that irresponsible attacks on the schools are not successful where citizens participate actively in school affairs, but that even a good program cannot survive in a crisis if it does not represent a genuine consensus of the people. Many constructive suggestions for involvement of citizens in total school planning.

"Parents and the Schools," *The National Elementary Principal,* Bulletin of the Department of Elementary School Principals, Volume XXXVII, No. 1. Washington, D.C.: National Education Association, September 1957 • An extensive series of short articles covering almost every phase of home-school relationships. Particularly pertinent to the elementary school.

Olsen, Edward G., editor, *School and Community Programs.* Englewood Cliffs, N. J.: Prentice-Hall, Inc., 1949 • Based on an earlier volume, *School and Community,* which pictures the school as an island separated by a moat from the community and describes ten "bridges" to eliminate the gap. The current volume presents practical projects carried out in various communities to develop more effective cooperation.

Part VI. Evaluation

Corey, Stephen M., *Action Research to Improve School Practices.* New York: Bureau of Publications, Teachers College, Columbia University, 1953 • Contrasts traditional educational research with "action research." Clear analysis of the action research process with illustrations of specific programs.

Hatch, Raymond N. and Buford Stefflre, *Administration of Guidance Services.* Englewood Cliffs, N. J.: Prentice-Hall, Inc., 1958 • While this volume is concerned primarily with administrative problems, the chapter on evaluation presents much of service to teachers. The section on "realistic evaluation" is specially pertinent.

Pupil Self-Evaluation in the Classroom. Detroit: Evaluation Committee, Metropolitan Detroit Bureau of Cooperative School Studies, 1957 • A consideration of the significance of pupil self-evaluation and suggestions for procedure; includes a number of illustrations drawn from classroom practice.

Remmers, H. H. and N. L. Gage, *Educational Measurement and Evaluation,* Revised Edition. New York: Harper and Brothers, 1955 • This volume gives a comprehensive treatment of evaluation procedures. The chapters on "Evaluating Emotional and Social Adjustment," "Measuring Interests and Attitudes," and "Measuring Environment and Background" will be of special interest to the teacher concerned with the guidance aspects of his teaching.

Willey, Roy DeVerl, and Dean C. Andrew, *Modern Methods and Technique of Guidance.* New York: Harper and Brothers, 1955 • Includes illustrations of a variety of techniques and instruments for evaluating the effectiveness of the guidance program. The follow-up study as an evaluative technique is described and illustrated.

Wilson, Frances M., *Procedures in Evaluating a Guidance Program.* New York: Columbia University Press, 1945 • This study takes up the need for evaluation, use of the questionnaire, the interview, observation in the guidance program, and self-evaluation for the individual school. It considers the functions of guidance, criteria for determining success or failure of various programs, and summary of evaluation studies already made.

Wrightstone, J. Wayne, Joseph Justman, and Irving Robbins, *Evaluation in Modern Education.* New York: American Book Company, 1956 • Presents a broad overview of the newer developments in evaluation for modern schools. Includes illustrative samples of case studies and other instruments. The teacher will find it helpful for background reading as well as for help in specific situations.

INDEX